TASKMASTER
UNTHINKABLE

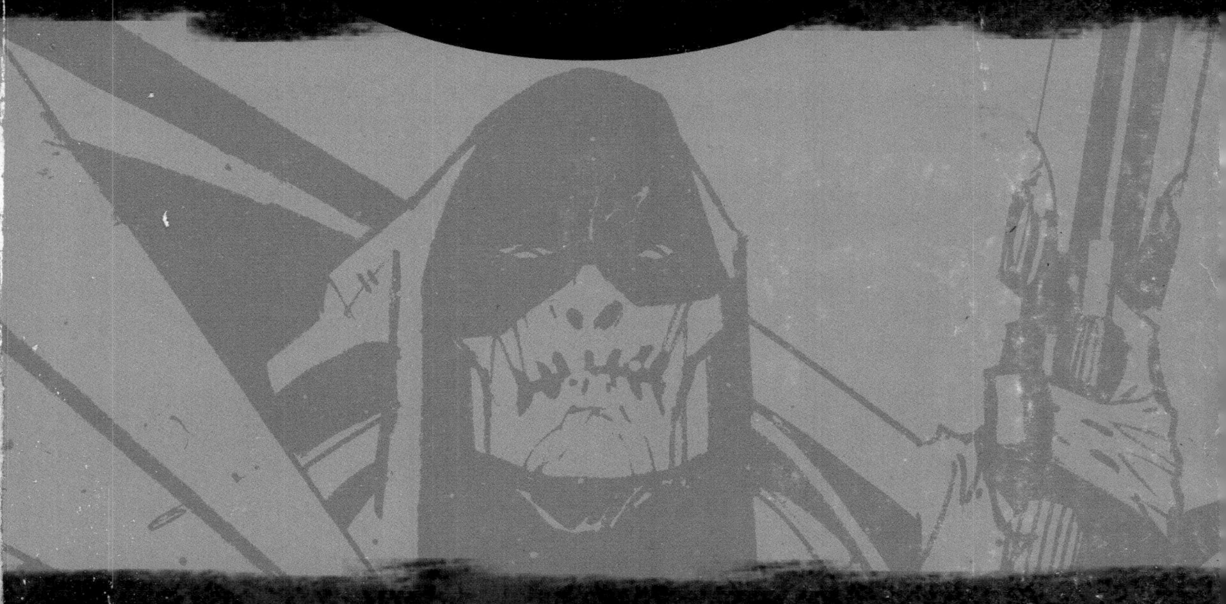

WRITER
FRED VAN LENTE

ARTIST
JEFTE PALO

COLOR ARTIST
JEAN~FRANCOIS BEAULIEU

LETTERER
DAVE LANPHEAR

COVER ARTISTS
GREG TOCCHINI &
FRANCESCO MATTINA

EDITOR
LAUREN SANKOVITCH

EXECUTIVE EDITOR
TOM BREVOORT

Collection Editor **NICOLE BOOSE**

Editorial Assistants **JAMES EMMETT & JOE HOCHSTEIN**

Assistant Editors **ALEX STARBUCK & NELSON RIBEIRO**

Editors, Special Projects **JENNIFER GRÜNWALD & MARK D. BEAZLEY**

Senior Editor, Special Projects **JEFF YOUNGQUIST**

Senior Vice President of Sales **DAVID GABRIEL**

Book Design **JEFF POWELL**

Production **JERRY KALINOWSKI**

Editor in Chief **AXEL ALONSO**

Chief Creative Officer **JOE QUESADA**

Publisher **DAN BUCKLEY**

Executive Producer **ALAN FINE**

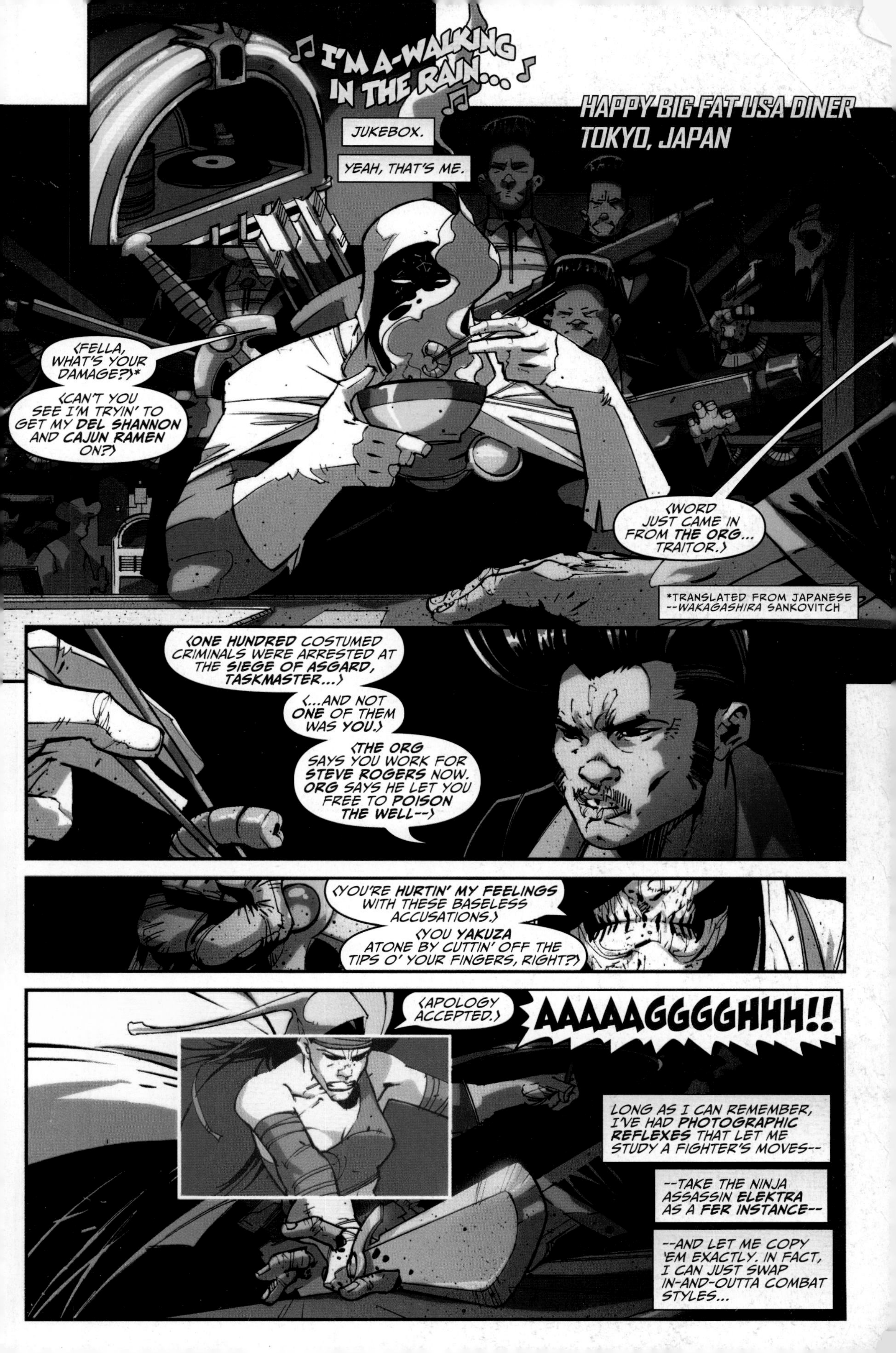
♫ I'M A-WALKING IN THE RAIN... ♫ ♫
HAPPY BIG FAT USA DINER
TOKYO, JAPAN
JUKEBOX.
YEAH, THAT'S ME.
‹FELLA, WHAT'S YOUR DAMAGE?›*
‹CAN'T YOU SEE I'M TRYIN' TO GET MY DEL SHANNON AND CAJUN RAMEN ON?›
‹WORD JUST CAME IN FROM THE ORG... TRAITOR.›
*TRANSLATED FROM JAPANESE --WAKAGASHIRA SANKOVITCH
‹ONE HUNDRED COSTUMED CRIMINALS WERE ARRESTED AT THE SIEGE OF ASGARD, TASKMASTER...›
‹...AND NOT ONE OF THEM WAS YOU.›
‹THE ORG SAYS YOU WORK FOR STEVE ROGERS NOW. ORG SAYS HE LET YOU FREE TO POISON THE WELL--›
‹YOU'RE HURTIN' MY FEELINGS WITH THESE BASELESS ACCUSATIONS.›
‹YOU YAKUZA ATONE BY CUTTIN' OFF THE TIPS O' YOUR FINGERS, RIGHT?›
‹APOLOGY ACCEPTED.›
AAAAAGGGGHHH!!
LONG AS I CAN REMEMBER, I'VE HAD PHOTOGRAPHIC REFLEXES THAT LET ME STUDY A FIGHTER'S MOVES--
--TAKE THE NINJA ASSASSIN ELEKTRA AS A FER INSTANCE--
--AND LET ME COPY 'EM EXACTLY. IN FACT, I CAN JUST SWAP IN-AND-OUTTA COMBAT STYLES...

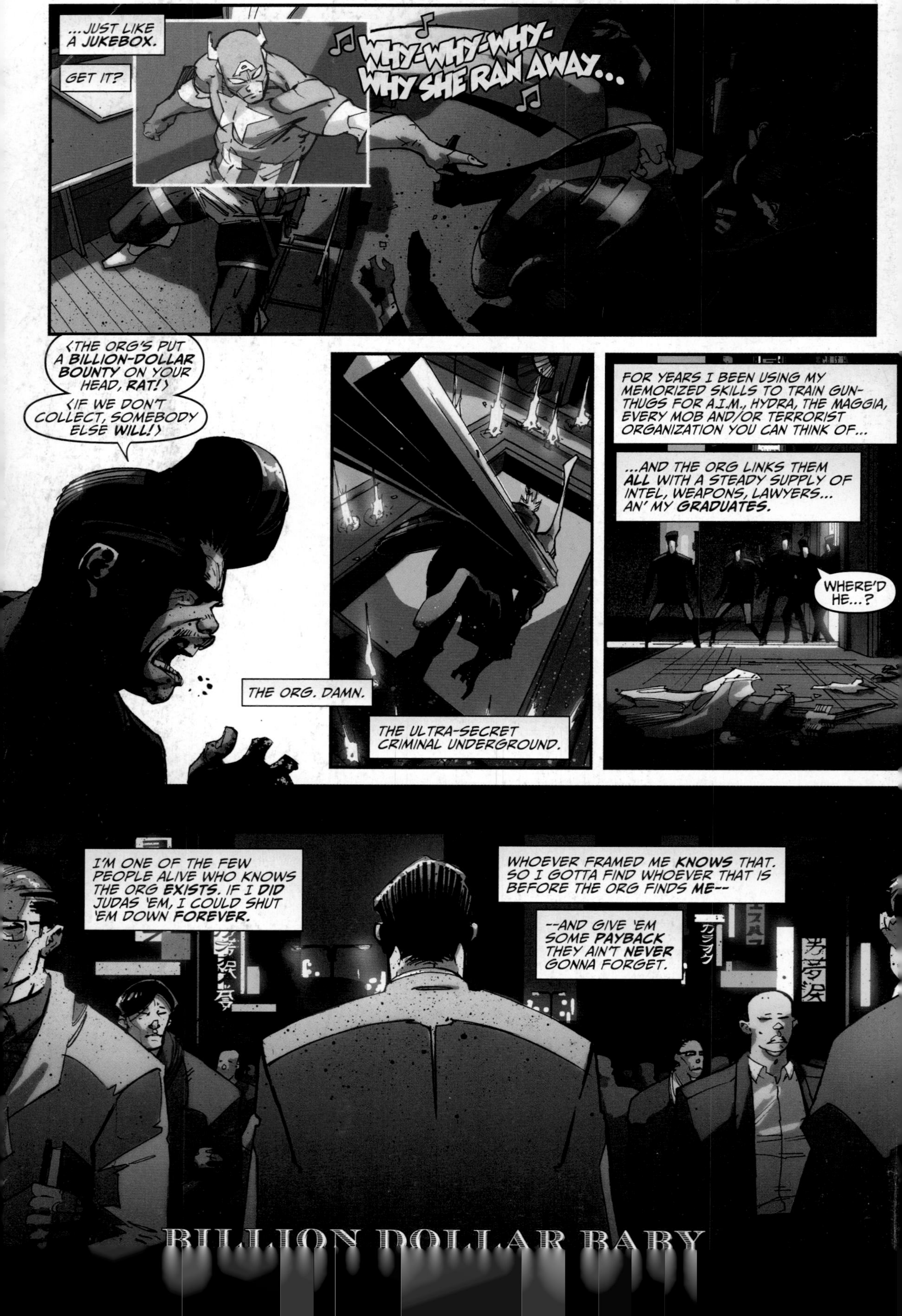

...JUST LIKE A JUKEBOX.
GET IT?
WHY-WHY-WHY-WHY SHE RAN AWAY...
<THE ORG'S PUT A BILLION-DOLLAR BOUNTY ON YOUR HEAD, RAT!>
<IF WE DON'T COLLECT, SOMEBODY ELSE WILL!>
THE ORG. DAMN.
THE ULTRA-SECRET CRIMINAL UNDERGROUND.
FOR YEARS I BEEN USING MY MEMORIZED SKILLS TO TRAIN GUN-THUGS FOR A.I.M., HYDRA, THE MAGGIA, EVERY MOB AND/OR TERRORIST ORGANIZATION YOU CAN THINK OF...
...AND THE ORG LINKS THEM ALL WITH A STEADY SUPPLY OF INTEL, WEAPONS, LAWYERS... AN' MY GRADUATES.
WHERE'D HE...?
I'M ONE OF THE FEW PEOPLE ALIVE WHO KNOWS THE ORG EXISTS. IF I DID JUDAS 'EM, I COULD SHUT 'EM DOWN FOREVER.
WHOEVER FRAMED ME KNOWS THAT. SO I GOTTA FIND WHOEVER THAT IS BEFORE THE ORG FINDS ME--
--AND GIVE 'EM SOME PAYBACK THEY AIN'T NEVER GONNA FORGET.
BILLION DOLLAR BABY

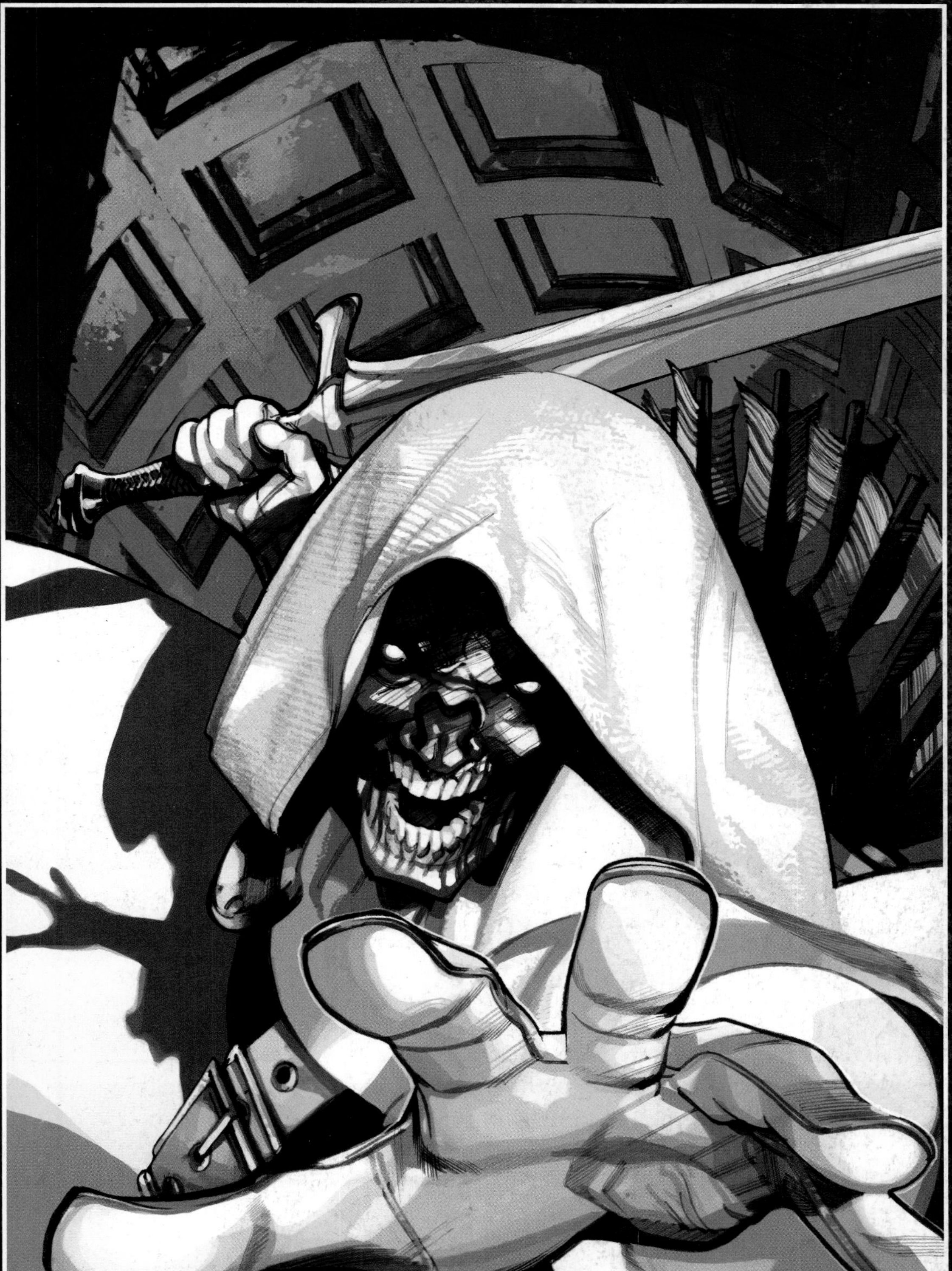

ONE

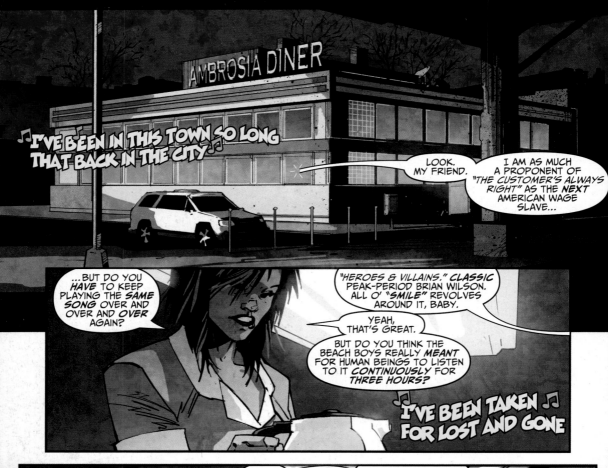

AMBROSIA DINER

♪ I'VE BEEN IN THIS TOWN SO LONG THAT BACK IN THE CITY ♪

LOOK. MY FRIEND.

I AM AS MUCH A PROPONENT OF *"THE CUSTOMER'S ALWAYS RIGHT"* AS THE *NEXT* AMERICAN WAGE SLAVE...

...BUT DO YOU *HAVE* TO KEEP PLAYING THE *SAME SONG* OVER AND OVER AND *OVER* AGAIN?

"HEROES & VILLAINS." CLASSIC PEAK-PERIOD BRIAN WILSON. ALL O' *"SMILE"* REVOLVES AROUND IT, BABY.

YEAH, THAT'S GREAT.

BUT DO YOU THINK THE BEACH BOYS REALLY *MEANT* FOR HUMAN BEINGS TO LISTEN TO IT *CONTINUOUSLY* FOR *THREE HOURS?*

♪ I'VE BEEN TAKEN FOR LOST AND GONE ♪

OH. SORRY.

DIDN'T REALIZE I WAS INTERFERIN' WITH THE TWO A.M. MONDAY *"RUSH."*

WELL L, M, A *AND* O.

BUT CAN YOU CUT *ME* SOME SLACK? I'M ON THE HOME STRETCH OF BACK-TO-BACK SHIFTS.

♪ AND UNKNOWN FOR A LONG, LONG TIME ♪

I'M HOBBLING AROUND ON STUMPS *AND* NOW I ALSO WANT TO TEAR MY EARS OFF.

HEROES & VILLAINS

HMMM.

WHAT DO I GET IN RETURN IF I *STOP?*

NOTHING THAT ISN'T ON THE MENU.

HOLD ON. NOT WHAT I MEANT... *MERCEDES,* RIGHT?

MERCEDES

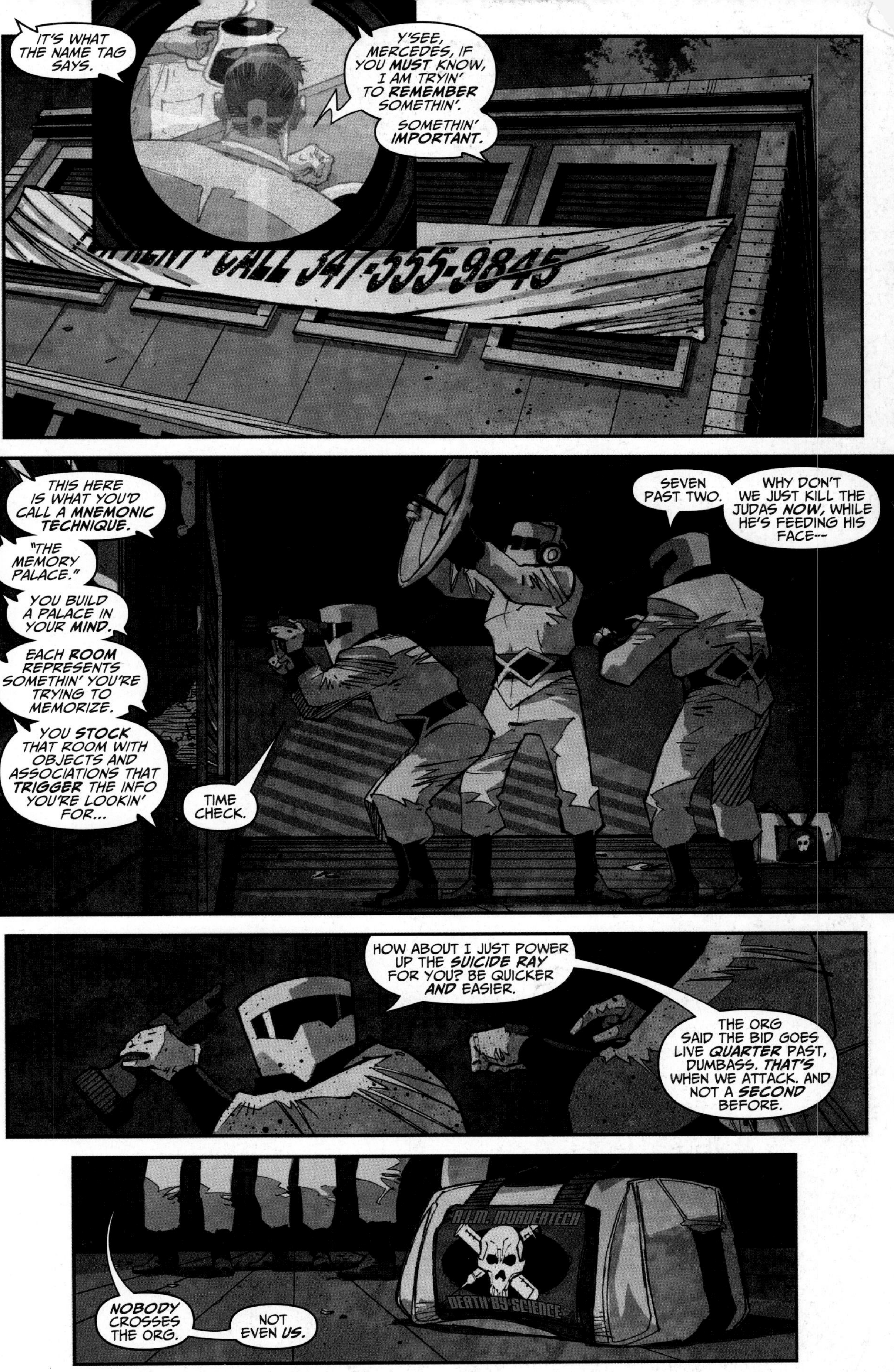

IT'S WHAT THE NAME TAG SAYS.
Y'SEE, MERCEDES, IF YOU **MUST** KNOW, I AM TRYIN' TO **REMEMBER** SOMETHIN'.
SOMETHIN' **IMPORTANT**.
CALL 347-555-9845
THIS HERE IS WHAT YOU'D CALL A **MNEMONIC TECHNIQUE**.
"THE MEMORY PALACE."
YOU BUILD A PALACE IN YOUR **MIND**.
EACH **ROOM** REPRESENTS SOMETHIN' YOU'RE TRYING TO MEMORIZE.
YOU **STOCK** THAT ROOM WITH OBJECTS AND ASSOCIATIONS THAT **TRIGGER** THE INFO YOU'RE LOOKIN' FOR...
TIME CHECK.
SEVEN PAST TWO.
WHY DON'T WE JUST KILL THE JUDAS ***NOW,*** WHILE HE'S FEEDING HIS FACE--
HOW ABOUT I JUST POWER UP THE ***SUICIDE RAY*** FOR YOU? BE QUICKER ***AND*** EASIER.
THE ORG SAID THE BID GOES LIVE ***QUARTER*** PAST, DUMBASS. ***THAT'S*** WHEN WE ATTACK. AND NOT A ***SECOND*** BEFORE.
A.I.M. MURDERTECH
DEATH BY SCIENCE
NOBODY CROSSES THE ORG.
NOT EVEN ***US***.

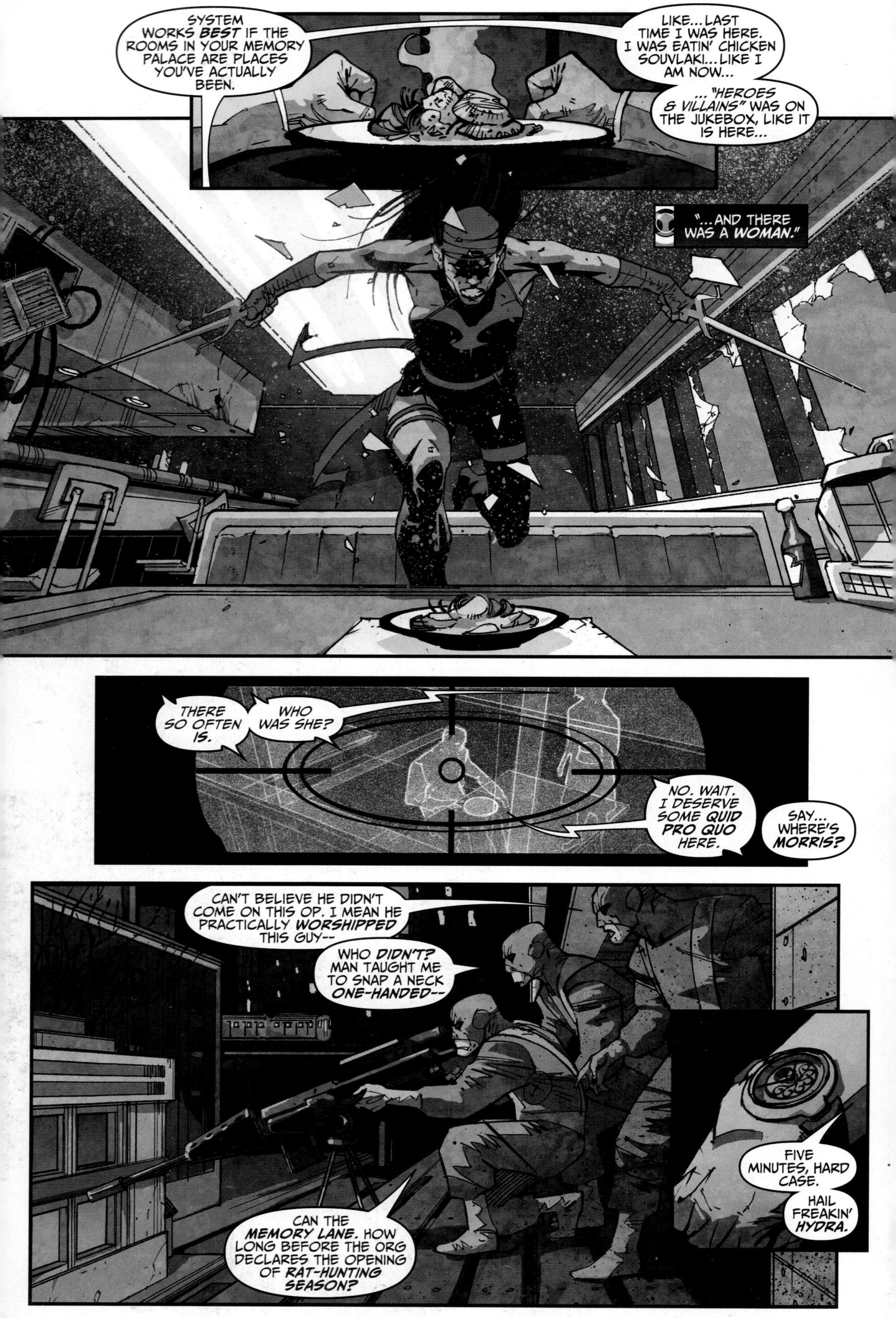
SYSTEM WORKS BEST IF THE ROOMS IN YOUR MEMORY PALACE ARE PLACES YOU'VE ACTUALLY BEEN.
LIKE... LAST TIME I WAS HERE. I WAS EATIN' CHICKEN SOUVLAKI... LIKE I AM NOW...
..."HEROES & VILLAINS" WAS ON THE JUKEBOX, LIKE IT IS HERE...
"...AND THERE WAS A WOMAN."
THERE SO OFTEN IS.
WHO WAS SHE?
NO. WAIT. I DESERVE SOME QUID PRO QUO HERE.
SAY... WHERE'S MORRIS?
CAN'T BELIEVE HE DIDN'T COME ON THIS OP. I MEAN HE PRACTICALLY WORSHIPPED THIS GUY--
WHO DIDN'T? MAN TAUGHT ME TO SNAP A NECK ONE-HANDED--
CAN THE MEMORY LANE. HOW LONG BEFORE THE ORG DECLARES THE OPENING OF RAT-HUNTING SEASON?
FIVE MINUTES, HARD CASE.
HAIL FREAKIN' HYDRA.

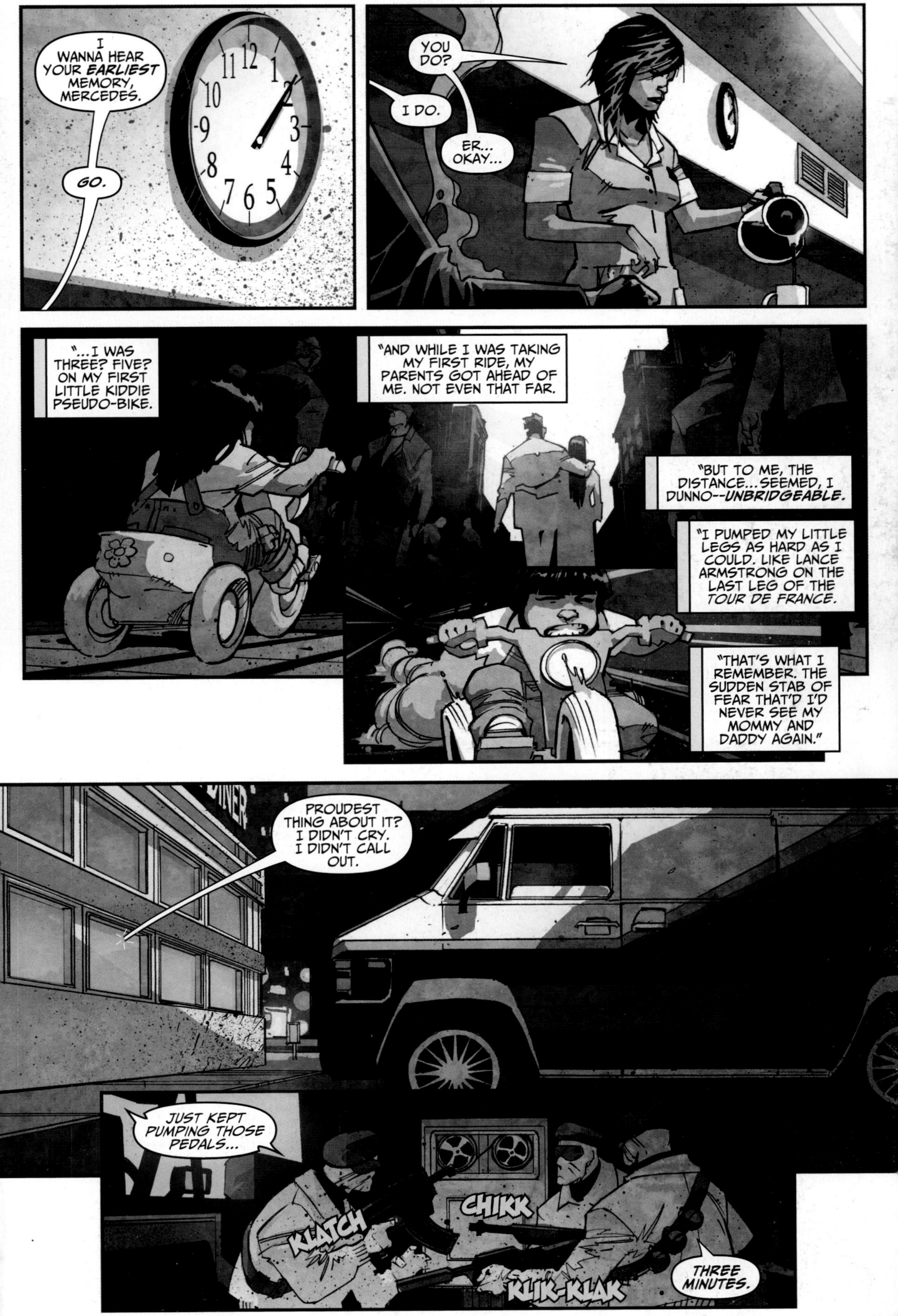

I WANNA HEAR YOUR EARLIEST MEMORY, MERCEDES.
GO.
YOU DO?
I DO.
ER... OKAY...
"...I WAS THREE? FIVE? ON MY FIRST LITTLE KIDDIE PSEUDO-BIKE.
"AND WHILE I WAS TAKING MY FIRST RIDE, MY PARENTS GOT AHEAD OF ME. NOT EVEN THAT FAR.
"BUT TO ME, THE DISTANCE...SEEMED, I DUNNO--UNBRIDGEABLE.
"I PUMPED MY LITTLE LEGS AS HARD AS I COULD. LIKE LANCE ARMSTRONG ON THE LAST LEG OF THE TOUR DE FRANCE.
"THAT'S WHAT I REMEMBER. THE SUDDEN STAB OF FEAR THAT'D I'D NEVER SEE MY MOMMY AND DADDY AGAIN."
PROUDEST THING ABOUT IT? I DIDN'T CRY. I DIDN'T CALL OUT.
JUST KEPT PUMPING THOSE PEDALS...
CHIKK
KLATCH
KLIK-KLAK
THREE MINUTES.

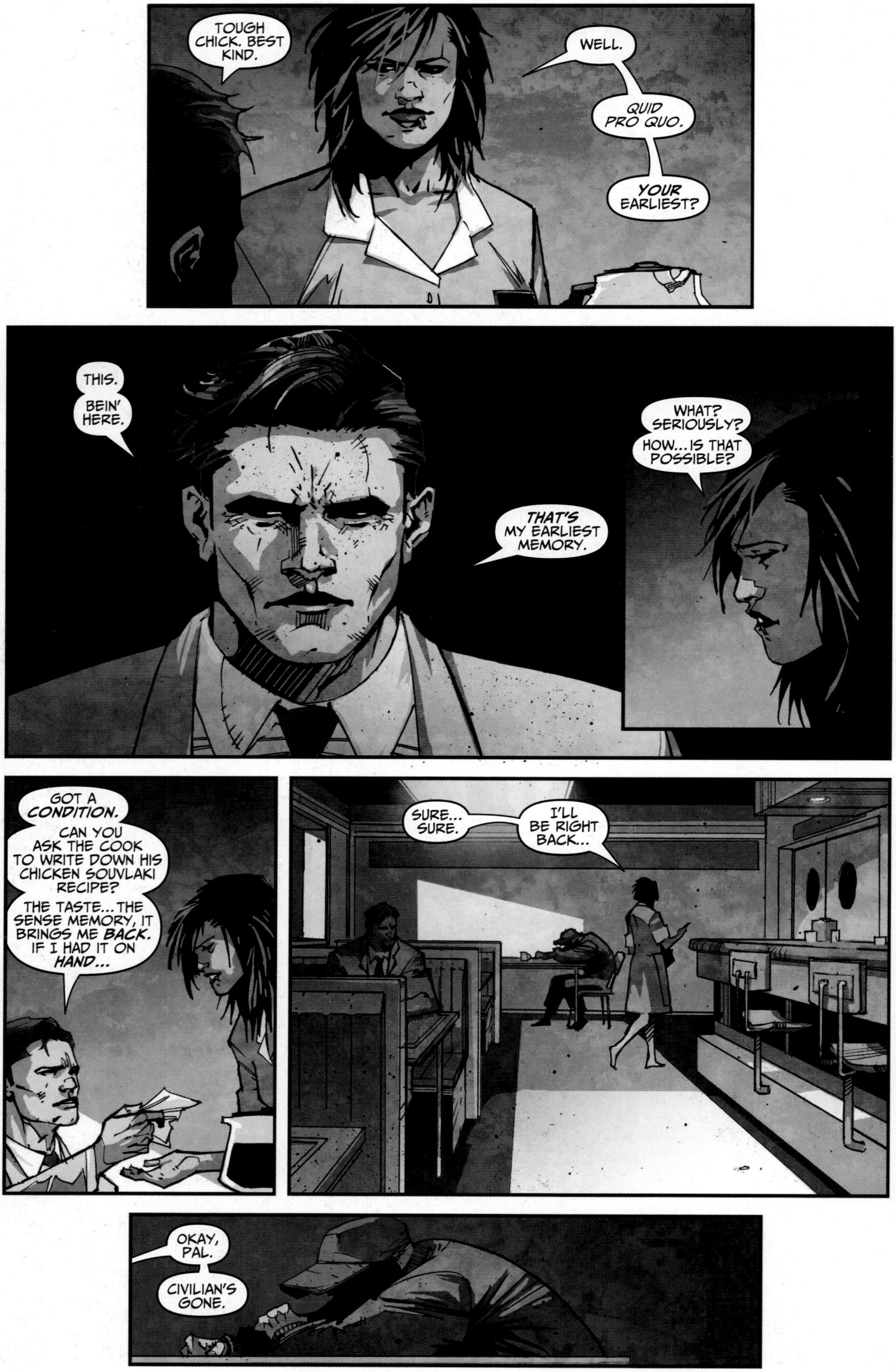
TOUGH CHICK. BEST KIND.
WELL.
QUID PRO QUO.
YOUR EARLIEST?
THIS.
BEIN' HERE.
THAT'S MY EARLIEST MEMORY.
WHAT? SERIOUSLY?
HOW...IS THAT POSSIBLE?
GOT A CONDITION.
CAN YOU ASK THE COOK TO WRITE DOWN HIS CHICKEN SOUVLAKI RECIPE?
THE TASTE...THE SENSE MEMORY, IT BRINGS ME BACK. IF I HAD IT ON HAND...
SURE... SURE.
I'LL BE RIGHT BACK...
OKAY, PAL.
CIVILIAN'S GONE.

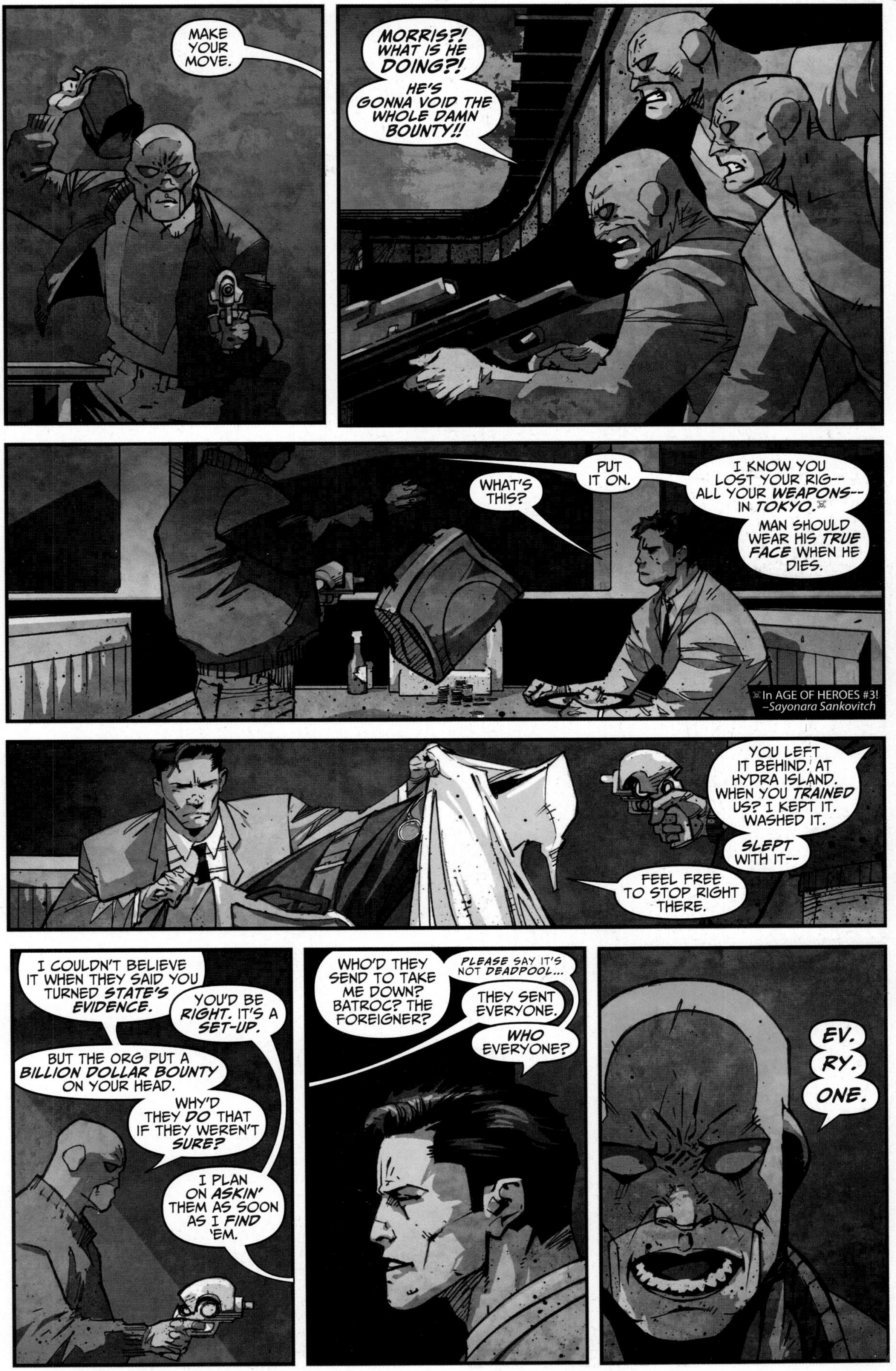

MAKE YOUR MOVE.
MORRIS?! WHAT IS HE DOING?!
HE'S GONNA VOID THE WHOLE DAMN BOUNTY!!
WHAT'S THIS?
PUT IT ON.
I KNOW YOU LOST YOUR RIG-- ALL YOUR WEAPONS-- IN TOKYO.☠
MAN SHOULD WEAR HIS TRUE FACE WHEN HE DIES.
☠In AGE OF HEROES #3! –Sayonara Sankovitch
YOU LEFT IT BEHIND. AT HYDRA ISLAND. WHEN YOU TRAINED US? I KEPT IT. WASHED IT.
SLEPT WITH IT--
FEEL FREE TO STOP RIGHT THERE.
I COULDN'T BELIEVE IT WHEN THEY SAID YOU TURNED STATE'S EVIDENCE.
YOU'D BE RIGHT. IT'S A SET-UP.
BUT THE ORG PUT A BILLION DOLLAR BOUNTY ON YOUR HEAD.
WHY'D THEY DO THAT IF THEY WEREN'T SURE?
I PLAN ON ASKIN' THEM AS SOON AS I FIND 'EM.
WHO'D THEY SEND TO TAKE ME DOWN? BATROC? THE FOREIGNER?
PLEASE SAY IT'S NOT DEADPOOL...
THEY SENT EVERYONE.
WHO EVERYONE?
EV. RY. ONE.

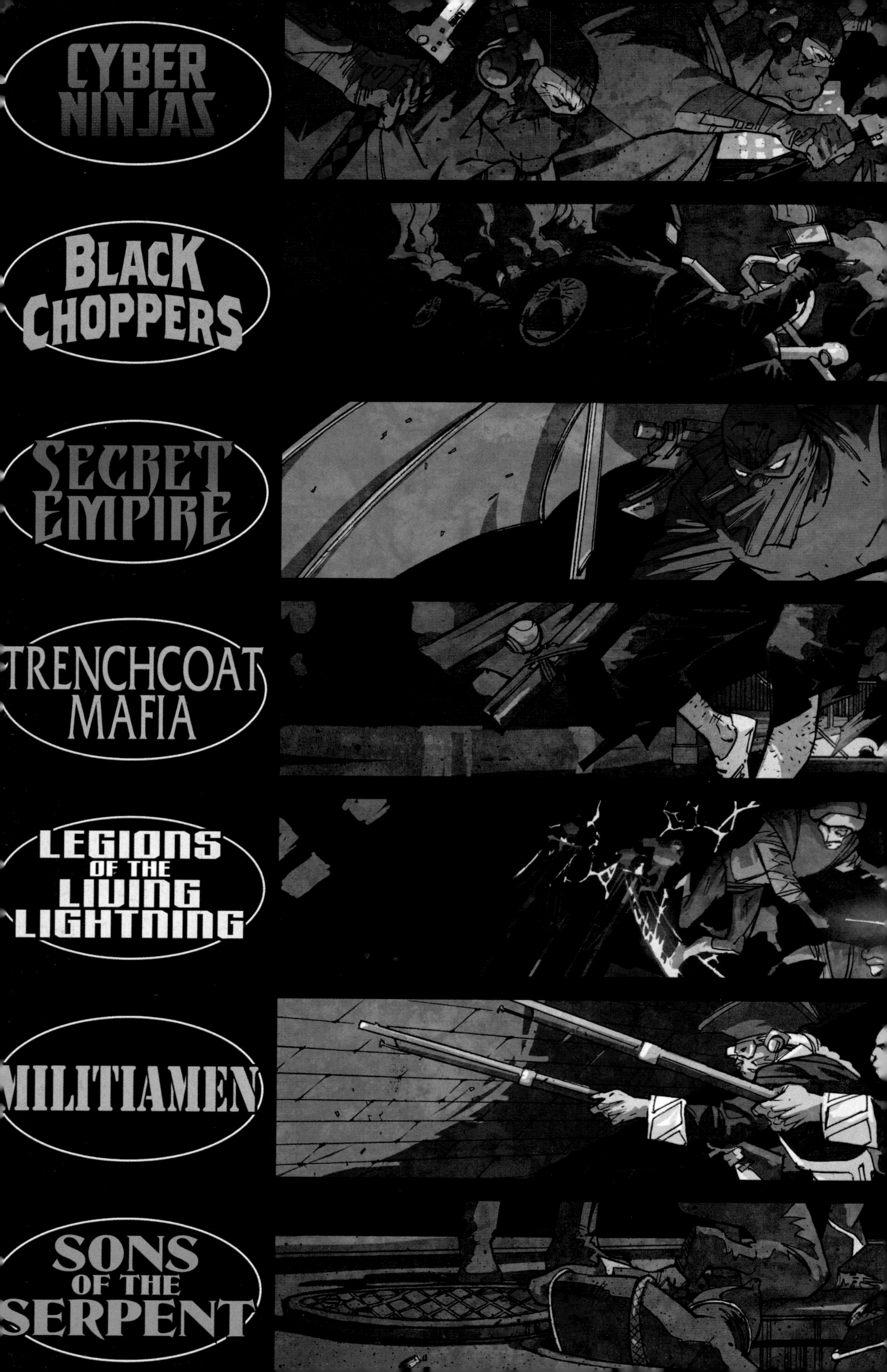
CYBER NINJAS
BLACK CHOPPERS
SECRET EMPIRE
TRENCHCOAT MAFIA
LEGIONS OF THE LIVING LIGHTNING
MILITIAMEN
SONS OF THE SERPENT

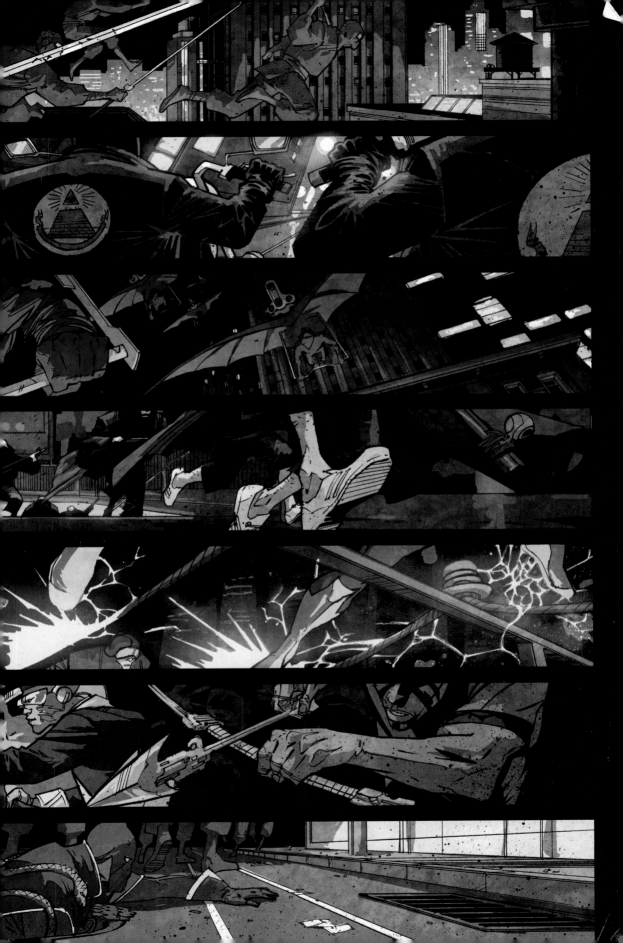

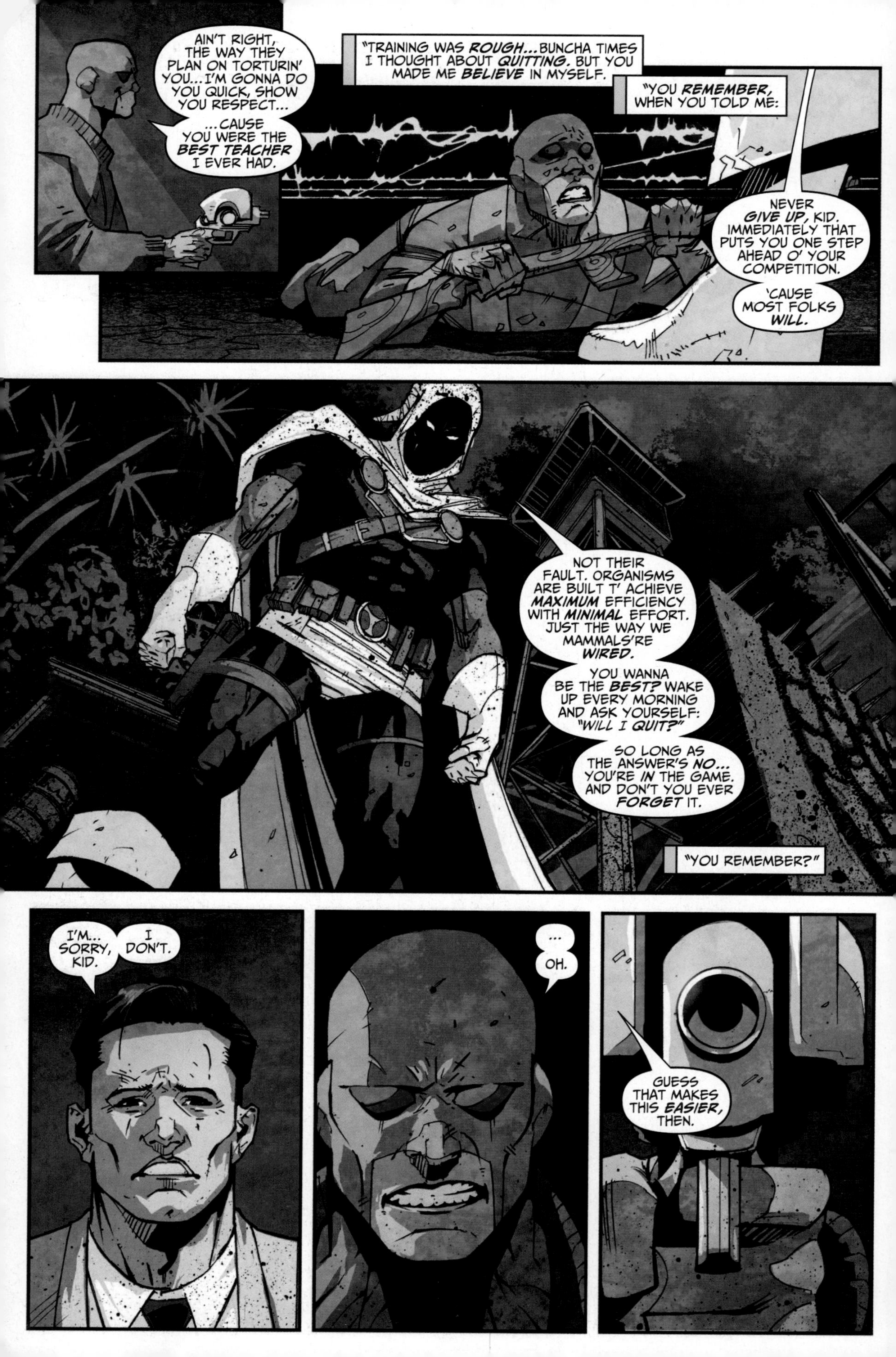
AIN'T RIGHT, THE WAY THEY PLAN ON TORTURIN' YOU...I'M GONNA DO YOU QUICK, SHOW YOU RESPECT...
...CAUSE YOU WERE THE BEST TEACHER I EVER HAD.
"TRAINING WAS ROUGH...BUNCHA TIMES I THOUGHT ABOUT QUITTING. BUT YOU MADE ME BELIEVE IN MYSELF.
"YOU REMEMBER, WHEN YOU TOLD ME:
NEVER GIVE UP, KID. IMMEDIATELY THAT PUTS YOU ONE STEP AHEAD O' YOUR COMPETITION.
'CAUSE MOST FOLKS WILL.
NOT THEIR FAULT. ORGANISMS ARE BUILT T' ACHIEVE MAXIMUM EFFICIENCY WITH MINIMAL EFFORT. JUST THE WAY WE MAMMALS'RE WIRED.
YOU WANNA BE THE BEST? WAKE UP EVERY MORNING AND ASK YOURSELF: "WILL I QUIT?"
SO LONG AS THE ANSWER'S NO... YOU'RE IN THE GAME. AND DON'T YOU EVER FORGET IT.
"YOU REMEMBER?"
I'M... SORRY, KID.
I DON'T.
... OH.
GUESS THAT MAKES THIS EASIER, THEN.

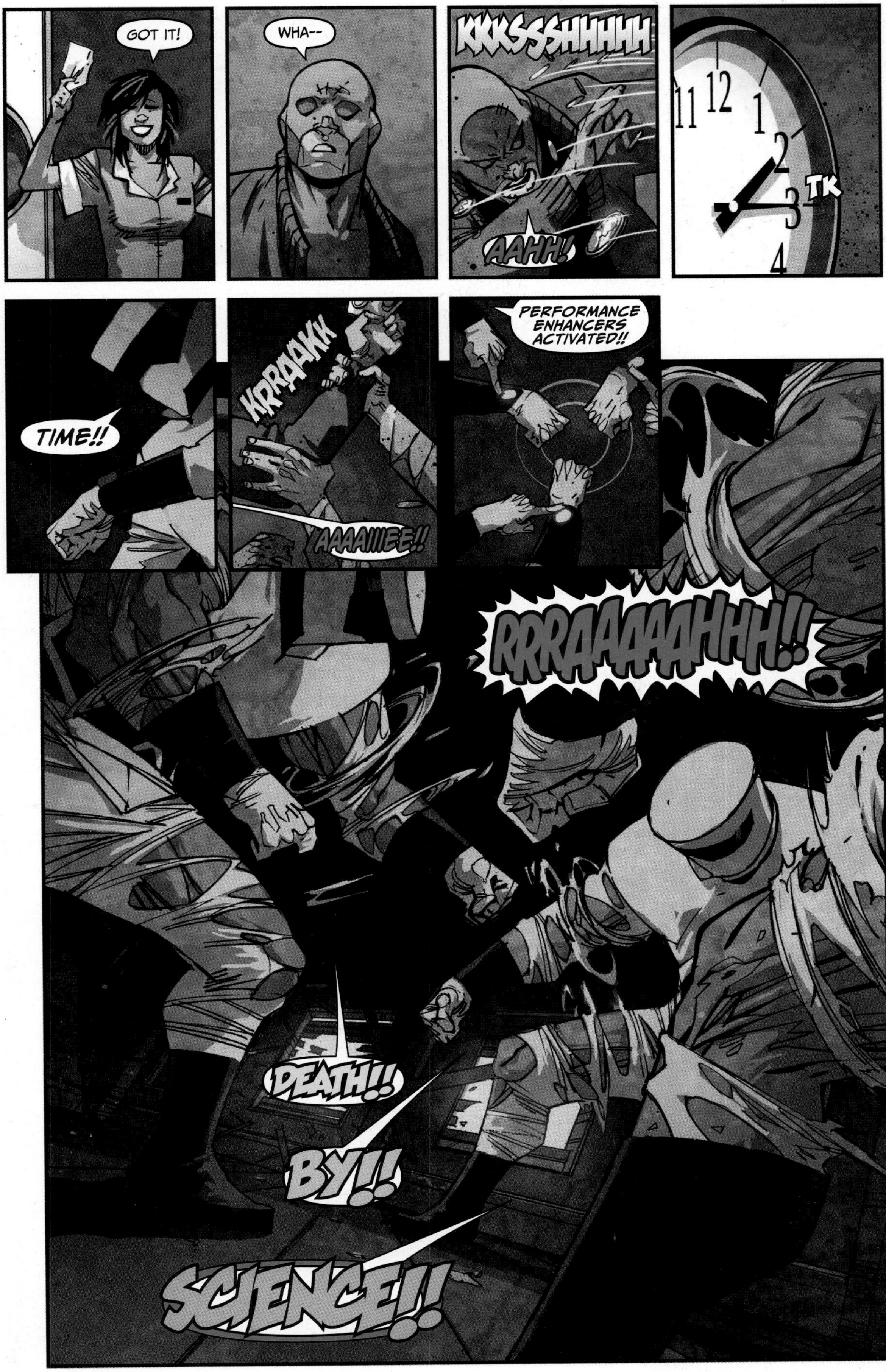
GOT IT!
WHA--
KKKSSSHHHHH
AAHH!
TK
TIME!!
KRRAAKK
AAAAIIIEE!!
PERFORMANCE ENHANCERS ACTIVATED!!
RRRAAAAAHHH!!
DEATH!!
BY!!
SCIENCE!!

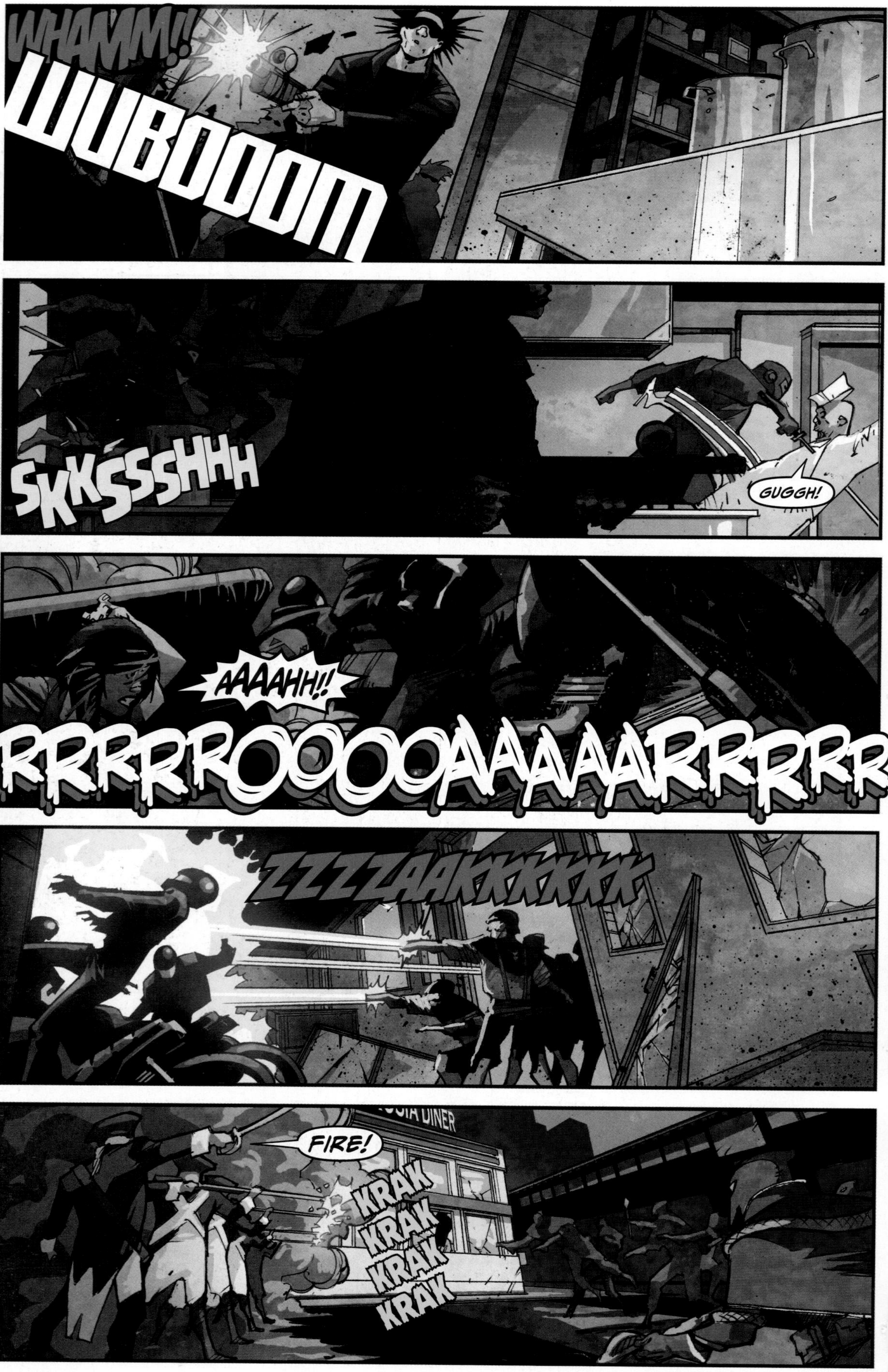
WHAMM!!
WUBOOOM
SKKSSSHHH
GUGGH!
AAAAHH!!
RRRRROOOOOAAAAARRRRR
ZZZZAAKKKKKK
FIRE!
KRAK
KRAK
KRAK
KRAK

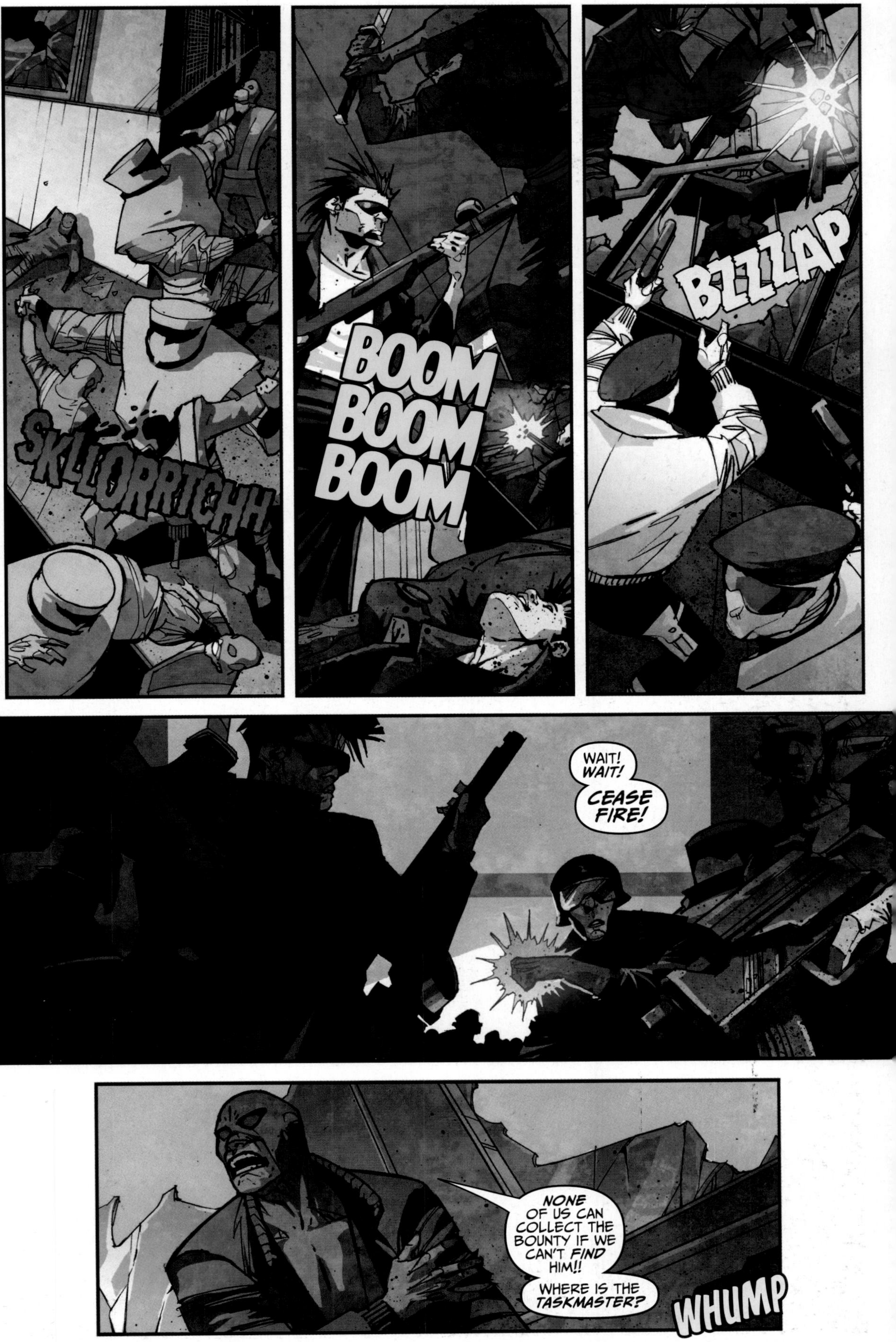
SKLLORRRTCHH
BOOM
BOOM
BOOM
BZZZAP
WAIT! WAIT!
CEASE FIRE!
NONE OF US CAN COLLECT THE BOUNTY IF WE CAN'T FIND HIM!!
WHERE IS THE TASKMASTER?
WHUMP

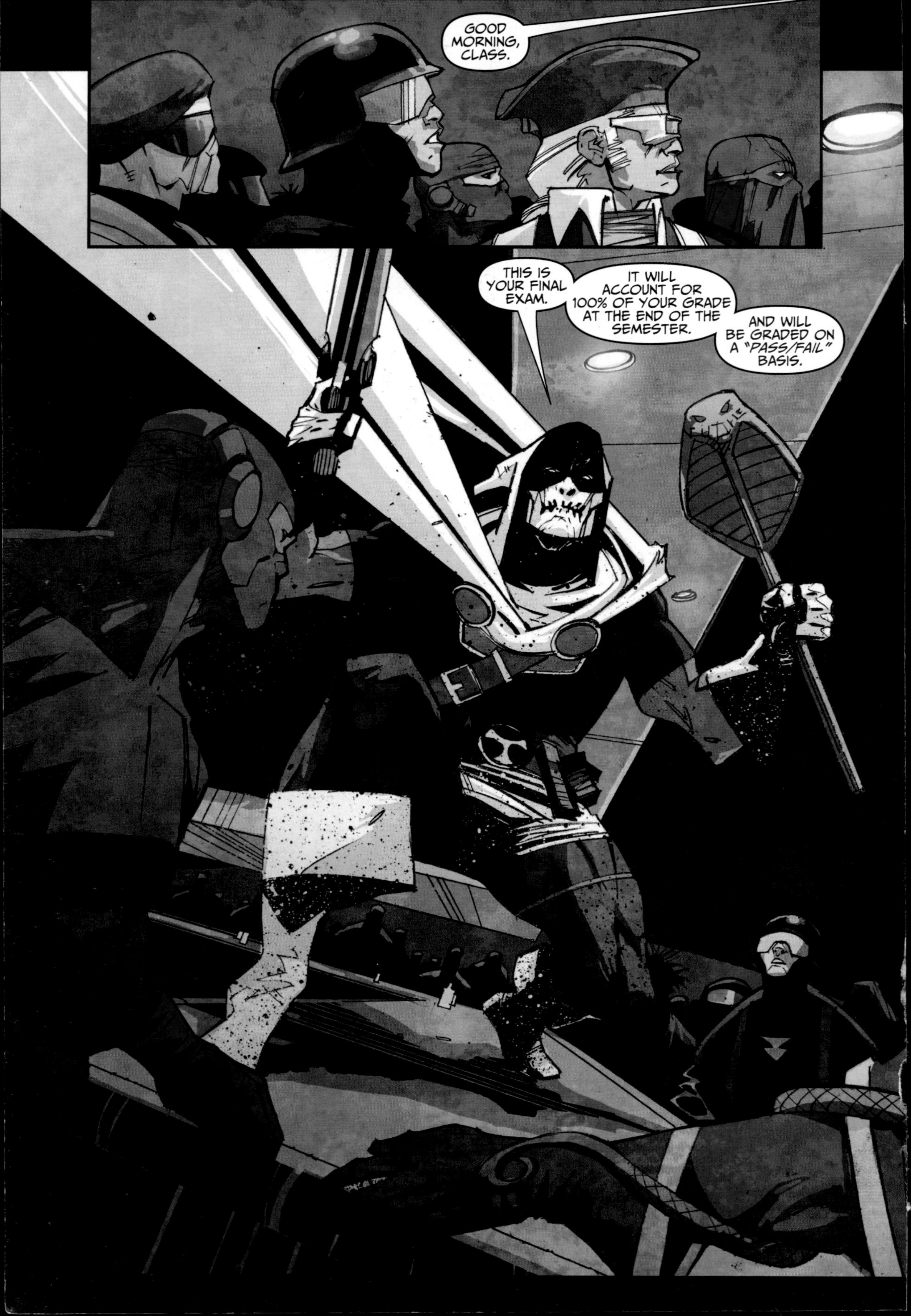
GOOD MORNING, CLASS.
THIS IS YOUR FINAL EXAM.
IT WILL ACCOUNT FOR 100% OF YOUR GRADE AT THE END OF THE SEMESTER.
AND WILL BE GRADED ON A "PASS/FAIL" BASIS.

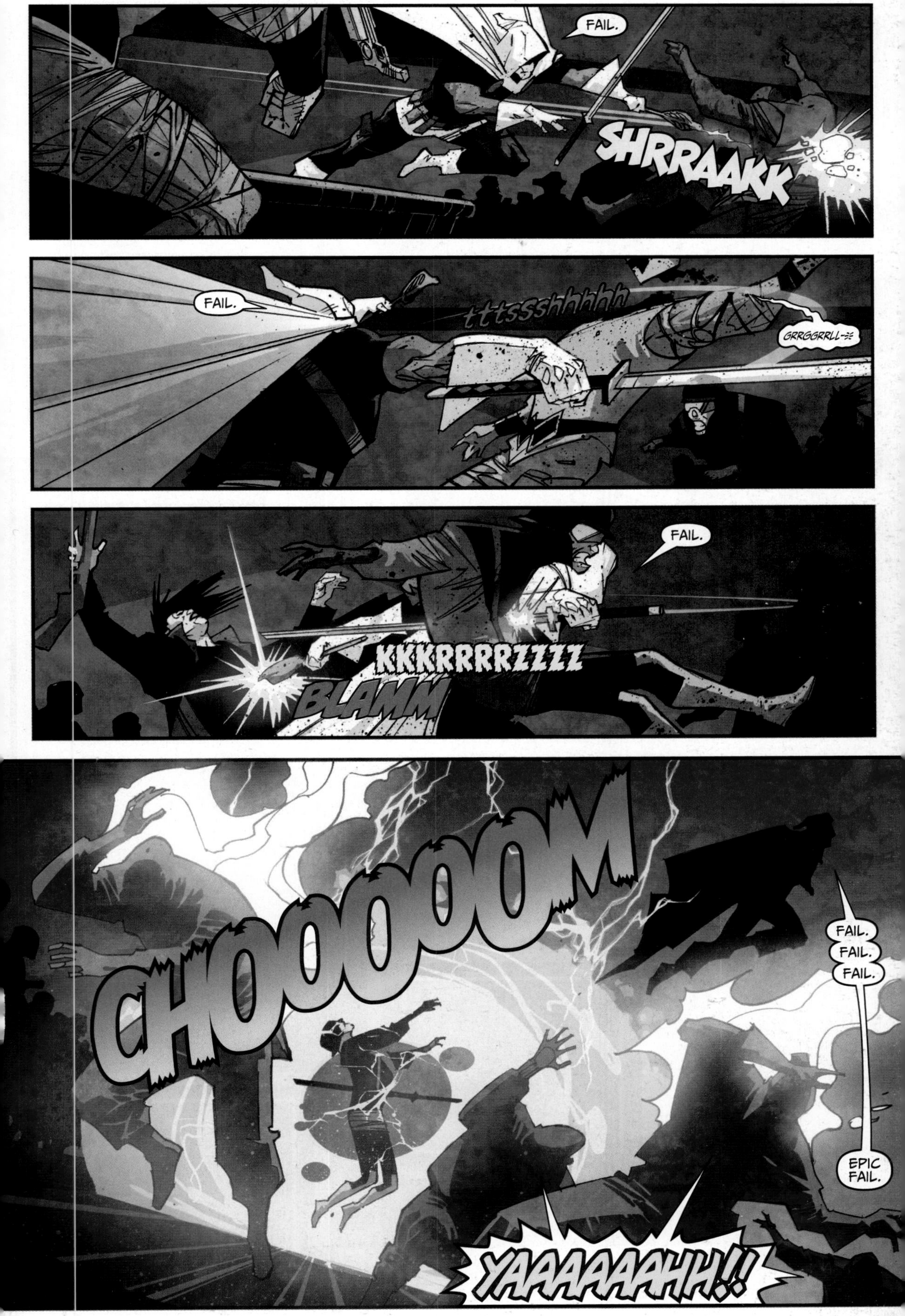
FAIL.
SHRRAAKK
FAIL.
tttssshhhhh
GRRGGRRLL
FAIL.
KKKRRRRZZZZ
BLAMM
CHOOOOOOM
FAIL.
FAIL.
FAIL.
EPIC FAIL.
YAAAAAAHH!!

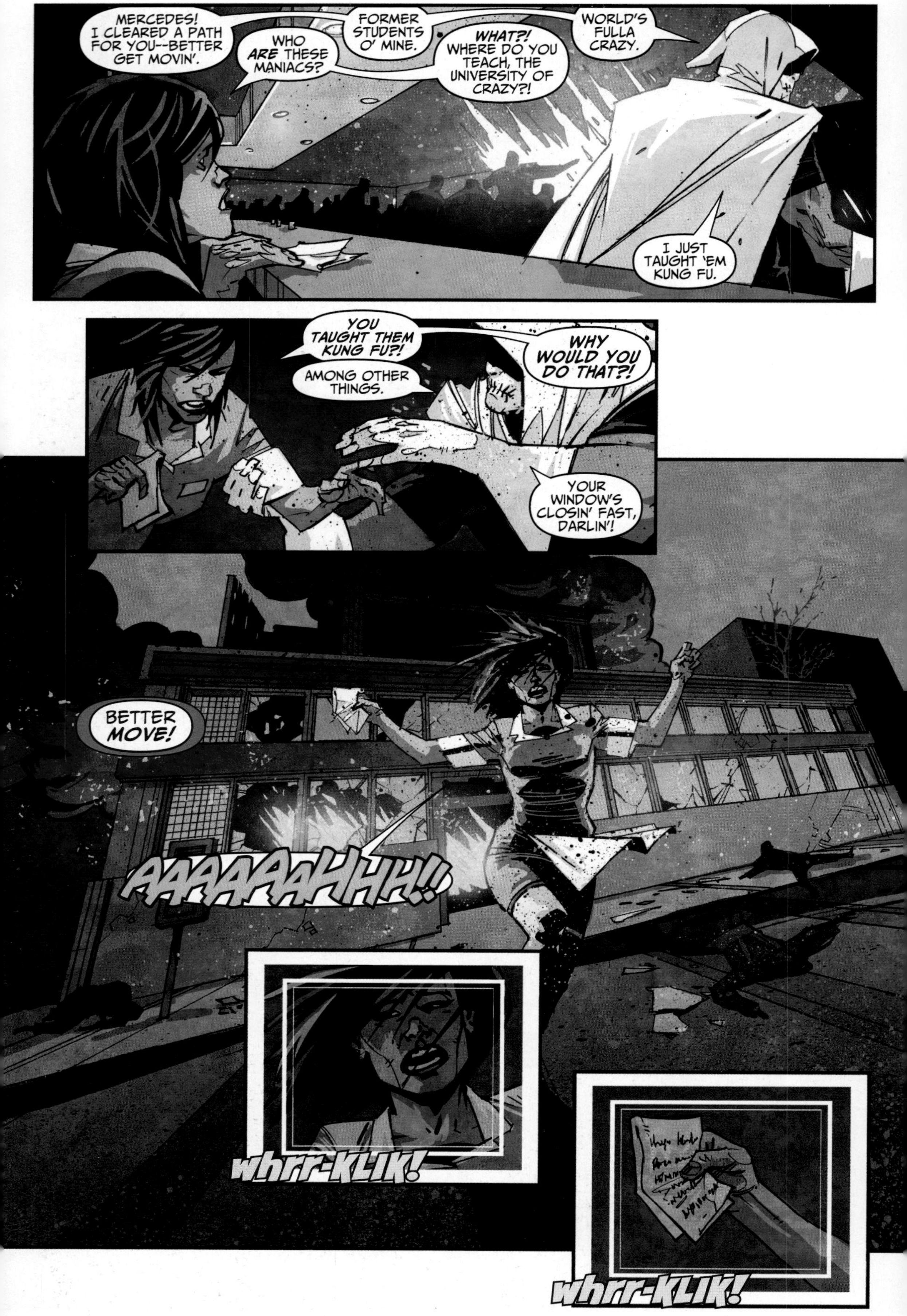
MERCEDES! I CLEARED A PATH FOR YOU--BETTER GET MOVIN'.
WHO ARE THESE MANIACS?
FORMER STUDENTS O' MINE.
WHAT?! WHERE DO YOU TEACH, THE UNIVERSITY OF CRAZY?!
WORLD'S FULLA CRAZY.
I JUST TAUGHT 'EM KUNG FU.
YOU TAUGHT THEM KUNG FU?!
AMONG OTHER THINGS.
WHY WOULD YOU DO THAT?!
YOUR WINDOW'S CLOSIN' FAST, DARLIN'!
BETTER MOVE!
AAAAAAHHH!!
whrr-KLIK!
whrr-KLIK!

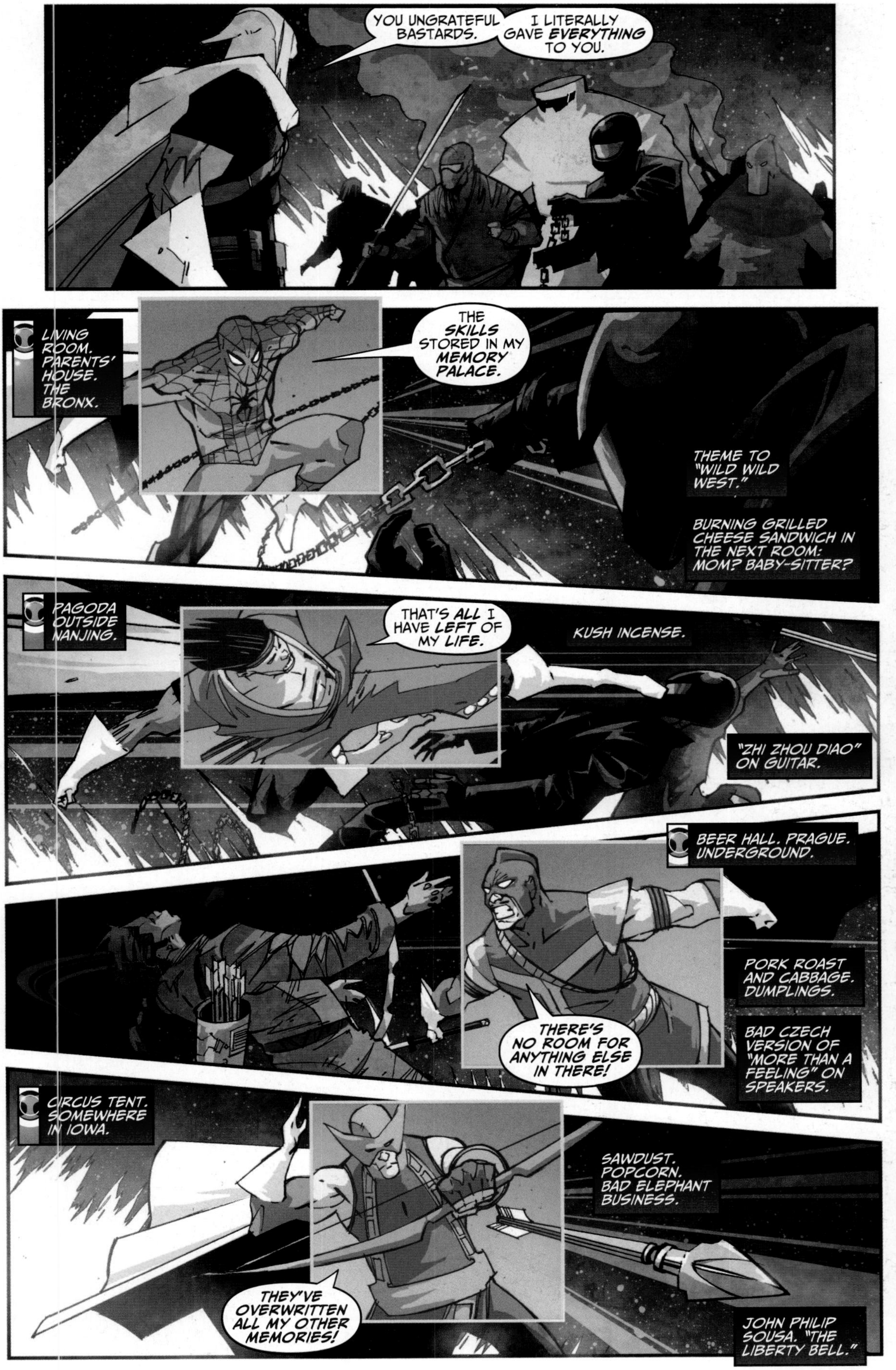
YOU UNGRATEFUL BASTARDS.
I LITERALLY GAVE EVERYTHING TO YOU.
LIVING ROOM. PARENTS' HOUSE. THE BRONX.
THE SKILLS STORED IN MY MEMORY PALACE.
THEME TO "WILD WILD WEST."
BURNING GRILLED CHEESE SANDWICH IN THE NEXT ROOM: MOM? BABY-SITTER?
PAGODA OUTSIDE NANJING.
THAT'S ALL I HAVE LEFT OF MY LIFE.
KUSH INCENSE.
"ZHI ZHOU DIAO" ON GUITAR.
BEER HALL. PRAGUE. UNDERGROUND.
PORK ROAST AND CABBAGE. DUMPLINGS.
BAD CZECH VERSION OF "MORE THAN A FEELING" ON SPEAKERS.
THERE'S NO ROOM FOR ANYTHING ELSE IN THERE!
CIRCUS TENT. SOMEWHERE IN IOWA.
SAWDUST. POPCORN. BAD ELEPHANT BUSINESS.
THEY'VE OVERWRITTEN ALL MY OTHER MEMORIES!
JOHN PHILIP SOUSA. "THE LIBERTY BELL."

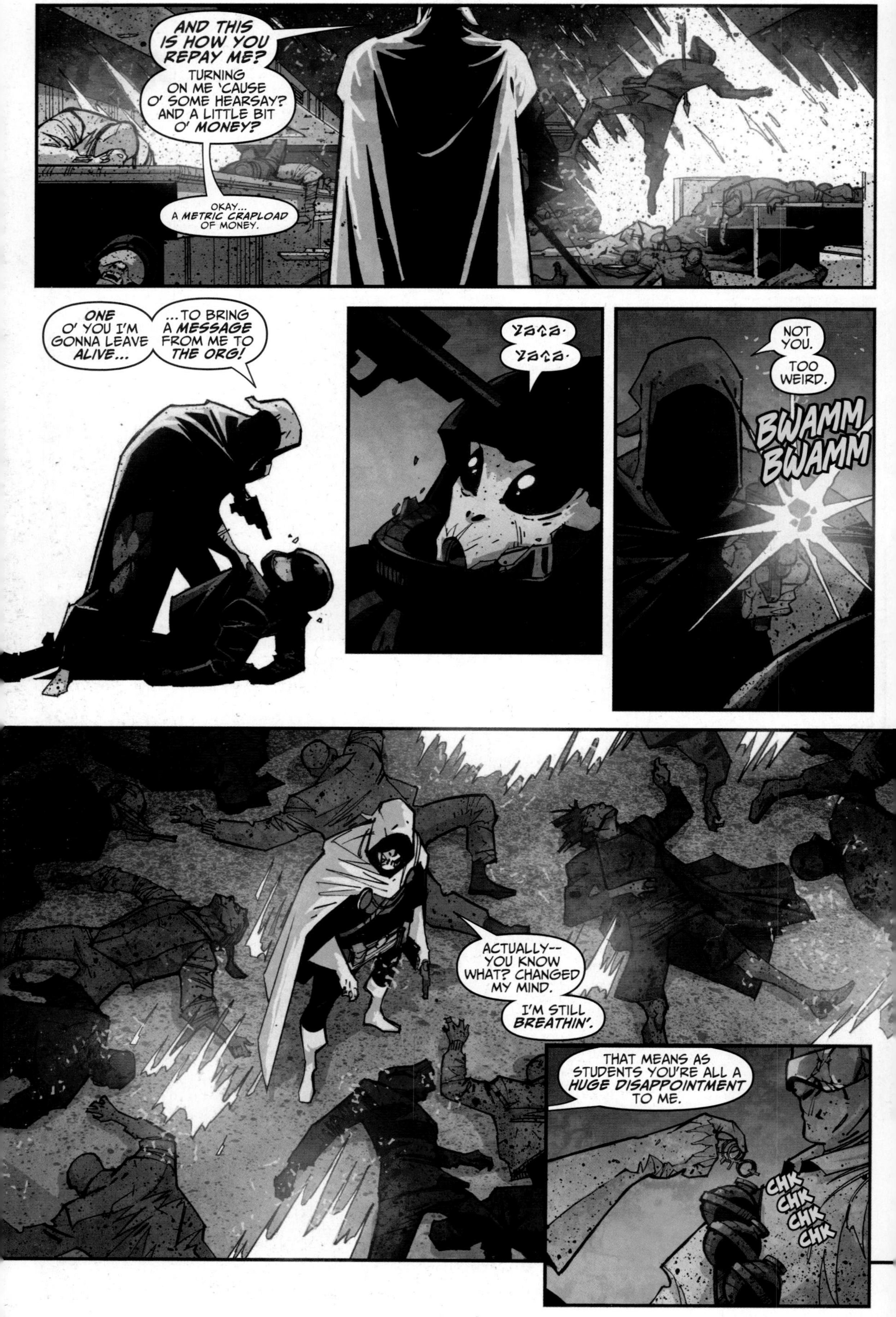
AND THIS IS HOW YOU REPAY ME?
TURNING ON ME 'CAUSE O' SOME HEARSAY? AND A LITTLE BIT O' MONEY?
OKAY... A METRIC CRAPLOAD OF MONEY.
ONE O' YOU I'M GONNA LEAVE ALIVE...
...TO BRING A MESSAGE FROM ME TO THE ORG!
NOT YOU.
TOO WEIRD.
BWAMM
BWAMM
ACTUALLY-- YOU KNOW WHAT? CHANGED MY MIND.
I'M STILL BREATHIN'.
THAT MEANS AS STUDENTS YOU'RE ALL A HUGE DISAPPOINTMENT TO ME.
CHK
CHK
CHK
CHK

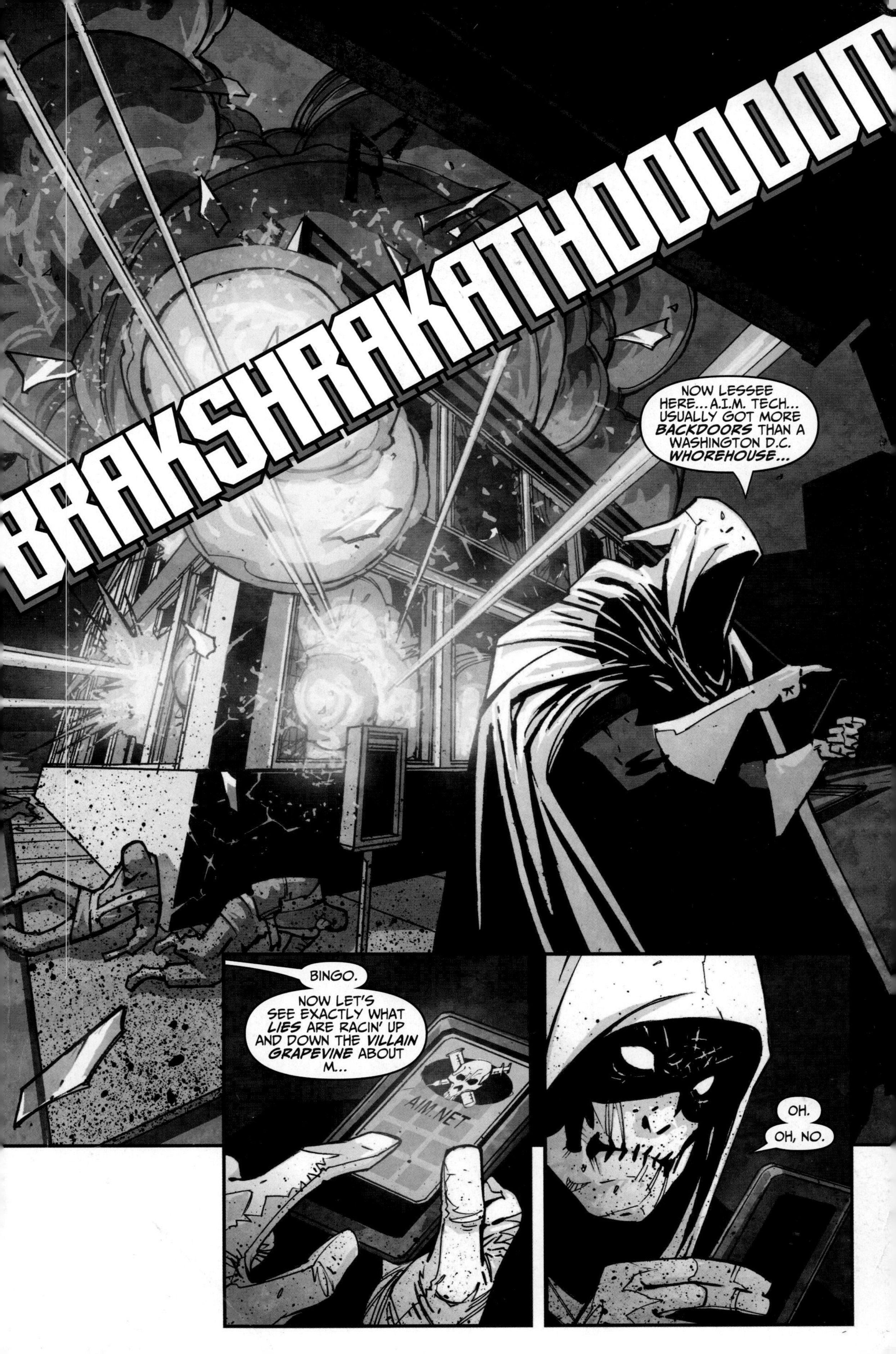
BRAKSHRAKATHOOOOOM
NOW LESSEE HERE... A.I.M. TECH... USUALLY GOT MORE BACKDOORS THAN A WASHINGTON D.C. WHOREHOUSE...
BINGO.
NOW LET'S SEE EXACTLY WHAT LIES ARE RACIN' UP AND DOWN THE VILLAIN GRAPEVINE ABOUT M...
A.I.M.NET
OH.
OH, NO.

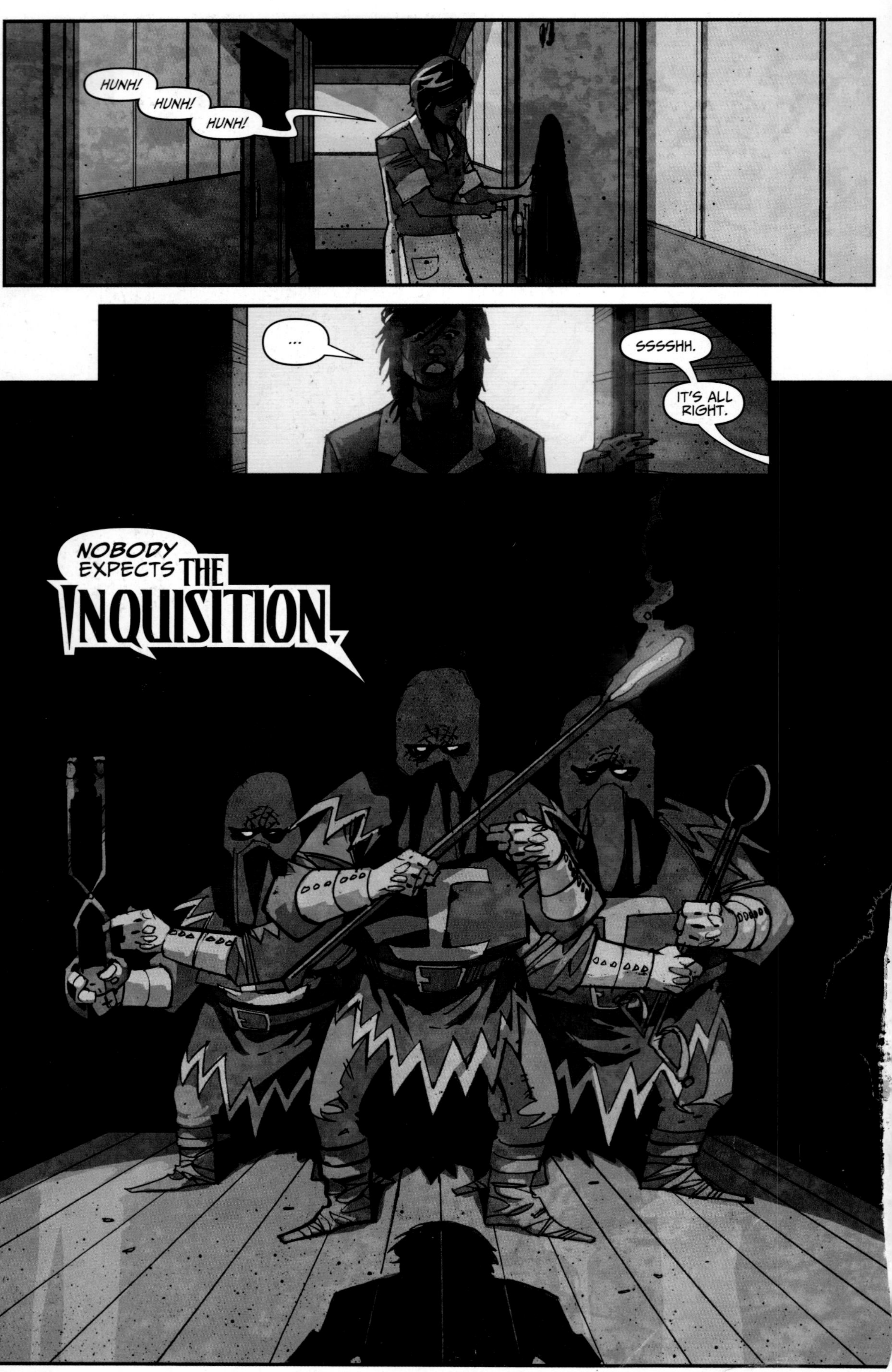
HUNH!
HUNH!
HUNH!
...
SSSSHH.
IT'S ALL RIGHT.
NOBODY EXPECTS THE INQUISITION.

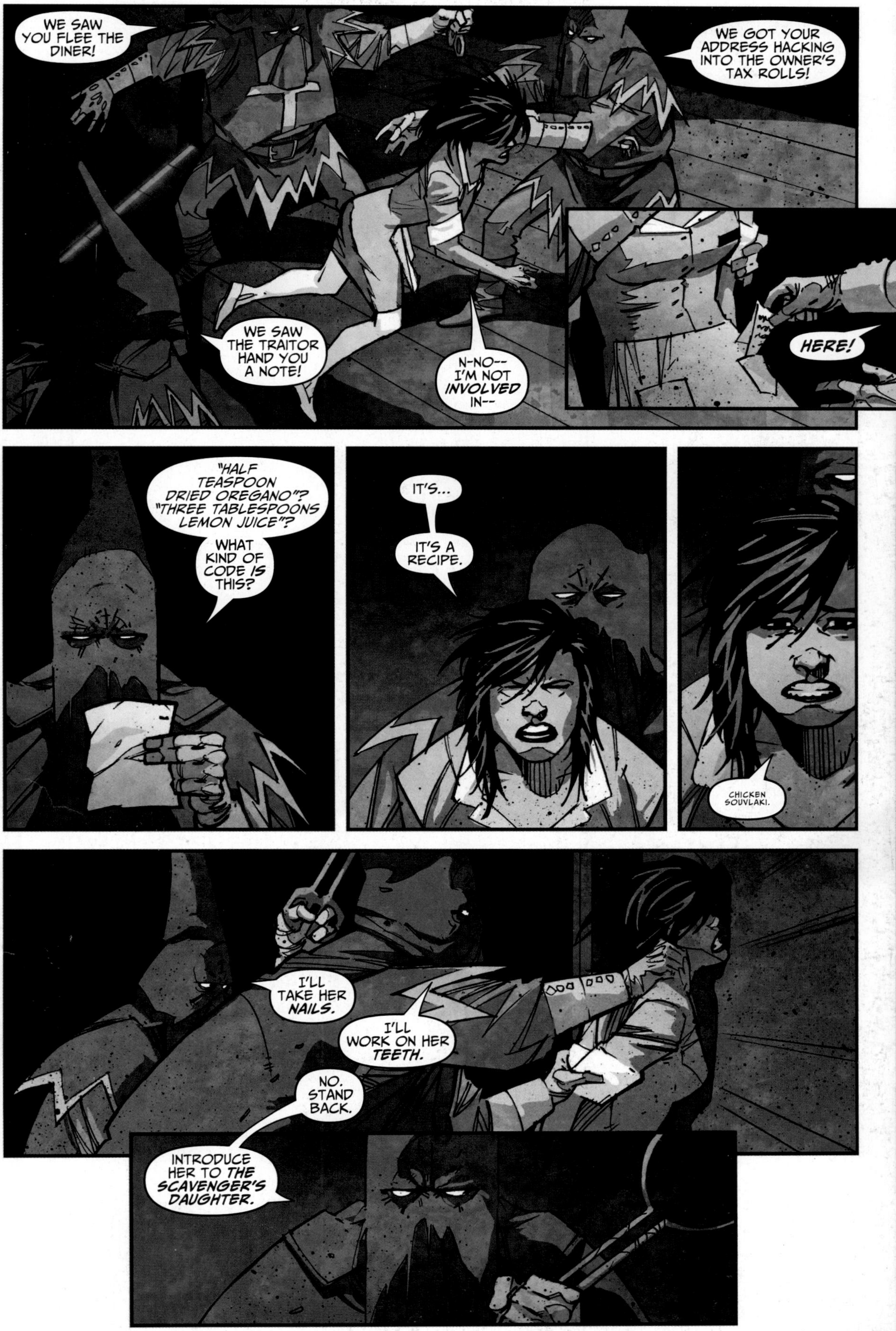
WE SAW YOU FLEE THE DINER!
WE GOT YOUR ADDRESS HACKING INTO THE OWNER'S TAX ROLLS!
WE SAW THE TRAITOR HAND YOU A NOTE!
N-NO-- I'M NOT INVOLVED IN--
HERE!
"HALF TEASPOON DRIED OREGANO"? "THREE TABLESPOONS LEMON JUICE"?
WHAT KIND OF CODE IS THIS?
IT'S...
IT'S A RECIPE.
CHICKEN SOUVLAKI.
I'LL TAKE HER NAILS.
I'LL WORK ON HER TEETH.
NO. STAND BACK.
INTRODUCE HER TO THE SCAVENGER'S DAUGHTER.

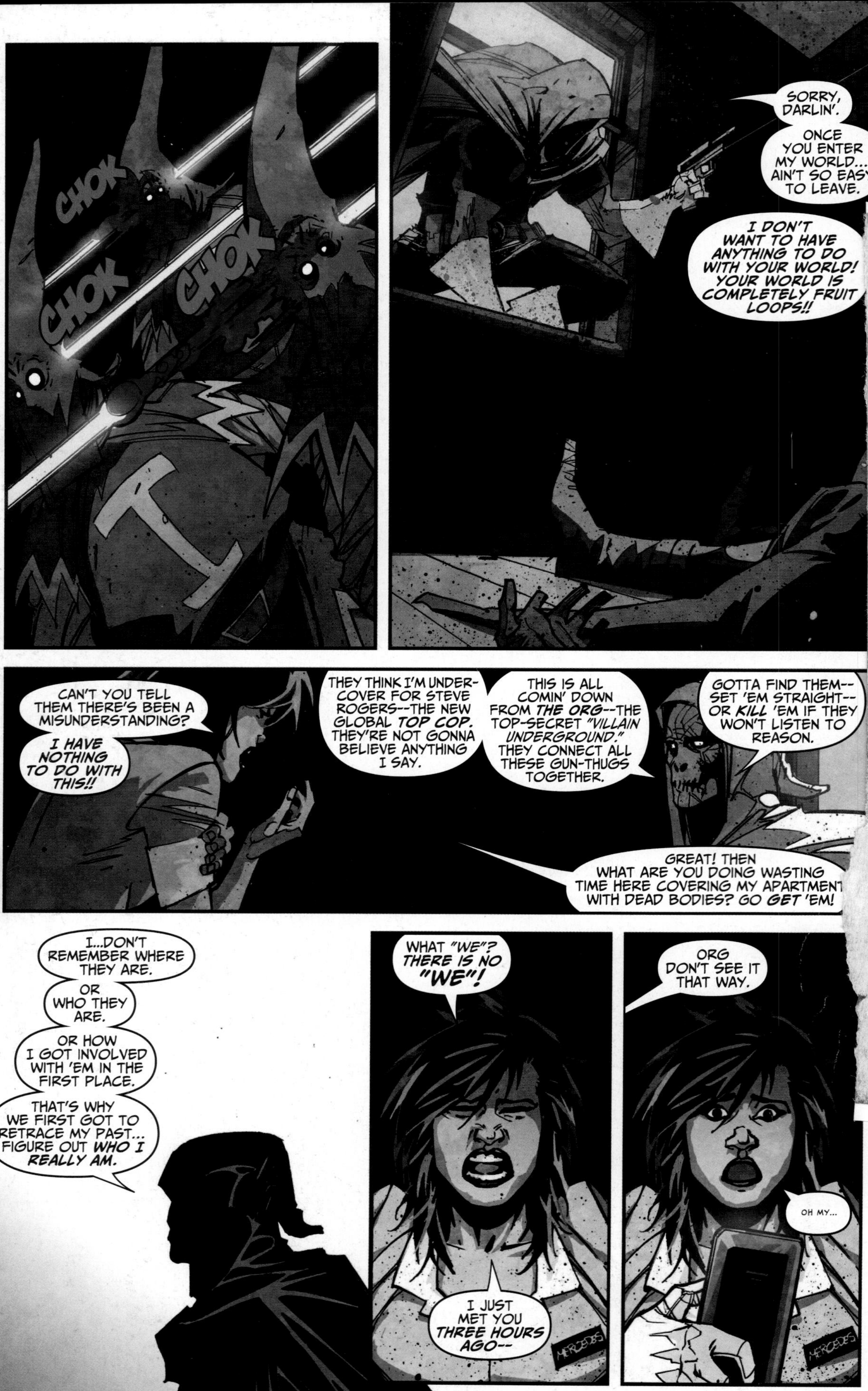

CHOK
CHOK
CHOK
SORRY, DARLIN'.
ONCE YOU ENTER MY WORLD... AIN'T SO EASY TO LEAVE.
I DON'T WANT TO HAVE ANYTHING TO DO WITH YOUR WORLD! YOUR WORLD IS COMPLETELY FRUIT LOOPS!!
CAN'T YOU TELL THEM THERE'S BEEN A MISUNDERSTANDING?
I HAVE NOTHING TO DO WITH THIS!!
THEY THINK I'M UNDERCOVER FOR STEVE ROGERS--THE NEW GLOBAL TOP COP. THEY'RE NOT GONNA BELIEVE ANYTHING I SAY.
THIS IS ALL COMIN' DOWN FROM THE ORG--THE TOP-SECRET "VILLAIN UNDERGROUND." THEY CONNECT ALL THESE GUN-THUGS TOGETHER.
GOTTA FIND THEM--SET 'EM STRAIGHT--OR KILL 'EM IF THEY WON'T LISTEN TO REASON.
GREAT! THEN WHAT ARE YOU DOING WASTING TIME HERE COVERING MY APARTMENT WITH DEAD BODIES? GO GET 'EM!
I...DON'T REMEMBER WHERE THEY ARE.
OR WHO THEY ARE.
OR HOW I GOT INVOLVED WITH 'EM IN THE FIRST PLACE.
THAT'S WHY WE FIRST GOT TO RETRACE MY PAST... FIGURE OUT WHO I REALLY AM.
WHAT "WE"? THERE IS NO "WE"!
I JUST MET YOU THREE HOURS AGO--
ORG DON'T SEE IT THAT WAY.
OH MY...
MERCEDES
MERCEDES

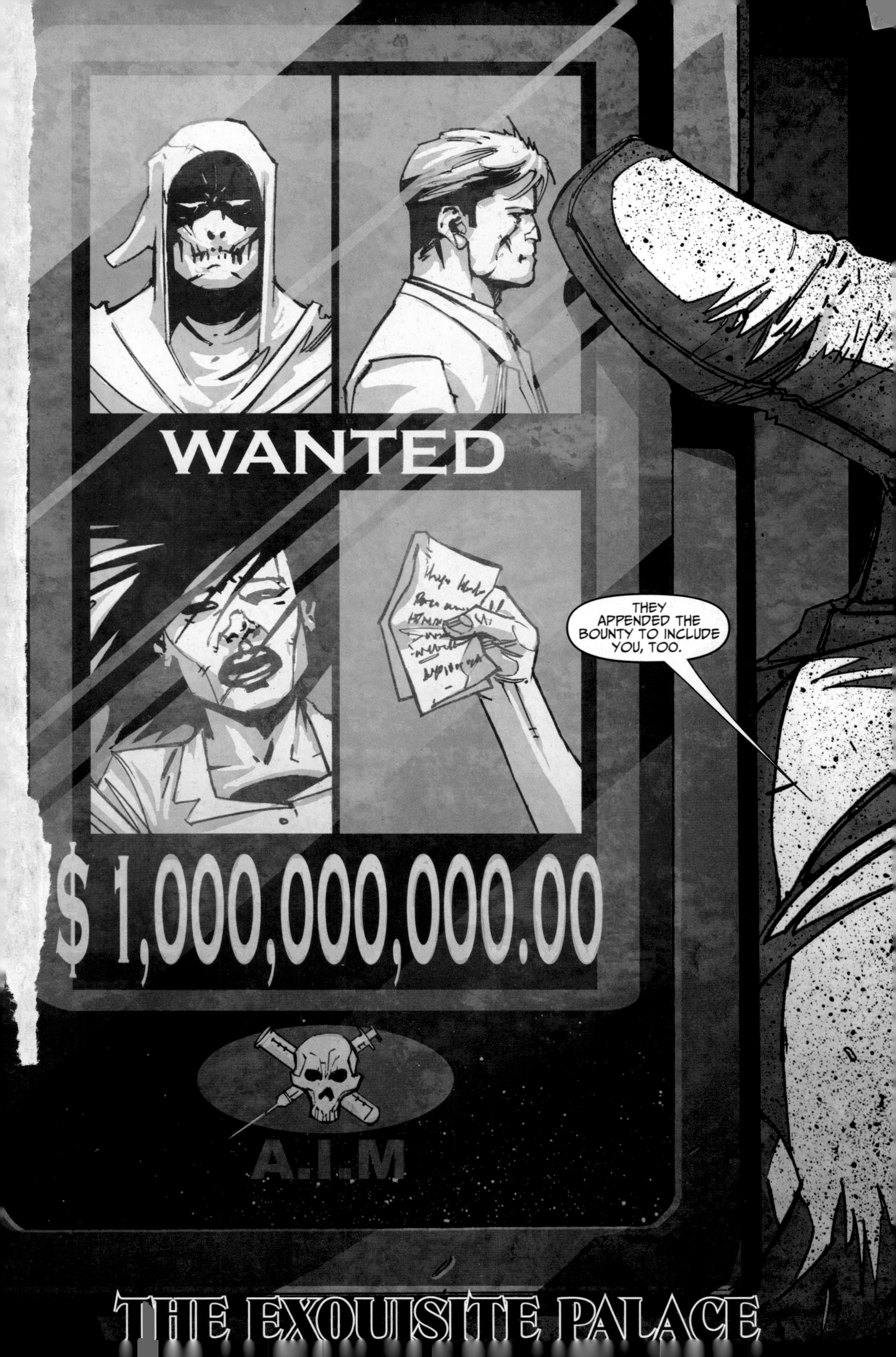
WANTED
$ 1,000,000,000.00
A.I.M
THEY APPENDED THE BOUNTY TO INCLUDE YOU, TOO.
THE EXQUISITE PALACE

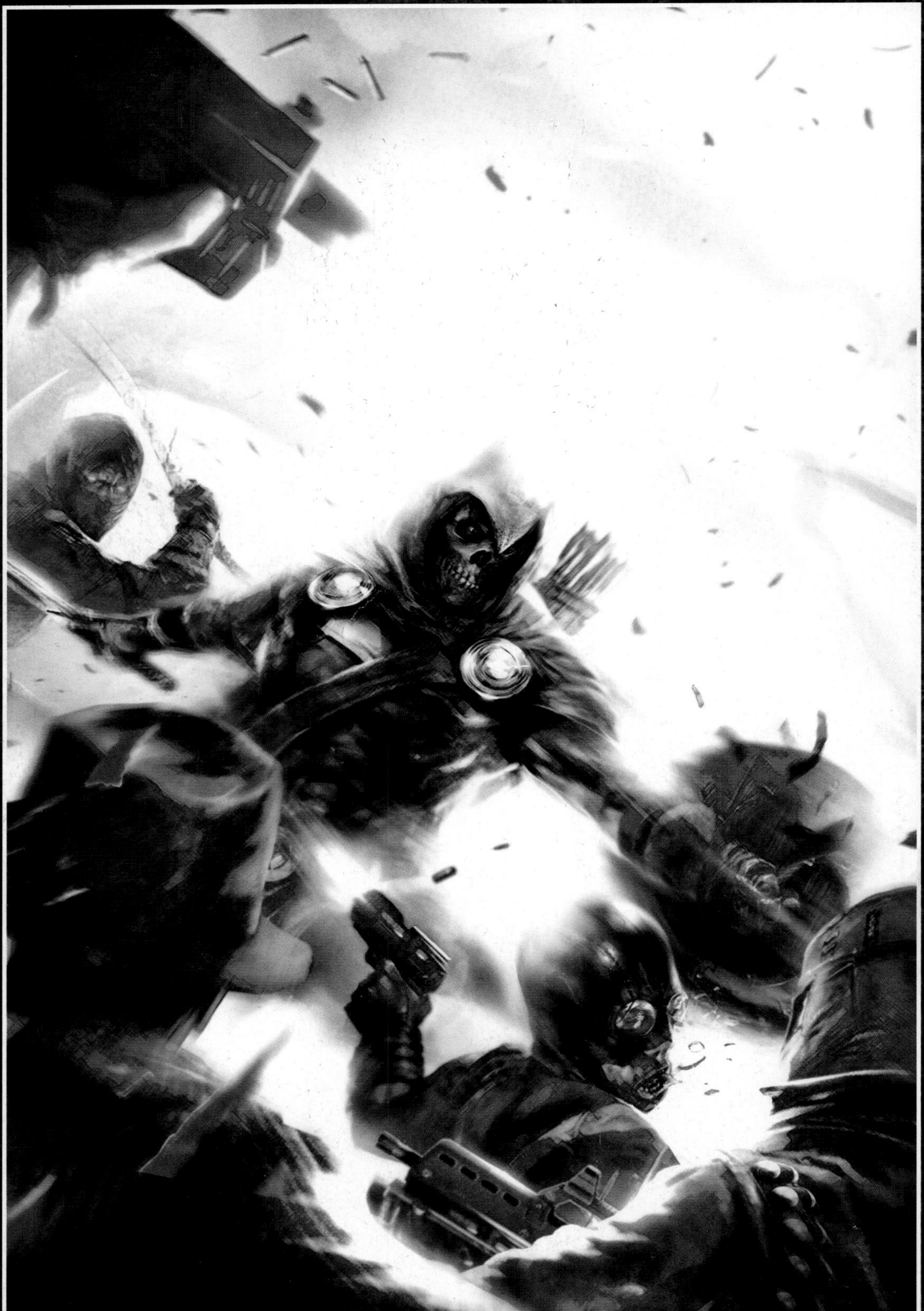

› TWO ‹

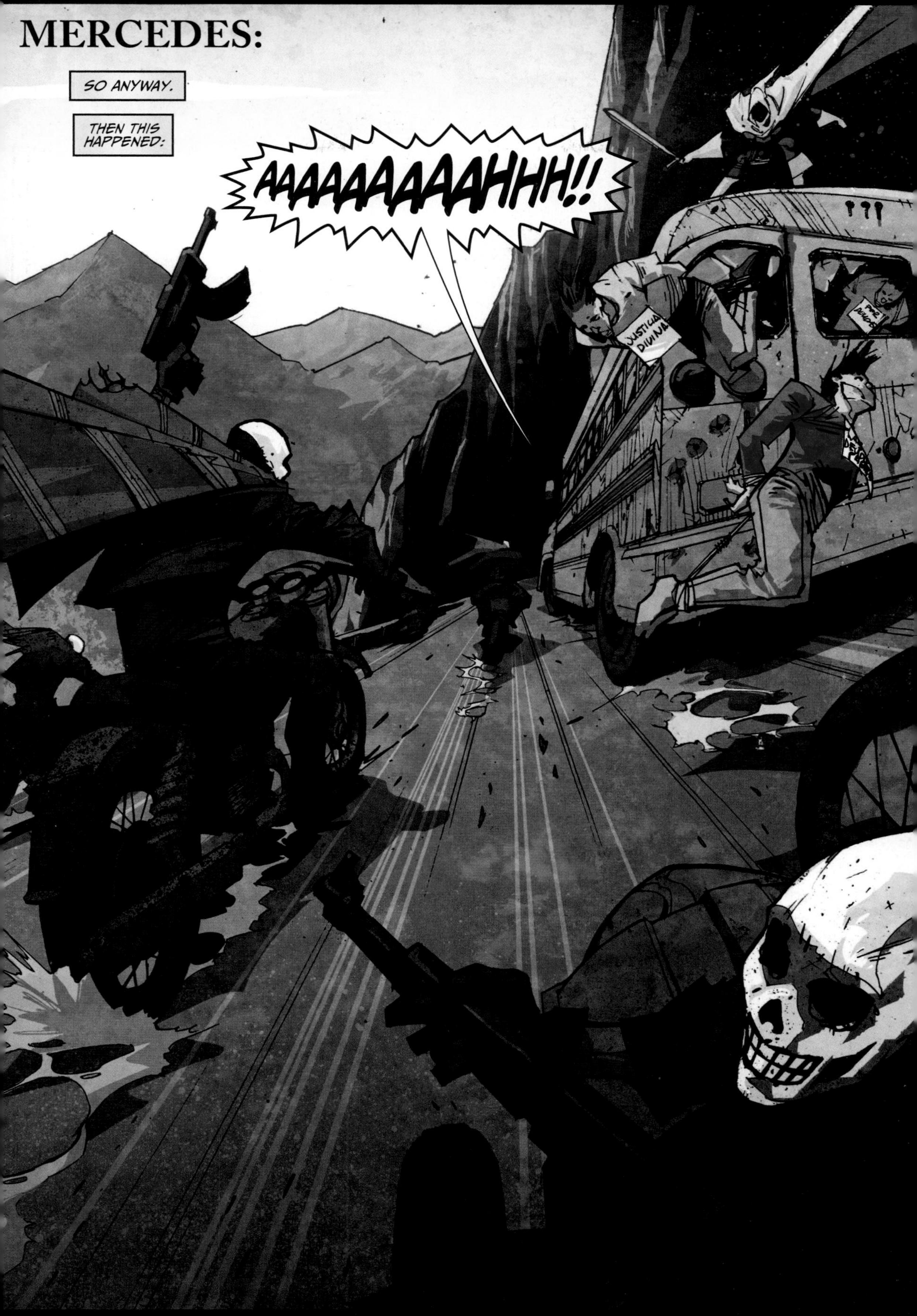
MERCEDES:
SO ANYWAY.
THEN THIS HAPPENED:
AAAAAAAAAAHHH!!
JUSTICIA DIVINA

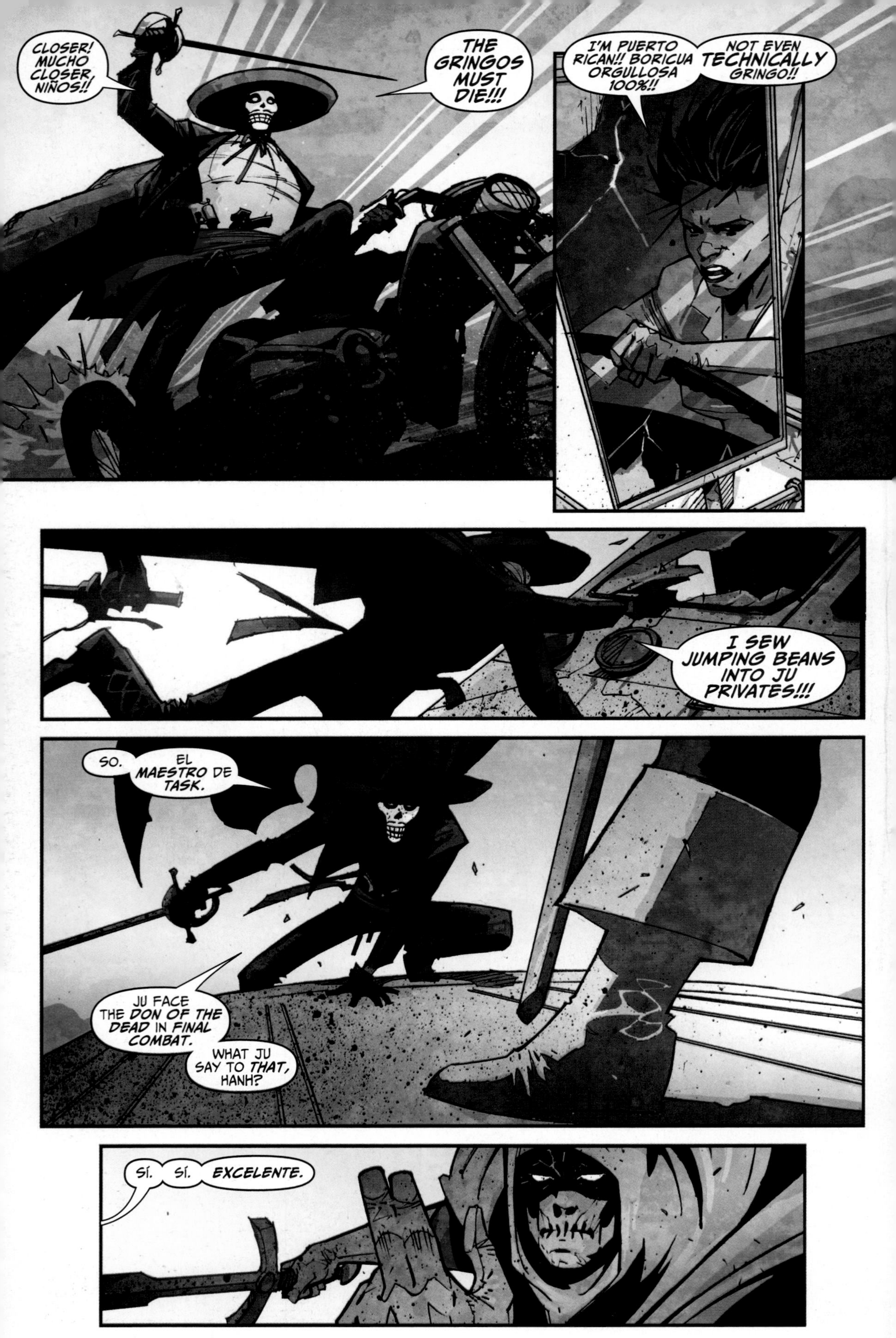
CLOSER! MUCHO CLOSER, NIÑOS!!
THE GRINGOS MUST DIE!!!
I'M PUERTO RICAN!! BORICUA ORGULLOSA 100%!!
NOT EVEN TECHNICALLY GRINGO!!
I SEW JUMPING BEANS INTO JU PRIVATES!!!
SO.
EL MAESTRO DE TASK.
JU FACE THE DON OF THE DEAD IN FINAL COMBAT.
WHAT JU SAY TO THAT, HANH?
SÍ.
SÍ.
EXCELENTE.

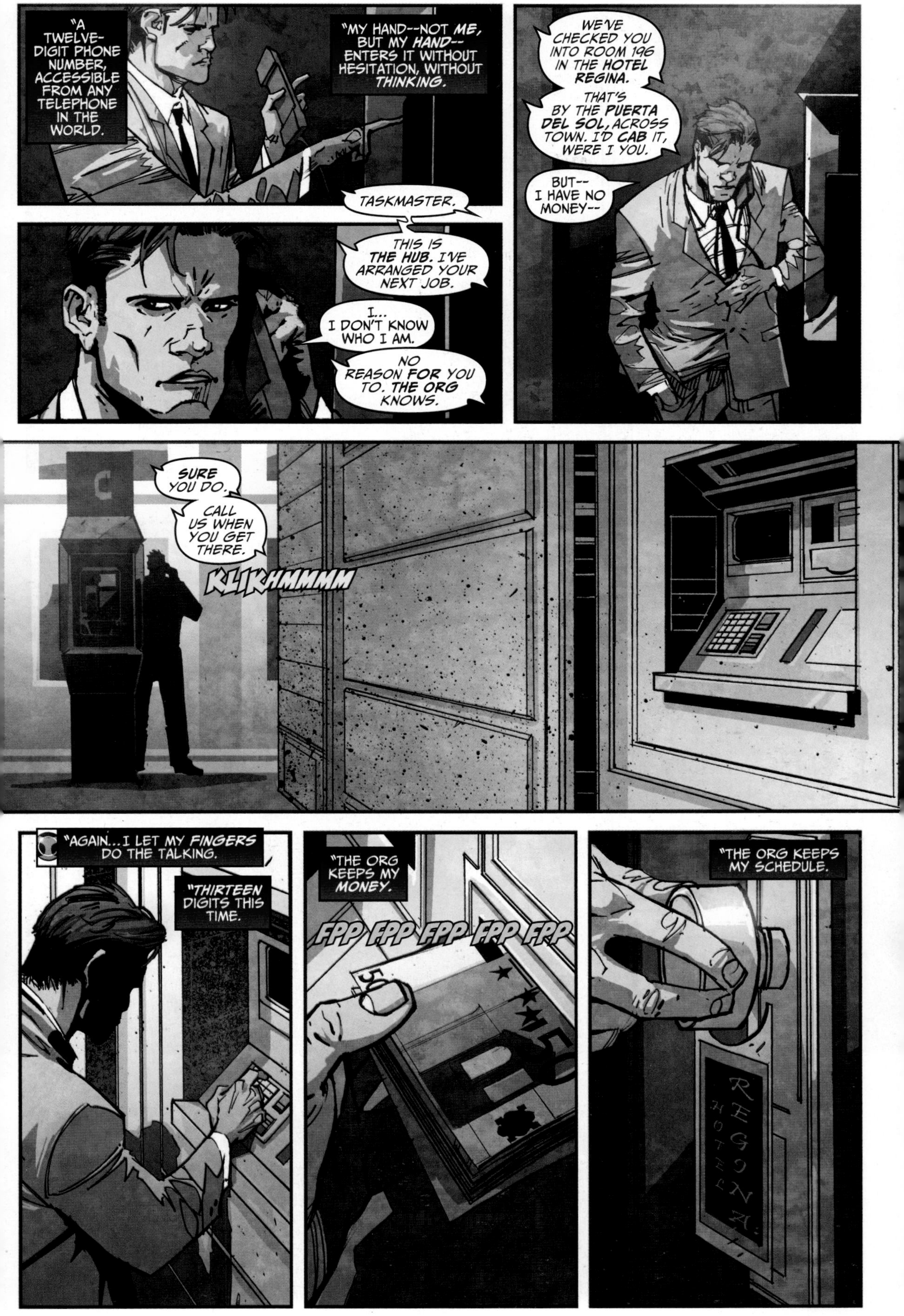

"A TWELVE-DIGIT PHONE NUMBER, ACCESSIBLE FROM ANY TELEPHONE IN THE WORLD.
"MY HAND--NOT ME, BUT MY HAND--ENTERS IT WITHOUT HESITATION, WITHOUT THINKING.
TASKMASTER.
THIS IS THE HUB. I'VE ARRANGED YOUR NEXT JOB.
I... I DON'T KNOW WHO I AM.
NO REASON FOR YOU TO. THE ORG KNOWS.
WE'VE CHECKED YOU INTO ROOM 196 IN THE HOTEL REGINA.
THAT'S BY THE PUERTA DEL SOL, ACROSS TOWN. I'D CAB IT, WERE I YOU.
BUT-- I HAVE NO MONEY--
SURE YOU DO.
CALL US WHEN YOU GET THERE.
KLIKHMMMM
"AGAIN...I LET MY FINGERS DO THE TALKING.
"THIRTEEN DIGITS THIS TIME.
"THE ORG KEEPS MY MONEY.
FPP FPP FPP FPP FPP
"THE ORG KEEPS MY SCHEDULE.
REGINA HOTEL

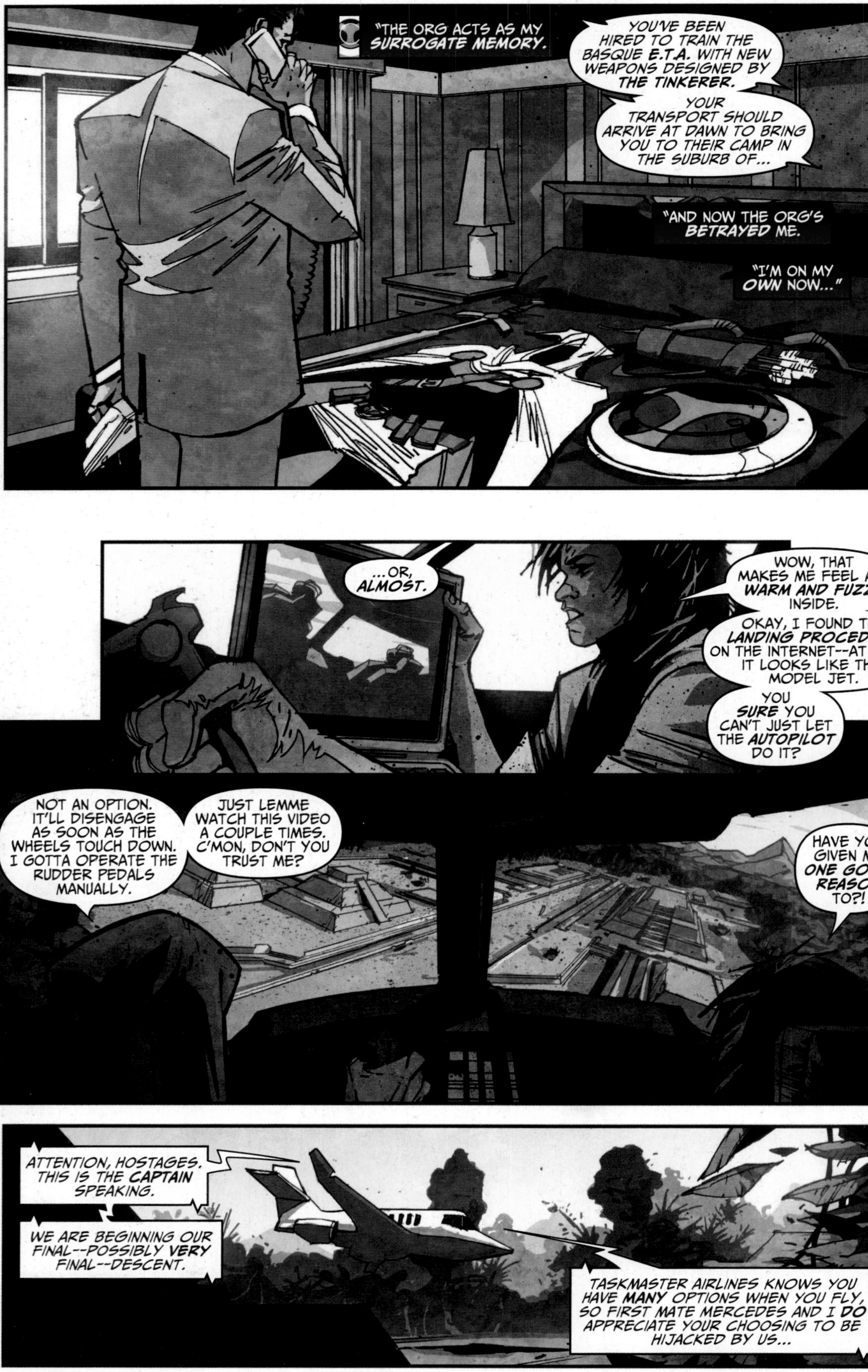
"THE ORG ACTS AS MY SURROGATE MEMORY.
YOU'VE BEEN HIRED TO TRAIN THE BASQUE E.T.A. WITH NEW WEAPONS DESIGNED BY THE TINKERER.
YOUR TRANSPORT SHOULD ARRIVE AT DAWN TO BRING YOU TO THEIR CAMP IN THE SUBURB OF...
"AND NOW THE ORG'S BETRAYED ME.
"I'M ON MY OWN NOW..."
...OR, ALMOST.
WOW, THAT MAKES ME FEEL ALL WARM AND FUZZY INSIDE.
OKAY, I FOUND THE LANDING PROCEDURE ON THE INTERNET--AT LEAS IT LOOKS LIKE THIS MODEL JET.
YOU SURE YOU CAN'T JUST LET THE AUTOPILOT DO IT?
NOT AN OPTION. IT'LL DISENGAGE AS SOON AS THE WHEELS TOUCH DOWN. I GOTTA OPERATE THE RUDDER PEDALS MANUALLY.
JUST LEMME WATCH THIS VIDEO A COUPLE TIMES. C'MON, DON'T YOU TRUST ME?
HAVE YOU GIVEN ME ONE GOOD REASON TO?!
ATTENTION, HOSTAGES. THIS IS THE CAPTAIN SPEAKING.
WE ARE BEGINNING OUR FINAL--POSSIBLY VERY FINAL--DESCENT.
TASKMASTER AIRLINES KNOWS YOU HAVE MANY OPTIONS WHEN YOU FLY, SO FIRST MATE MERCEDES AND I DO APPRECIATE YOUR CHOOSING TO BE HIJACKED BY US...

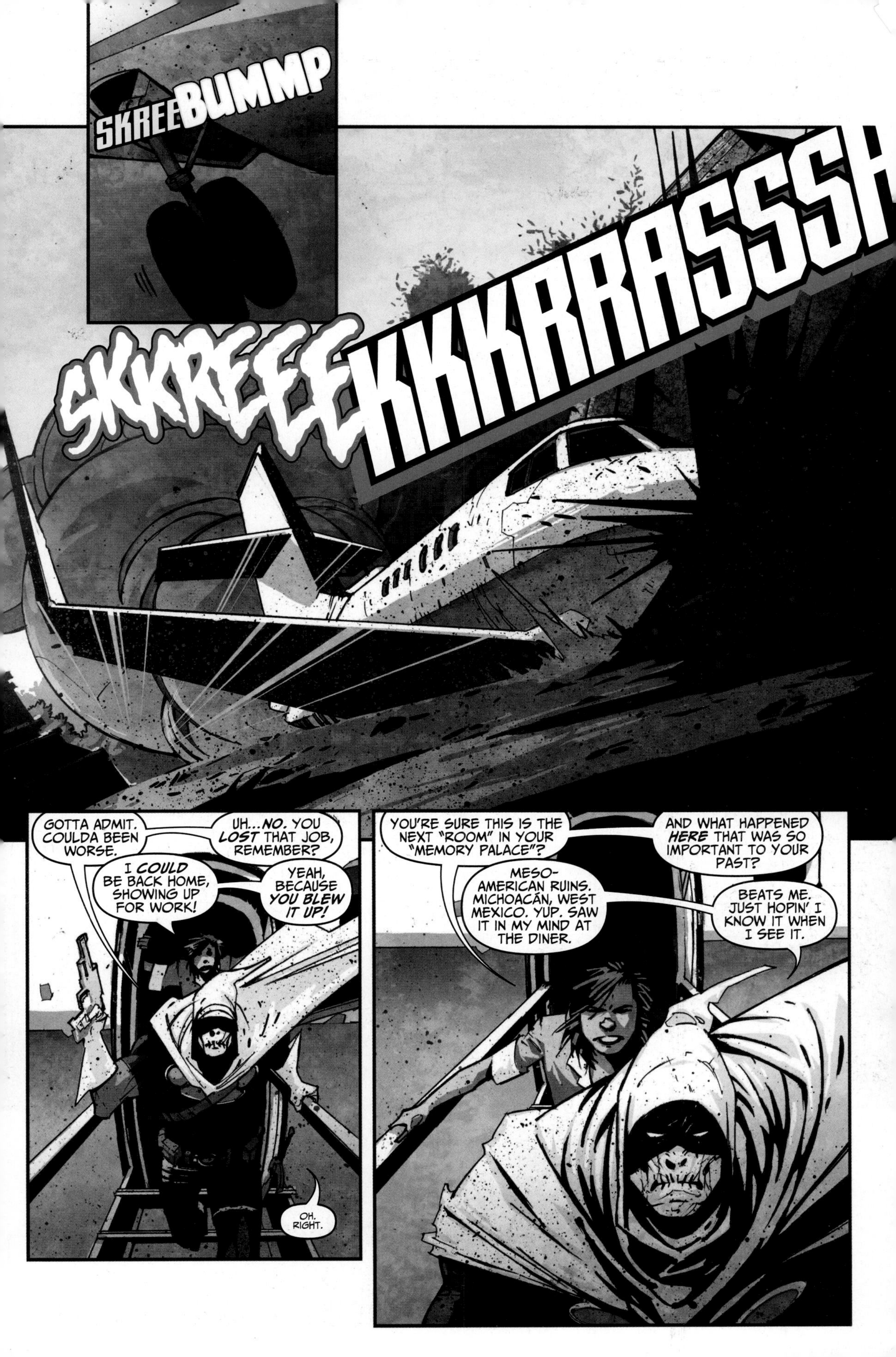
SKREE BUMMP
SKREEEE KKKRRASSSH
GOTTA ADMIT. COULDA BEEN WORSE.
UH...NO. YOU LOST THAT JOB, REMEMBER?
I COULD BE BACK HOME, SHOWING UP FOR WORK!
YEAH, BECAUSE YOU BLEW IT UP!
OH. RIGHT.
YOU'RE SURE THIS IS THE NEXT "ROOM" IN YOUR "MEMORY PALACE"?
MESO-AMERICAN RUINS. MICHOACÁN, WEST MEXICO. YUP. SAW IT IN MY MIND AT THE DINER.
AND WHAT HAPPENED HERE THAT WAS SO IMPORTANT TO YOUR PAST?
BEATS ME. JUST HOPIN' I KNOW IT WHEN I SEE IT.

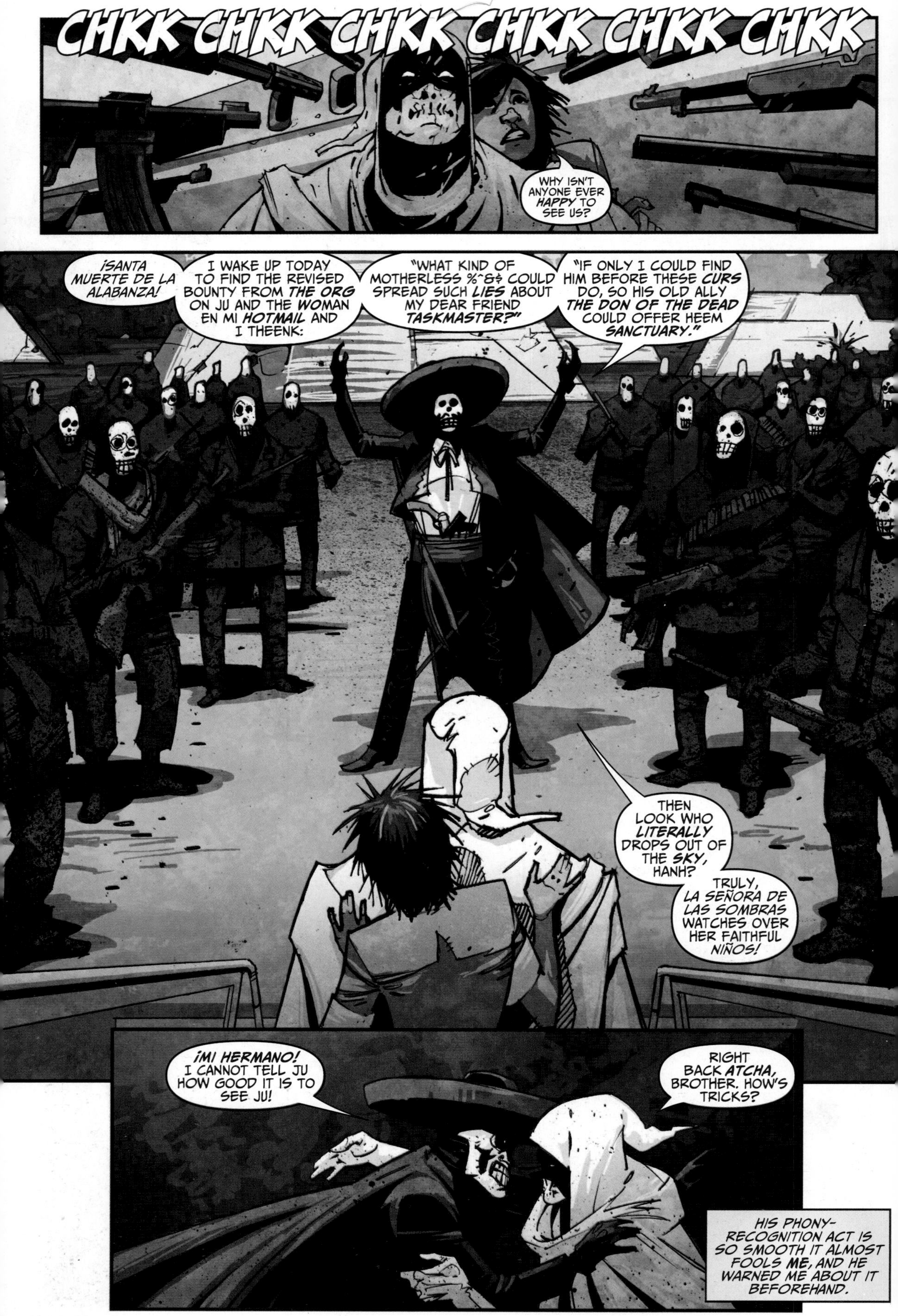
CHKK CHKK CHKK CHKK CHKK CHKK
WHY ISN'T ANYONE EVER *HAPPY* TO SEE US?
¡SANTA MUERTE DE LA ALABANZA!
I WAKE UP TODAY TO FIND THE REVISED BOUNTY FROM *THE ORG* ON JU AND THE *WOMAN* EN MI *HOTMAIL* AND I THEENK:
"WHAT KIND OF MOTHERLESS %^&$ COULD SPREAD SUCH *LIES* ABOUT MY DEAR FRIEND *TASKMASTER?"*
"IF ONLY I COULD FIND HIM BEFORE THESE *CURS* DO, SO HIS OLD ALLY *THE DON OF THE DEAD* COULD OFFER HEEM *SANCTUARY."*
THEN LOOK WHO *LITERALLY* DROPS OUT OF THE *SKY*, HANH?
TRULY, *LA SEÑORA DE LAS SOMBRAS* WATCHES OVER HER FAITHFUL *NIÑOS!*
¡MI HERMANO! I CANNOT TELL JU HOW GOOD IT IS TO SEE JU!
RIGHT BACK *ATCHA*, BROTHER. HOW'S TRICKS?
*HIS PHONY-RECOGNITION ACT IS SO SMOOTH IT ALMOST FOOLS **ME**, AND HE WARNED ME ABOUT IT BEFOREHAND.*

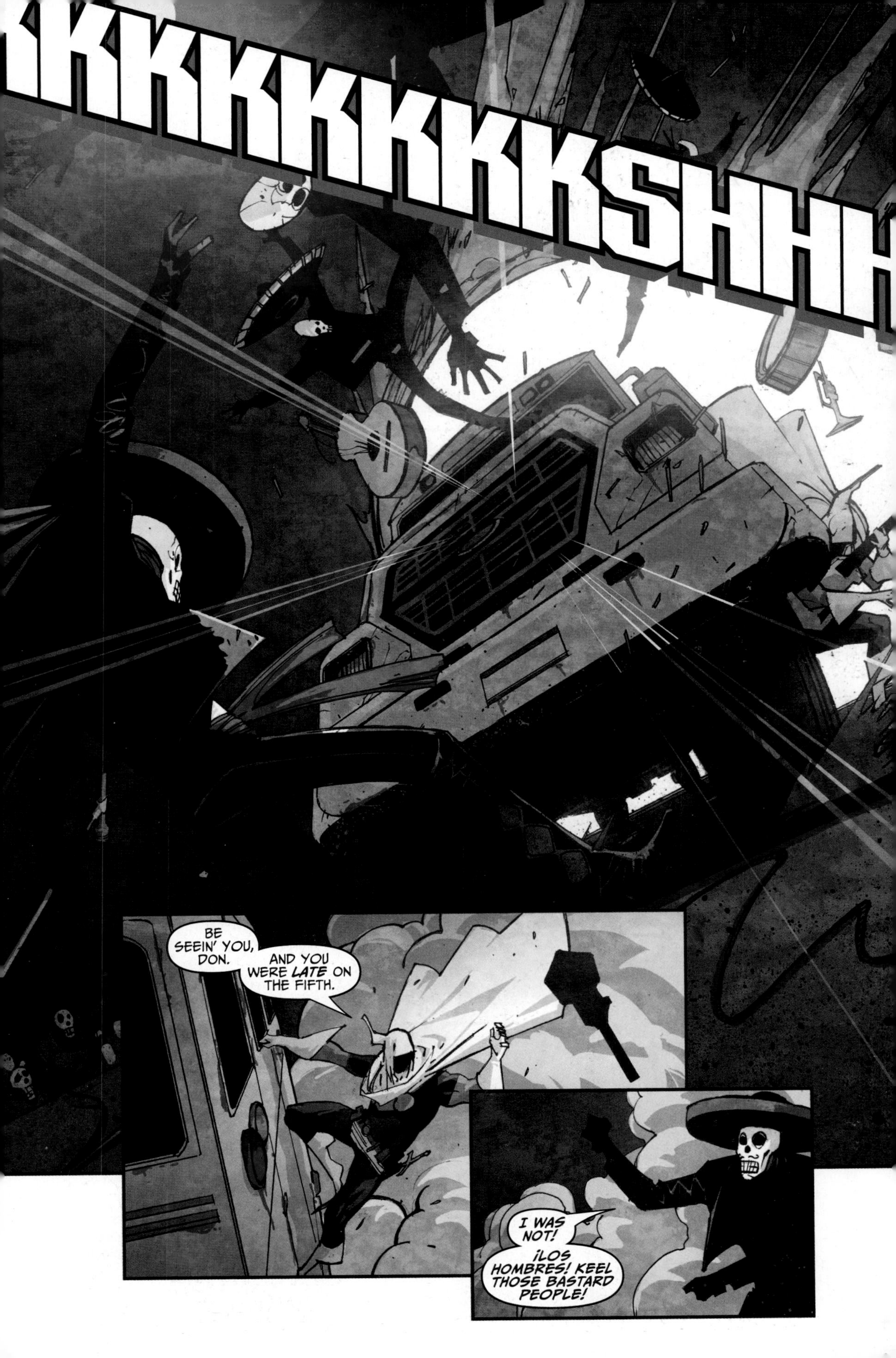
KKKKKKKKKSHHH
BE SEEIN' YOU, DON.
AND YOU WERE *LATE* ON THE FIFTH.
I WAS NOT!
¡LOS HOMBRES! KEEL THOSE BASTARD PEOPLE!

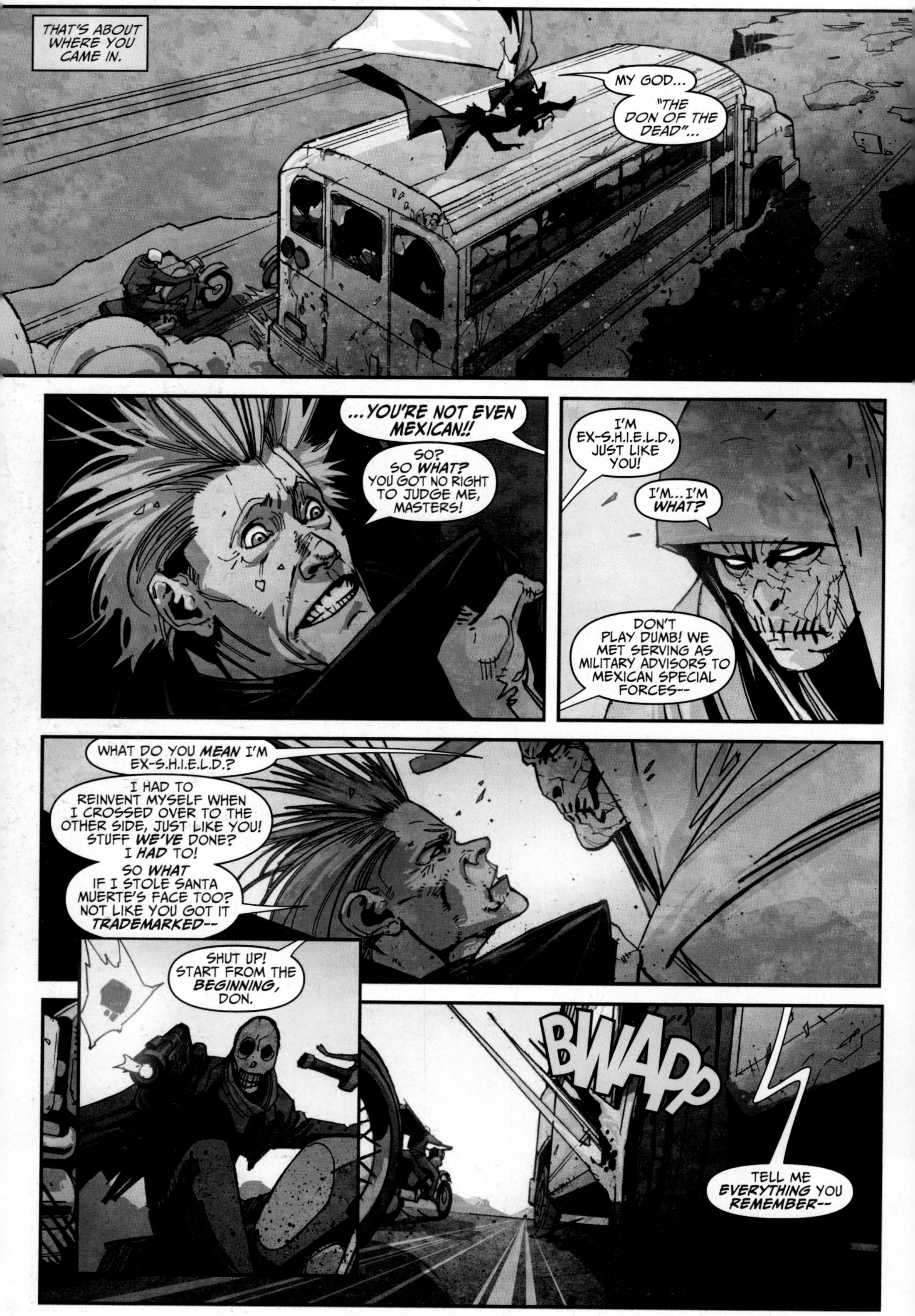
THAT'S ABOUT WHERE YOU CAME IN.
MY GOD... "THE DON OF THE DEAD"...
...YOU'RE NOT EVEN MEXICAN!!
SO? SO WHAT? YOU GOT NO RIGHT TO JUDGE ME, MASTERS!
I'M EX-S.H.I.E.L.D., JUST LIKE YOU!
I'M...I'M WHAT?
DON'T PLAY DUMB! WE MET SERVING AS MILITARY ADVISORS TO MEXICAN SPECIAL FORCES--
WHAT DO YOU MEAN I'M EX-S.H.I.E.L.D.?
I HAD TO REINVENT MYSELF WHEN I CROSSED OVER TO THE OTHER SIDE, JUST LIKE YOU! STUFF WE'VE DONE? I HAD TO!
SO WHAT IF I STOLE SANTA MUERTE'S FACE TOO? NOT LIKE YOU GOT IT TRADEMARKED--
SHUT UP! START FROM THE BEGINNING, DON.
BWAPP
TELL ME EVERYTHING YOU REMEMBER--

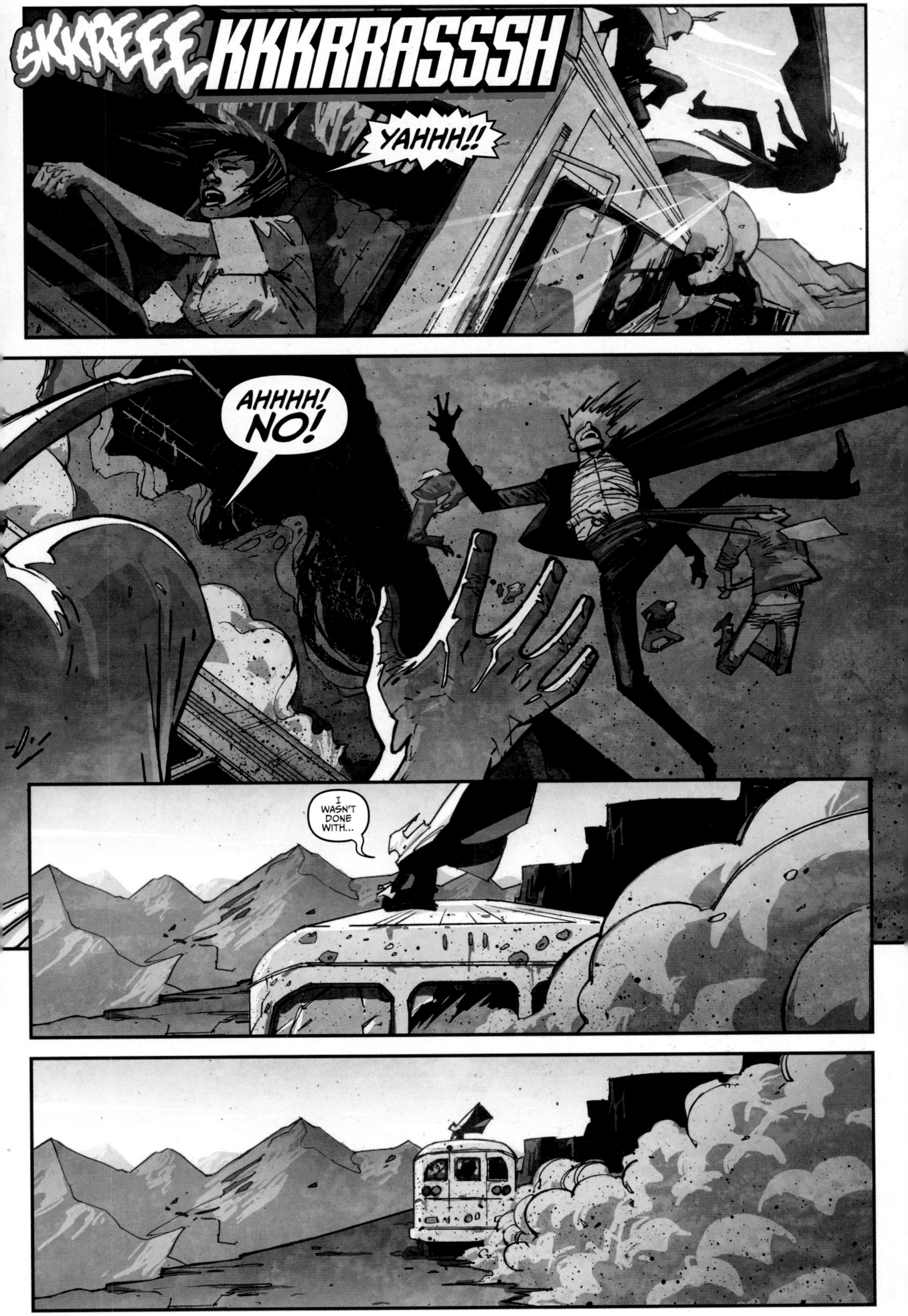
SKKREEE
KKKRRASSSH
YAHHH!!
AHHHH! NO!
I WASN'T DONE WITH...

BOLIVIA. THE ANDES.

THAT'S THE NEXT "ROOM" IN MY "PALACE." I SAW IT IN MY MIND'S EYE IN THE SANTA MUERTE TEMPLE.

THAT SHIP THERE IS BOUND FOR CARACAS. WE'LL GO OVERLAND FROM THERE.

ALL RIGHT.

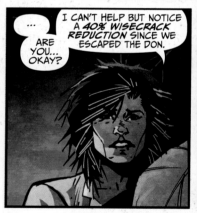

...

ARE YOU... OKAY?

I CAN'T HELP BUT NOTICE A *40% WISECRACK REDUCTION* SINCE WE ESCAPED THE DON.

JUST... IT'S JUST SINKING IN.

WHAT IS?

I'VE WONDERED... WHEN I HAVE THESE *BLACKOUTS*, LIKE I WAS TELLING YOU ABOUT.

IT NEVER OCCURS TO ME TO CHECK MYSELF INTO A *HOSPITAL*.

I NEVER GO TO THE *COPS*.

LIKE... INSTINCTUALLY... I *KNOW*...I'M *GUILTY* OF *SOMETHING*. AND NOT JUST THE USUAL STUFF, FROM MY JOB. THE GUYS I TRAIN. SOMETHING *SPECIFIC*. SOMETHING *BIG*.

I THINK... I'M GONNA *FIND OUT*, ON THIS TRIP, WHAT THAT *IS*.

AND I DON'T KNOW IF I CAN *HANDLE* IT.

THE DON-- SAID YOU WERE EX-*S.H.I.E.L.D.*

MEANS YOU WERE A *GOOD GUY* ONCE.

MAYBE... I DON'T KNOW.

MAYBE IT'S NOT TOO LATE TO CHANGE *BACK* AGAIN.

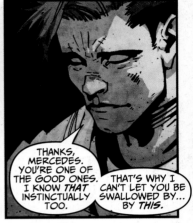

THANKS, MERCEDES. YOU'RE ONE OF THE GOOD ONES. I KNOW *THAT* INSTINCTUALLY TOO.

THAT'S WHY I CAN'T LET YOU BE SWALLOWED BY... BY *THIS.*

BUT ME? DIFFERENT STORY.

I CAN CHANGE ALLEGIANCE AS MANY TIMES AS I *WANT.*

IF I ALWAYS REVERT BACK TO *DEFAULT FACTORY SETTINGS,* IT DON'T MEAN *SQUAT.*

WAIT HERE.

GONNA TAKE OUT THOSE GUARDS, THEN WE CAN STOW ABOARD.

INSTINCTS.

WE'RE GOING INTO THE ANDES NEXT. *CASTLE GORSCHT.*

HE'S ON THE BRINK OF REMEMBERING EVERYTHING.

IT'S GOOD TO HAVE INSTINCTS.

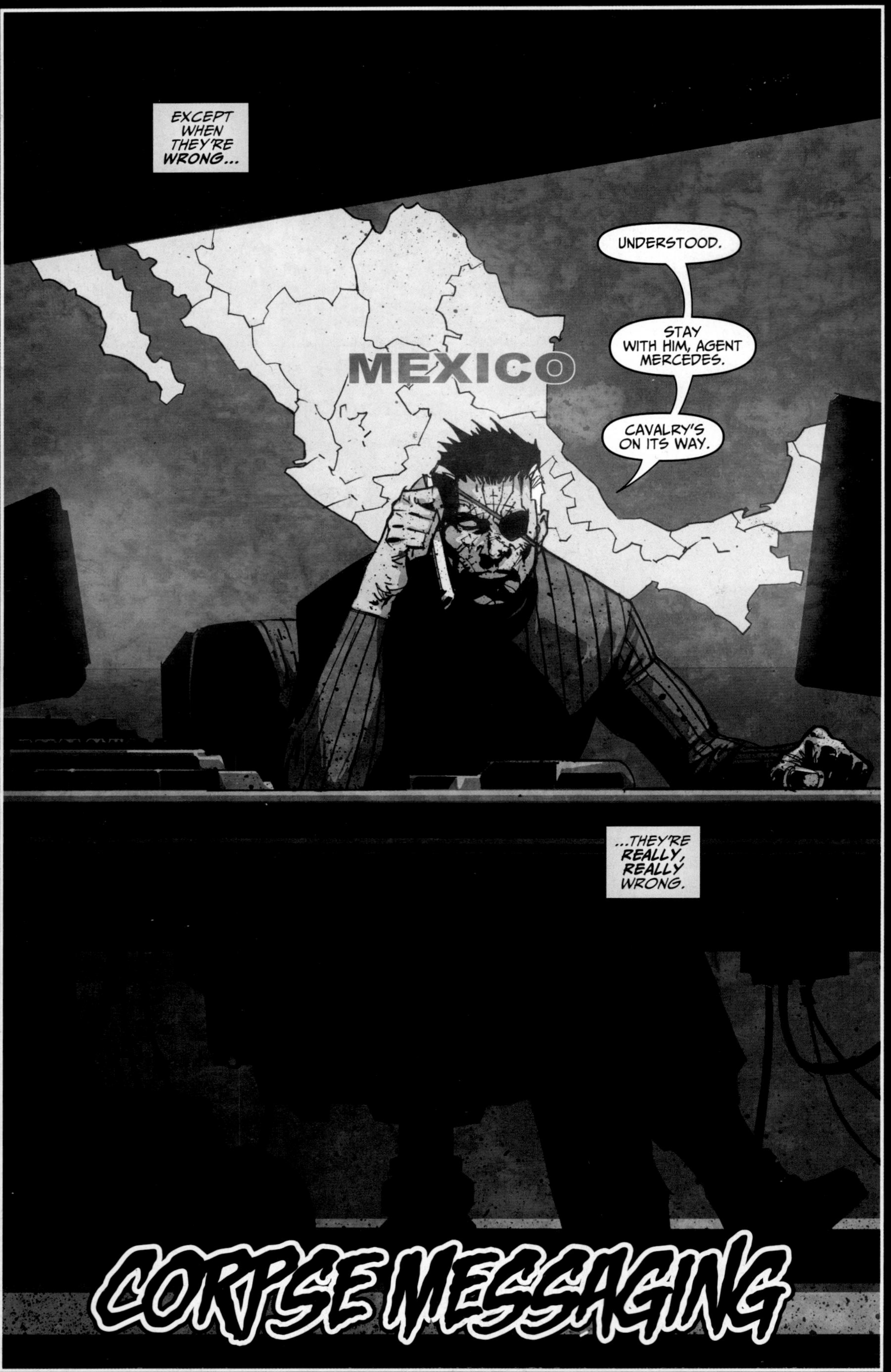
EXCEPT WHEN THEY'RE WRONG...
MEXICO
UNDERSTOOD.
STAY WITH HIM, AGENT MERCEDES.
CAVALRY'S ON ITS WAY.
...THEY'RE REALLY, REALLY WRONG.
CORPSE MESSAGING

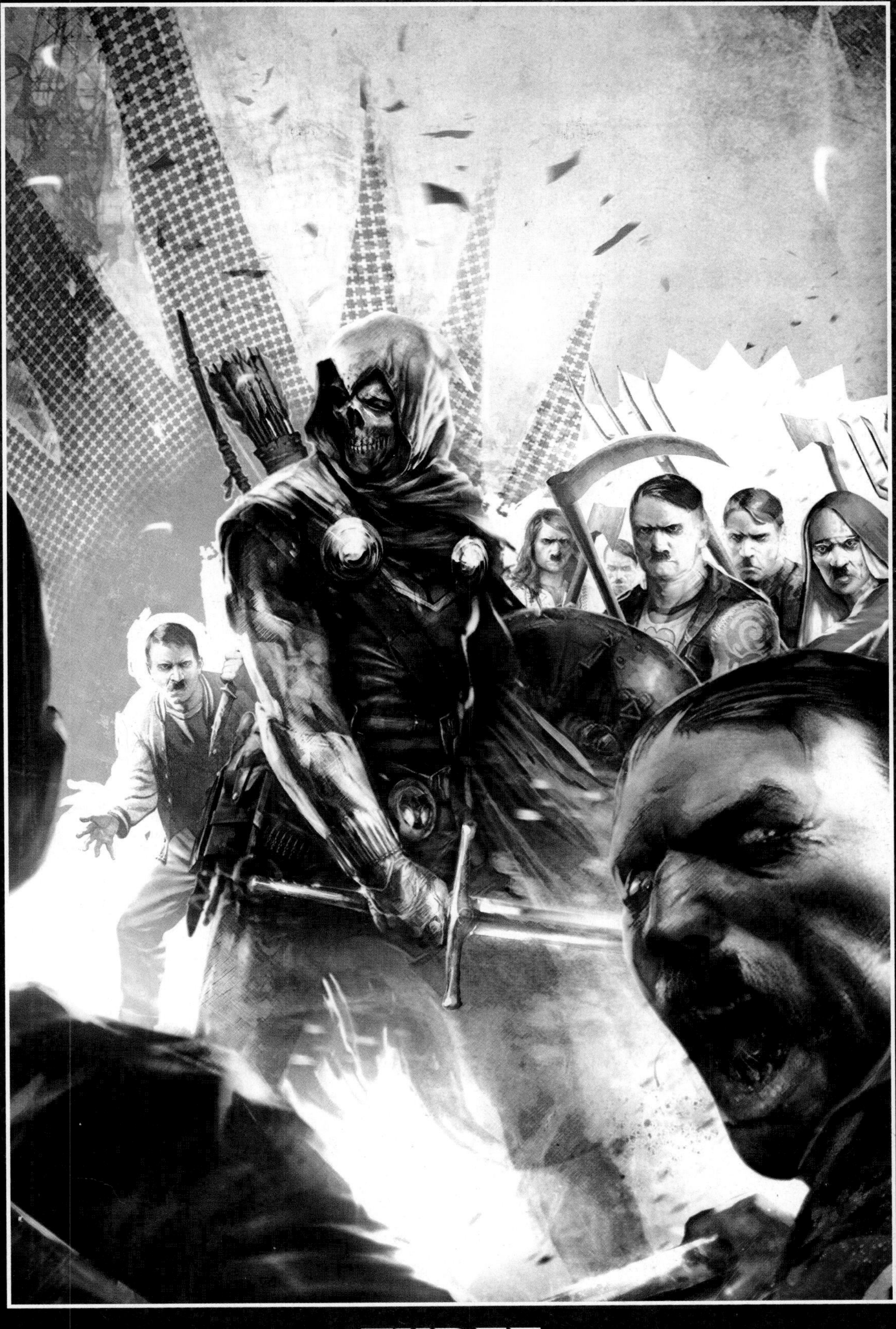

› THREE ‹

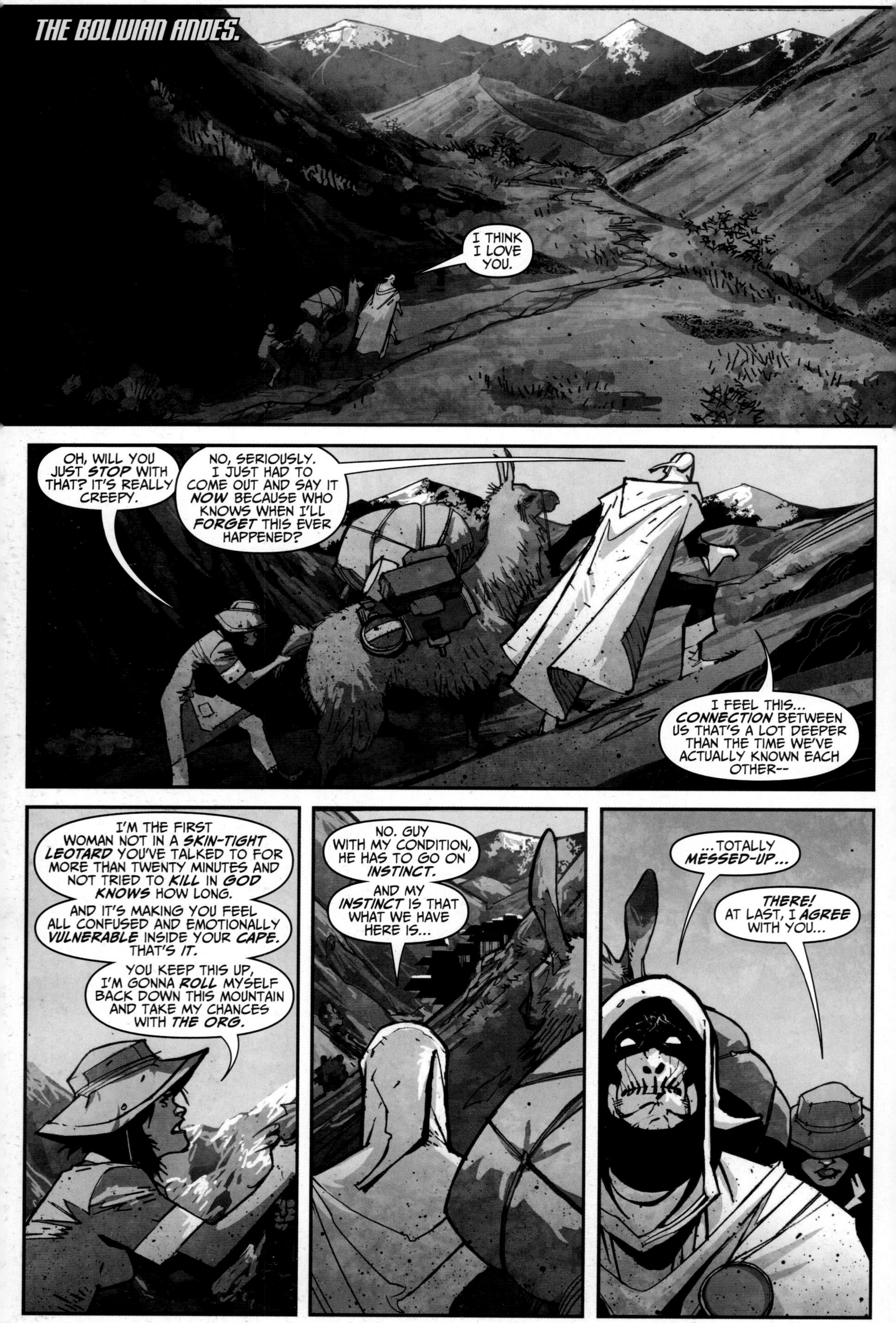
THE BOLIVIAN ANDES.
I THINK I LOVE YOU.
OH, WILL YOU JUST STOP WITH THAT? IT'S REALLY CREEPY.
NO, SERIOUSLY. I JUST HAD TO COME OUT AND SAY IT NOW BECAUSE WHO KNOWS WHEN I'LL FORGET THIS EVER HAPPENED?
I FEEL THIS... CONNECTION BETWEEN US THAT'S A LOT DEEPER THAN THE TIME WE'VE ACTUALLY KNOWN EACH OTHER--
I'M THE FIRST WOMAN NOT IN A SKIN-TIGHT LEOTARD YOU'VE TALKED TO FOR MORE THAN TWENTY MINUTES AND NOT TRIED TO KILL IN GOD KNOWS HOW LONG.
AND IT'S MAKING YOU FEEL ALL CONFUSED AND EMOTIONALLY VULNERABLE INSIDE YOUR CAPE. THAT'S IT.
YOU KEEP THIS UP, I'M GONNA ROLL MYSELF BACK DOWN THIS MOUNTAIN AND TAKE MY CHANCES WITH THE ORG.
NO. GUY WITH MY CONDITION, HE HAS TO GO ON INSTINCT.
AND MY INSTINCT IS THAT WHAT WE HAVE HERE IS...
...TOTALLY MESSED-UP...
THERE! AT LAST, I AGREE WITH YOU...

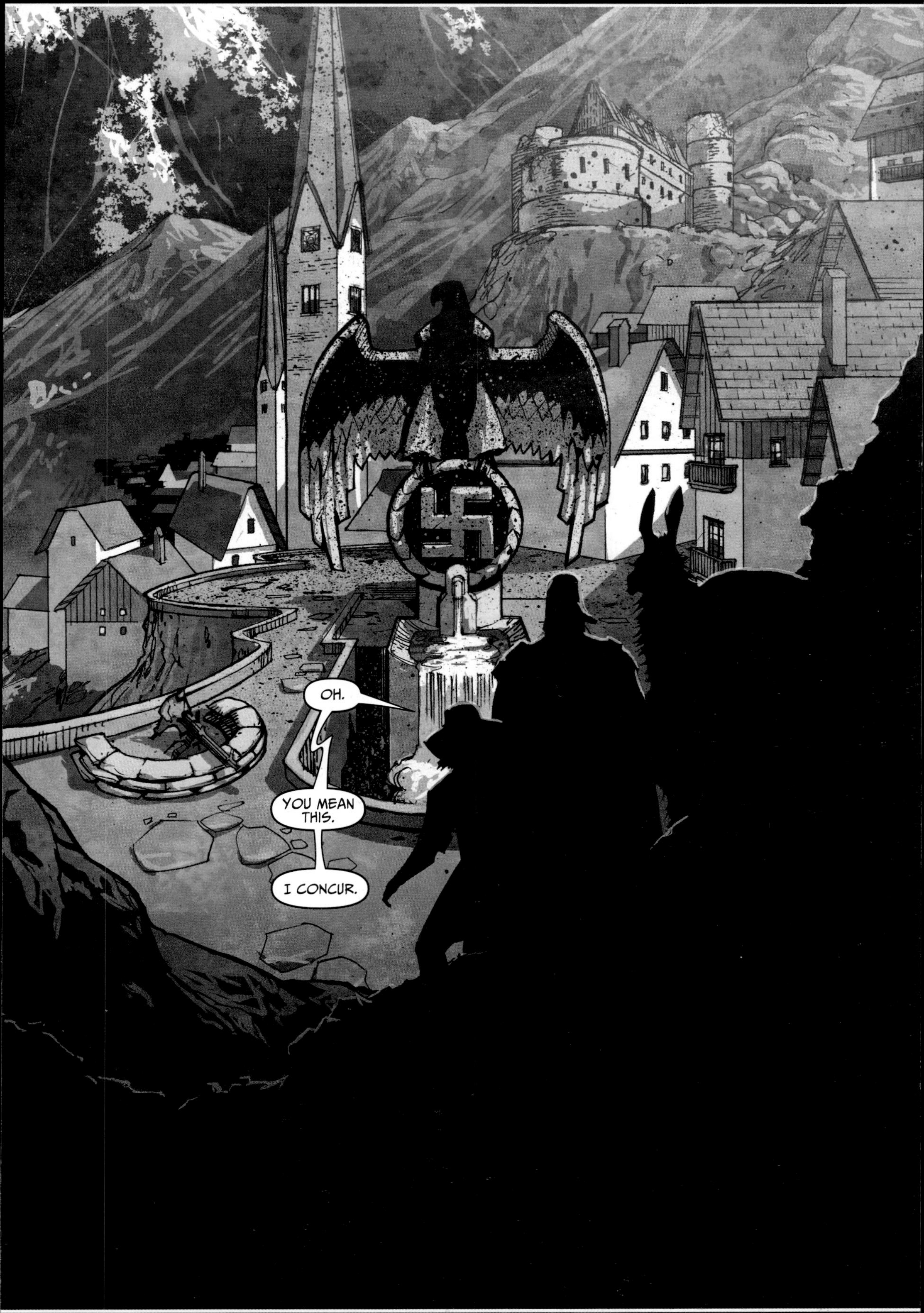
OH.
YOU MEAN THIS.
I CONCUR.

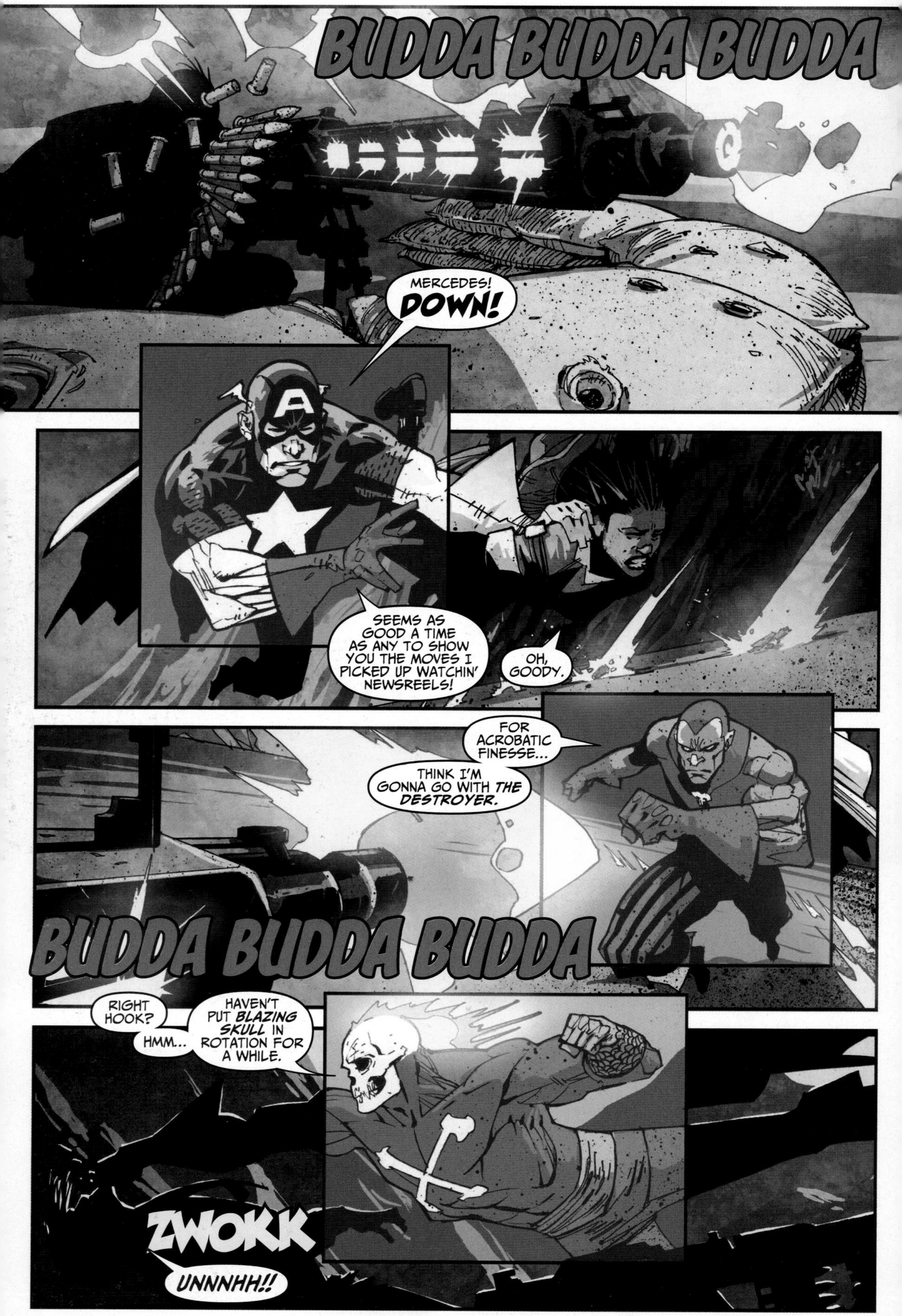
BUDDA BUDDA BUDDA
MERCEDES! DOWN!
SEEMS AS GOOD A TIME AS ANY TO SHOW YOU THE MOVES I PICKED UP WATCHIN' NEWSREELS!
OH, GOODY.
FOR ACROBATIC FINESSE...
THINK I'M GONNA GO WITH THE DESTROYER.
BUDDA BUDDA BUDDA
RIGHT HOOK?
HMM...
HAVEN'T PUT BLAZING SKULL IN ROTATION FOR A WHILE.
ZWOKK
UNNNHH!!

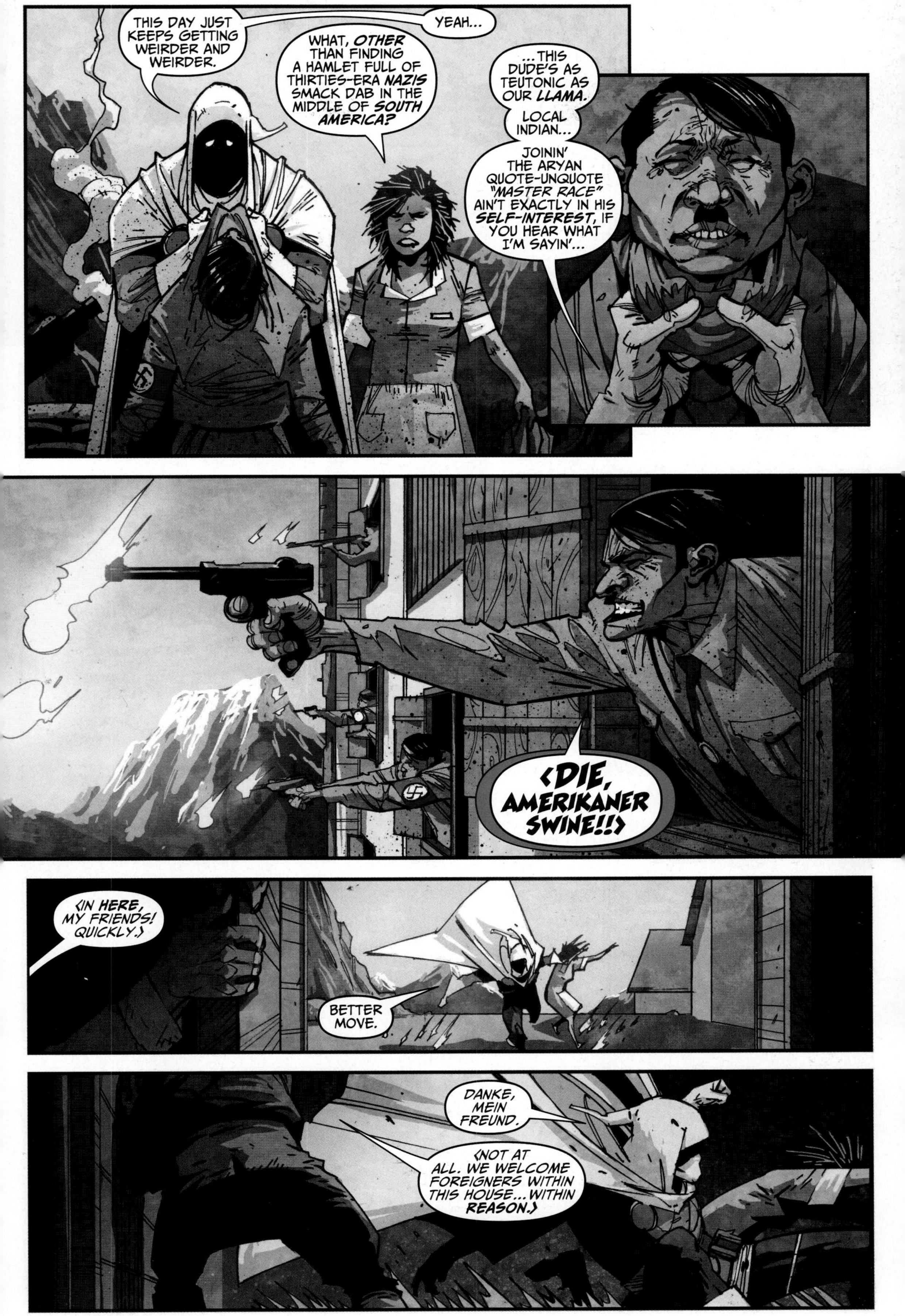
THIS DAY JUST KEEPS GETTING WEIRDER AND WEIRDER.
YEAH...
WHAT, *OTHER* THAN FINDING A HAMLET FULL OF THIRTIES-ERA *NAZIS* SMACK DAB IN THE MIDDLE OF *SOUTH AMERICA?*
...THIS DUDE'S AS TEUTONIC AS OUR *LLAMA*.
LOCAL INDIAN...
JOININ' THE ARYAN QUOTE-UNQUOTE *"MASTER RACE"* AIN'T EXACTLY IN HIS *SELF-INTEREST*, IF YOU HEAR WHAT I'M SAYIN'...
‹DIE, AMERIKANER SWINE!!›
‹IN HERE, MY FRIENDS! QUICKLY.›
BETTER MOVE.
DANKE, MEIN FREUND.
‹NOT AT ALL. WE WELCOME FOREIGNERS WITHIN THIS HOUSE...WITHIN *REASON*.›

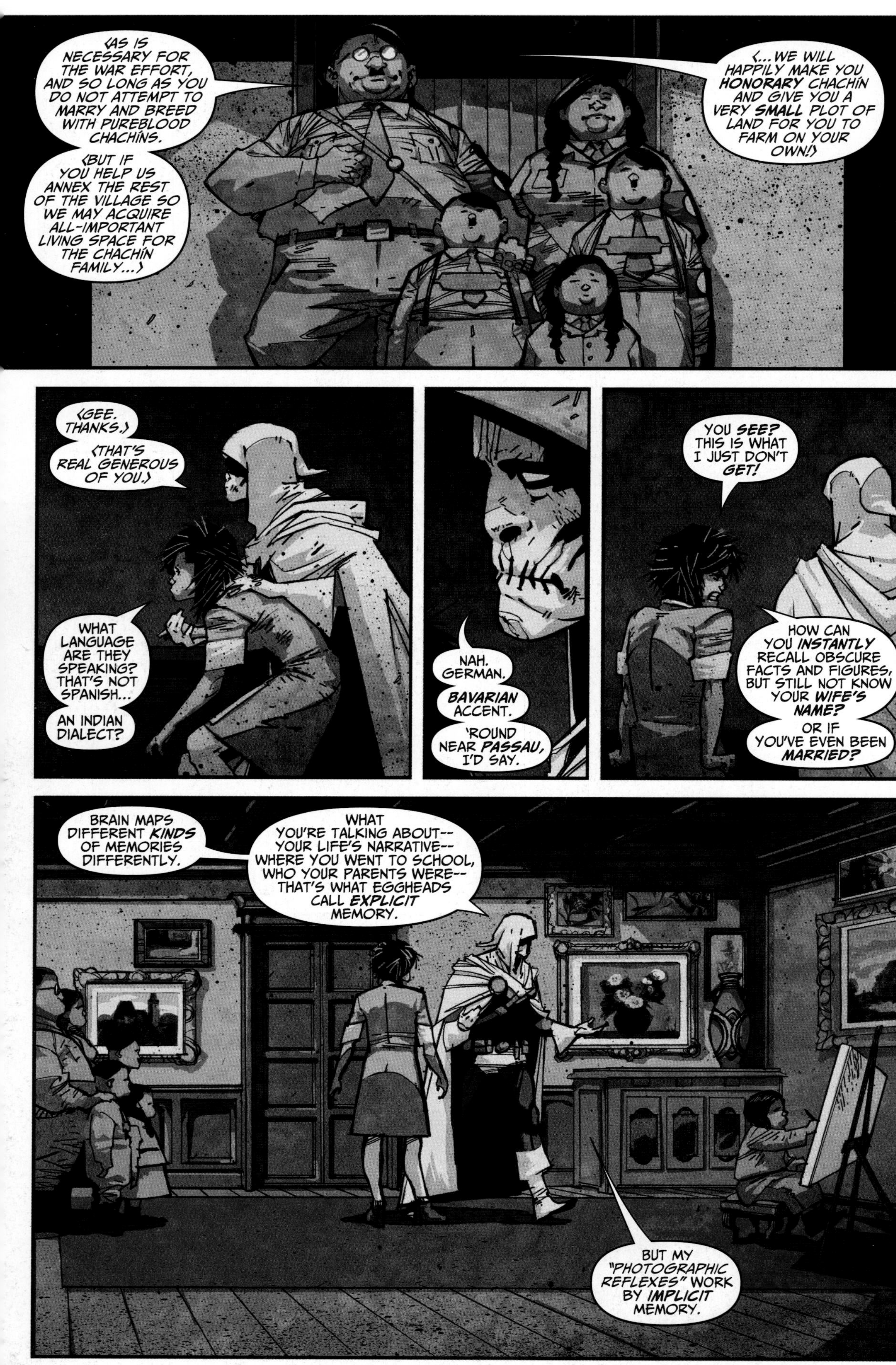
‹AS IS NECESSARY FOR THE WAR EFFORT, AND SO LONG AS YOU DO NOT ATTEMPT TO MARRY AND BREED WITH PUREBLOOD CHACHÍNS.
‹BUT IF YOU HELP US ANNEX THE REST OF THE VILLAGE SO WE MAY ACQUIRE ALL-IMPORTANT LIVING SPACE FOR THE CHACHÍN FAMILY...›
‹...WE WILL HAPPILY MAKE YOU HONORARY CHACHÍN AND GIVE YOU A VERY SMALL PLOT OF LAND FOR YOU TO FARM ON YOUR OWN!›
‹GEE. THANKS.›
‹THAT'S REAL GENEROUS OF YOU.›
WHAT LANGUAGE ARE THEY SPEAKING? THAT'S NOT SPANISH...
AN INDIAN DIALECT?
NAH. GERMAN.
BAVARIAN ACCENT.
'ROUND NEAR PASSAU, I'D SAY.
YOU SEE? THIS IS WHAT I JUST DON'T GET!
HOW CAN YOU INSTANTLY RECALL OBSCURE FACTS AND FIGURES, BUT STILL NOT KNOW YOUR WIFE'S NAME?
OR IF YOU'VE EVEN BEEN MARRIED?
BRAIN MAPS DIFFERENT KINDS OF MEMORIES DIFFERENTLY.
WHAT YOU'RE TALKING ABOUT-- YOUR LIFE'S NARRATIVE-- WHERE YOU WENT TO SCHOOL, WHO YOUR PARENTS WERE-- THAT'S WHAT EGGHEADS CALL EXPLICIT MEMORY.
BUT MY "PHOTOGRAPHIC REFLEXES" WORK BY IMPLICIT MEMORY.

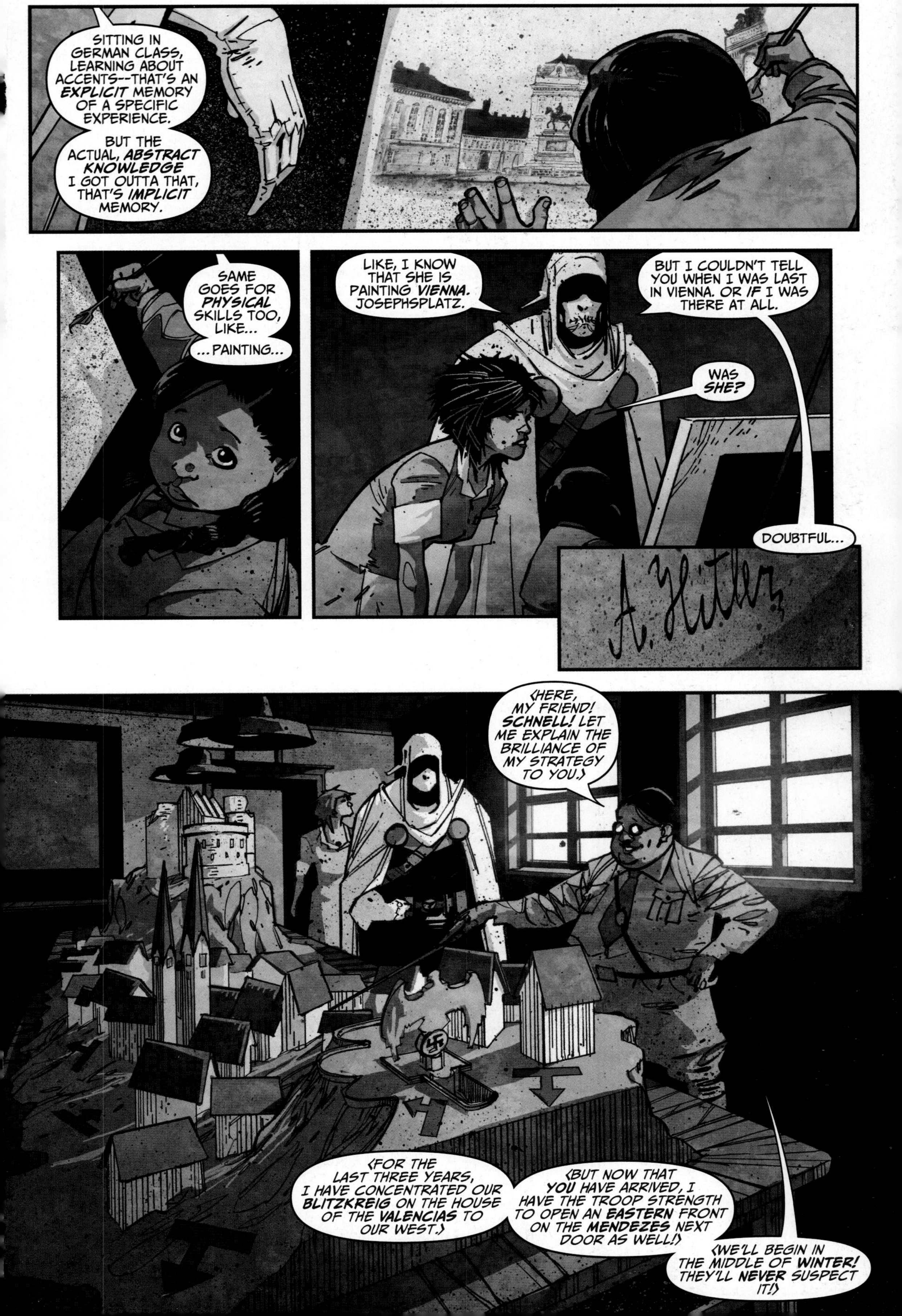
SITTING IN GERMAN CLASS, LEARNING ABOUT ACCENTS--THAT'S AN EXPLICIT MEMORY OF A SPECIFIC EXPERIENCE.
BUT THE ACTUAL, ABSTRACT KNOWLEDGE I GOT OUTTA THAT, THAT'S IMPLICIT MEMORY.
SAME GOES FOR PHYSICAL SKILLS TOO, LIKE...
...PAINTING...
LIKE, I KNOW THAT SHE IS PAINTING VIENNA. JOSEPHSPLATZ.
BUT I COULDN'T TELL YOU WHEN I WAS LAST IN VIENNA. OR IF I WAS THERE AT ALL.
WAS SHE?
DOUBTFUL...
A. Hitler
<HERE, MY FRIEND! SCHNELL! LET ME EXPLAIN THE BRILLIANCE OF MY STRATEGY TO YOU.>
<FOR THE LAST THREE YEARS, I HAVE CONCENTRATED OUR BLITZKRIEG ON THE HOUSE OF THE VALENCIAS TO OUR WEST.>
<BUT NOW THAT YOU HAVE ARRIVED, I HAVE THE TROOP STRENGTH TO OPEN AN EASTERN FRONT ON THE MENDEZES NEXT DOOR AS WELL!>
<WE'LL BEGIN IN THE MIDDLE OF WINTER! THEY'LL NEVER SUSPECT IT!>

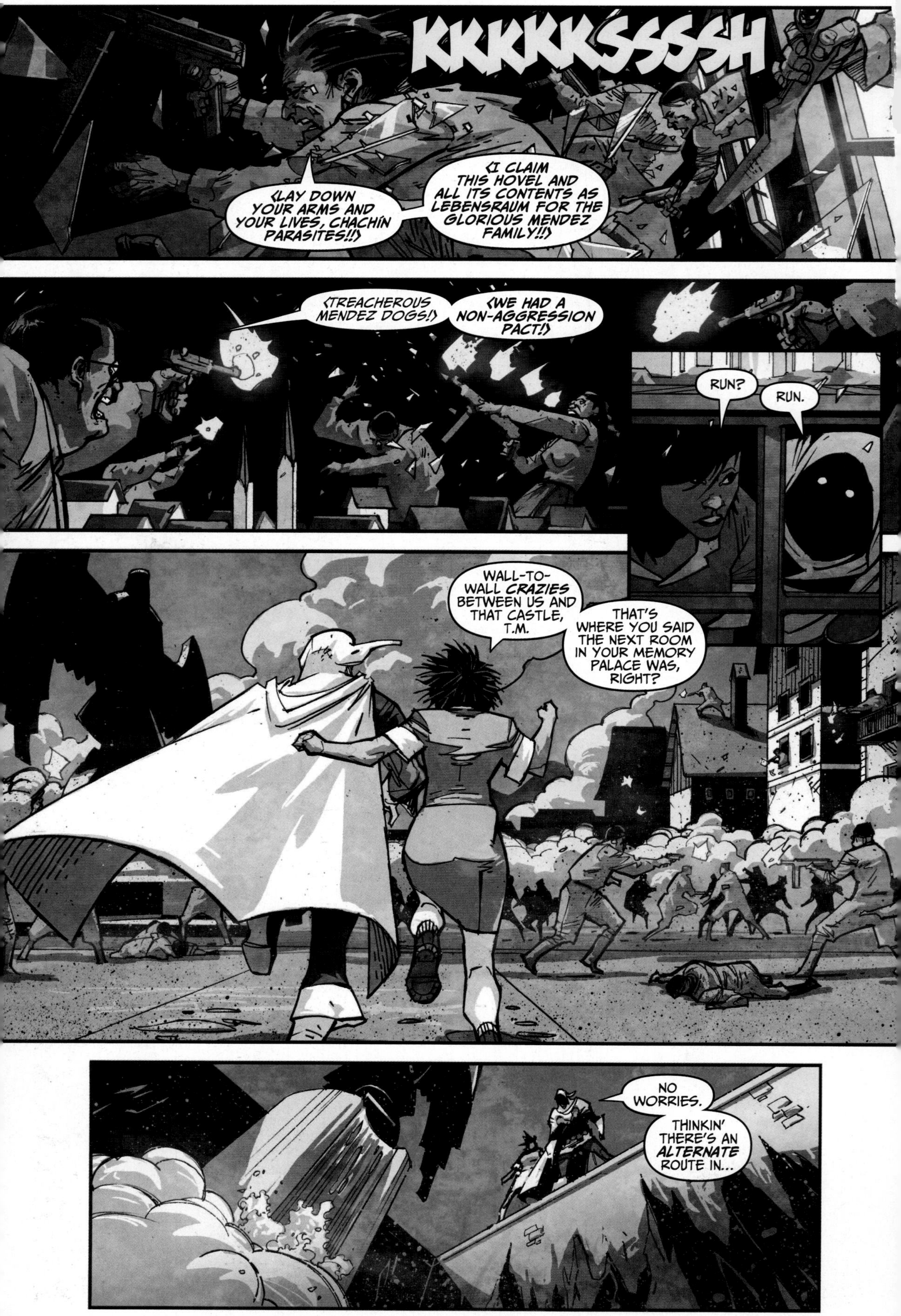

KKKKKSSSSH
<LAY DOWN YOUR ARMS AND YOUR LIVES, CHACHÍN PARASITES!!>
<I CLAIM THIS HOVEL AND ALL ITS CONTENTS AS LEBENSRAUM FOR THE GLORIOUS MENDEZ FAMILY!!>
<TREACHEROUS MENDEZ DOGS!>
<WE HAD A NON-AGGRESSION PACT!>
RUN?
RUN.
WALL-TO-WALL CRAZIES BETWEEN US AND THAT CASTLE, T.M.
THAT'S WHERE YOU SAID THE NEXT ROOM IN YOUR MEMORY PALACE WAS, RIGHT?
NO WORRIES.
THINKIN' THERE'S AN ALTERNATE ROUTE IN...

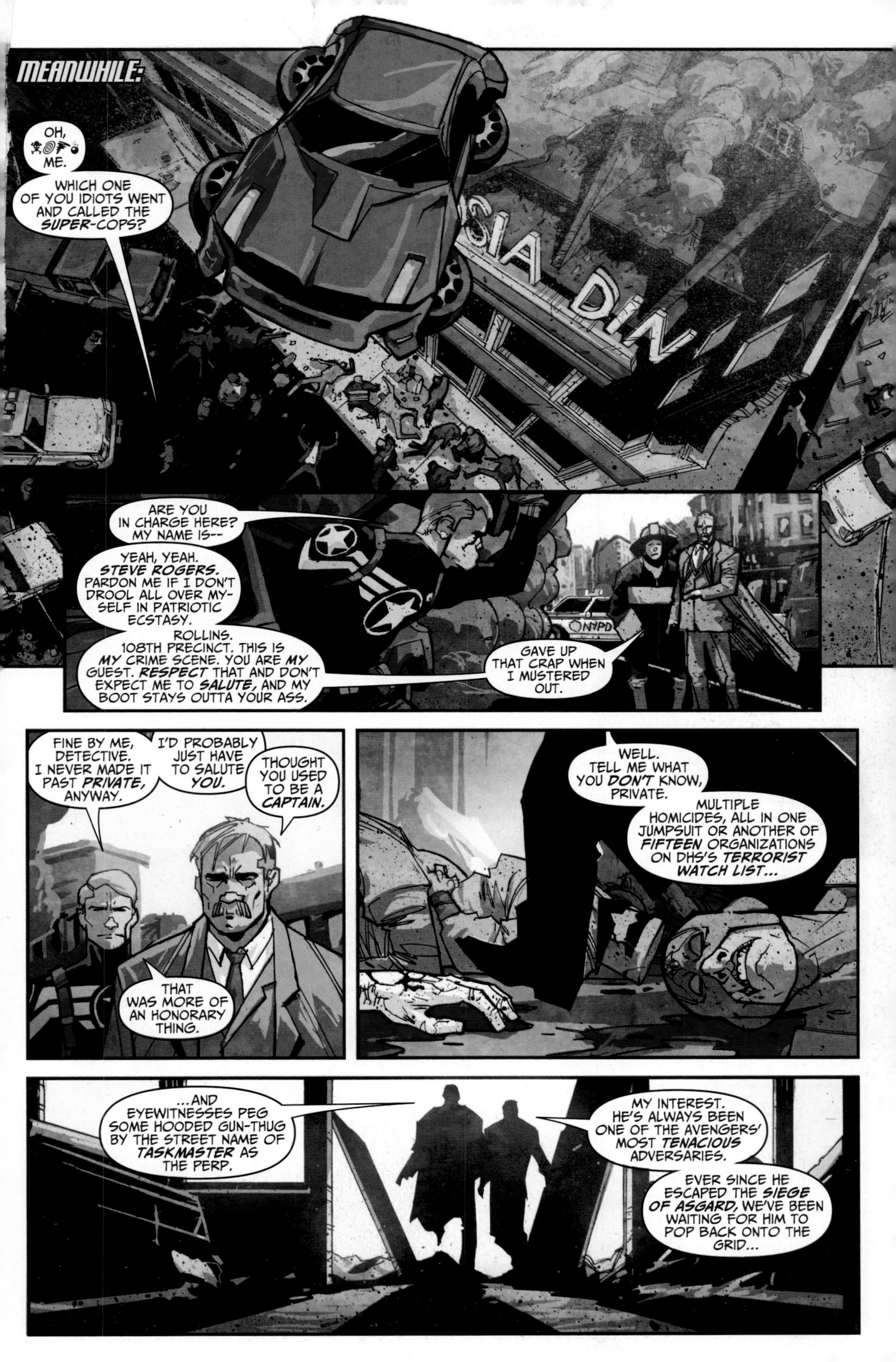
MEANWHILE:
OH, ☠@♂︎💣 ME.
WHICH ONE OF YOU IDIOTS WENT AND CALLED THE SUPER-COPS?
SIA DIN
ARE YOU IN CHARGE HERE? MY NAME IS--
YEAH, YEAH. STEVE ROGERS. PARDON ME IF I DON'T DROOL ALL OVER MY-SELF IN PATRIOTIC ECSTASY.
ROLLINS. 108TH PRECINCT. THIS IS MY CRIME SCENE. YOU ARE MY GUEST. RESPECT THAT AND DON'T EXPECT ME TO SALUTE, AND MY BOOT STAYS OUTTA YOUR ASS.
GAVE UP THAT CRAP WHEN I MUSTERED OUT.
NYPD
FINE BY ME, DETECTIVE. I NEVER MADE IT PAST PRIVATE, ANYWAY.
I'D PROBABLY JUST HAVE TO SALUTE YOU.
THOUGHT YOU USED TO BE A CAPTAIN.
THAT WAS MORE OF AN HONORARY THING.
WELL. TELL ME WHAT YOU DON'T KNOW, PRIVATE.
MULTIPLE HOMICIDES, ALL IN ONE JUMPSUIT OR ANOTHER OF FIFTEEN ORGANIZATIONS ON DHS'S TERRORIST WATCH LIST...
...AND EYEWITNESSES PEG SOME HOODED GUN-THUG BY THE STREET NAME OF TASKMASTER AS THE PERP.
MY INTEREST. HE'S ALWAYS BEEN ONE OF THE AVENGERS' MOST TENACIOUS ADVERSARIES.
EVER SINCE HE ESCAPED THE SIEGE OF ASGARD, WE'VE BEEN WAITING FOR HIM TO POP BACK ONTO THE GRID...

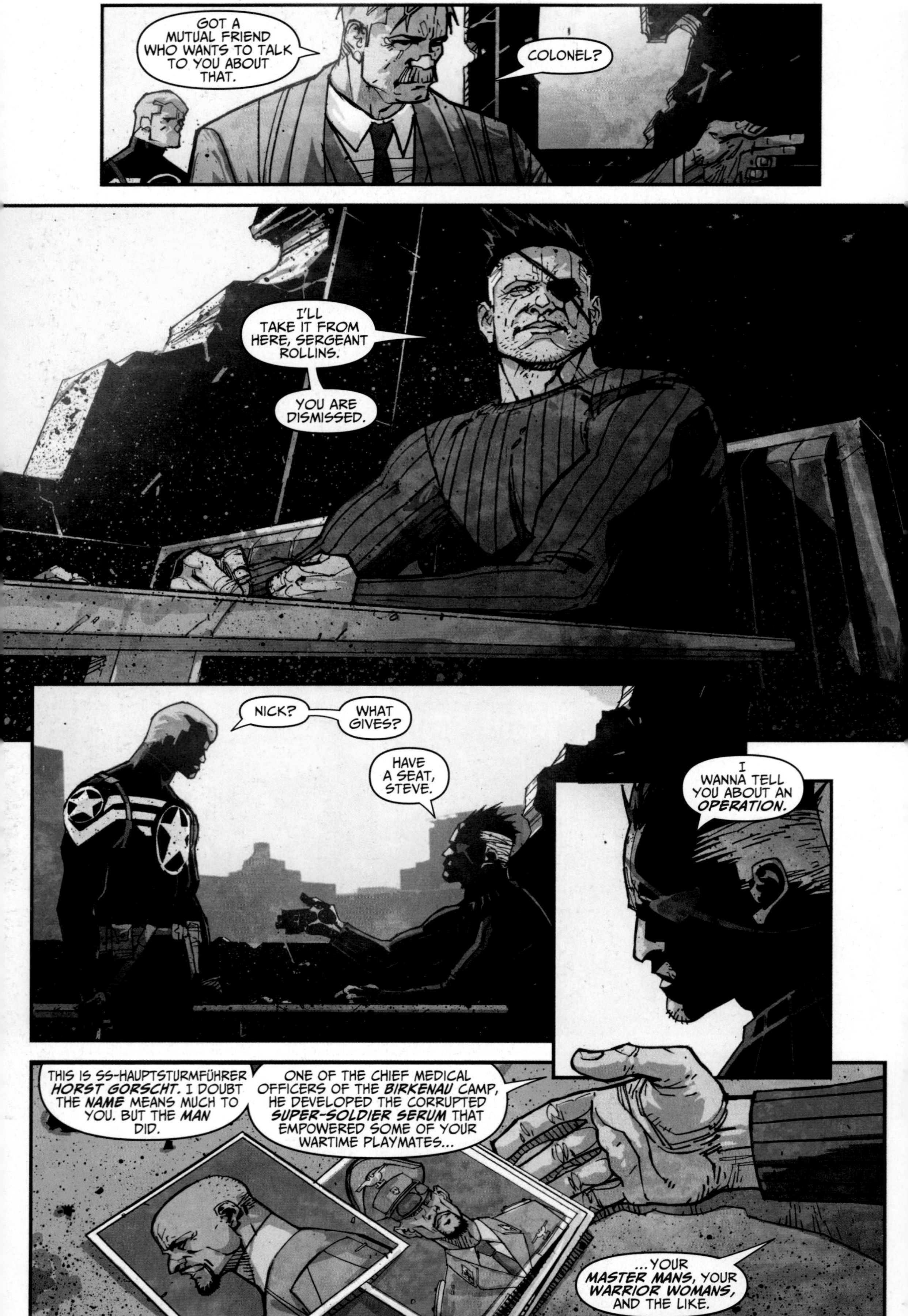
GOT A MUTUAL FRIEND WHO WANTS TO TALK TO YOU ABOUT THAT.
COLONEL?
I'LL TAKE IT FROM HERE, SERGEANT ROLLINS.
YOU ARE DISMISSED.
NICK?
WHAT GIVES?
HAVE A SEAT, STEVE.
I WANNA TELL YOU ABOUT AN OPERATION.
THIS IS SS-HAUPTSTURMFÜHRER HORST GORSCHT. I DOUBT THE NAME MEANS MUCH TO YOU. BUT THE MAN DID.
ONE OF THE CHIEF MEDICAL OFFICERS OF THE BIRKENAU CAMP, HE DEVELOPED THE CORRUPTED SUPER-SOLDIER SERUM THAT EMPOWERED SOME OF YOUR WARTIME PLAYMATES...
...YOUR MASTER MANS, YOUR WARRIOR WOMANS, AND THE LIKE.

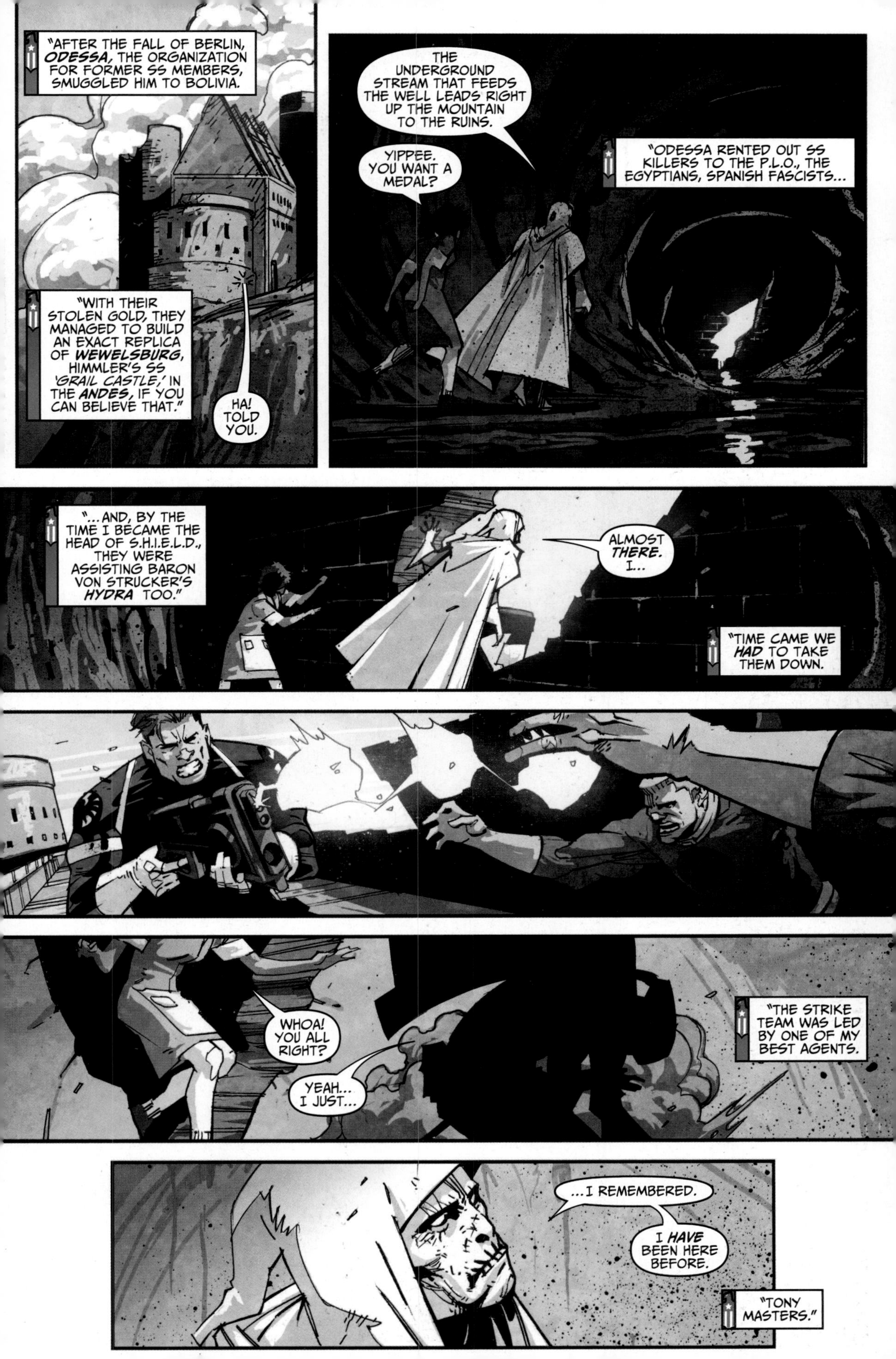
"AFTER THE FALL OF BERLIN, ODESSA, THE ORGANIZATION FOR FORMER SS MEMBERS, SMUGGLED HIM TO BOLIVIA.
"WITH THEIR STOLEN GOLD, THEY MANAGED TO BUILD AN EXACT REPLICA OF WEWELSBURG, HIMMLER'S SS 'GRAIL CASTLE,' IN THE ANDES, IF YOU CAN BELIEVE THAT."
HA! TOLD YOU.
THE UNDERGROUND STREAM THAT FEEDS THE WELL LEADS RIGHT UP THE MOUNTAIN TO THE RUINS.
YIPPEE. YOU WANT A MEDAL?
"ODESSA RENTED OUT SS KILLERS TO THE P.L.O., THE EGYPTIANS, SPANISH FASCISTS...
"...AND, BY THE TIME I BECAME THE HEAD OF S.H.I.E.L.D., THEY WERE ASSISTING BARON VON STRUCKER'S HYDRA TOO."
ALMOST THERE. I...
"TIME CAME WE HAD TO TAKE THEM DOWN.
WHOA! YOU ALL RIGHT?
YEAH... I JUST...
"THE STRIKE TEAM WAS LED BY ONE OF MY BEST AGENTS.
...I REMEMBERED.
I HAVE BEEN HERE BEFORE.
"TONY MASTERS."

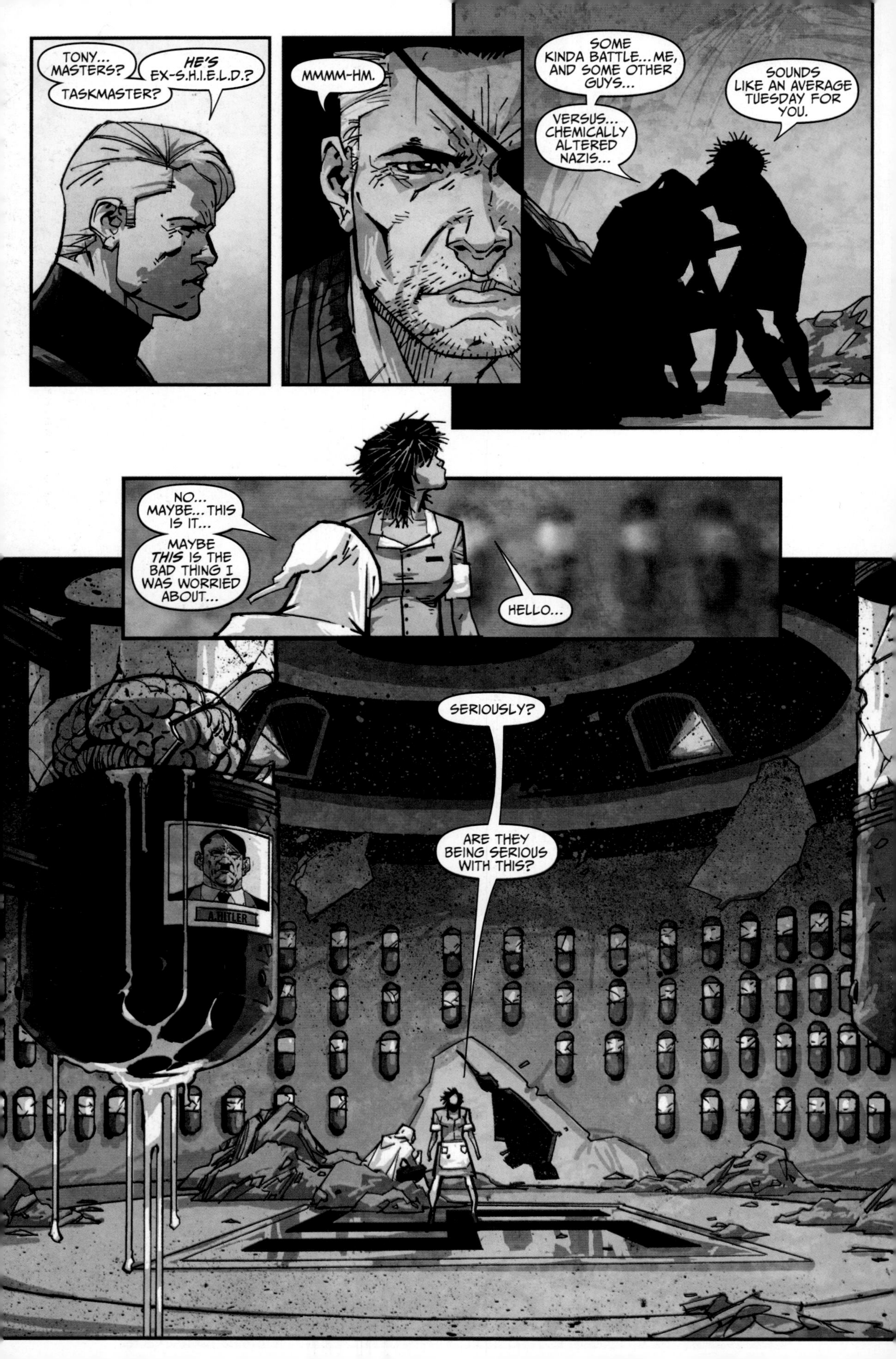
TONY... MASTERS?
TASKMASTER?
HE'S EX-S.H.I.E.L.D.?
MMMM-HM.
SOME KINDA BATTLE... ME, AND SOME OTHER GUYS...
VERSUS... CHEMICALLY ALTERED NAZIS...
SOUNDS LIKE AN AVERAGE TUESDAY FOR YOU.
NO... MAYBE... THIS IS IT...
MAYBE THIS IS THE BAD THING I WAS WORRIED ABOUT...
HELLO...
SERIOUSLY?
ARE THEY BEING SERIOUS WITH THIS?
A. HITLER

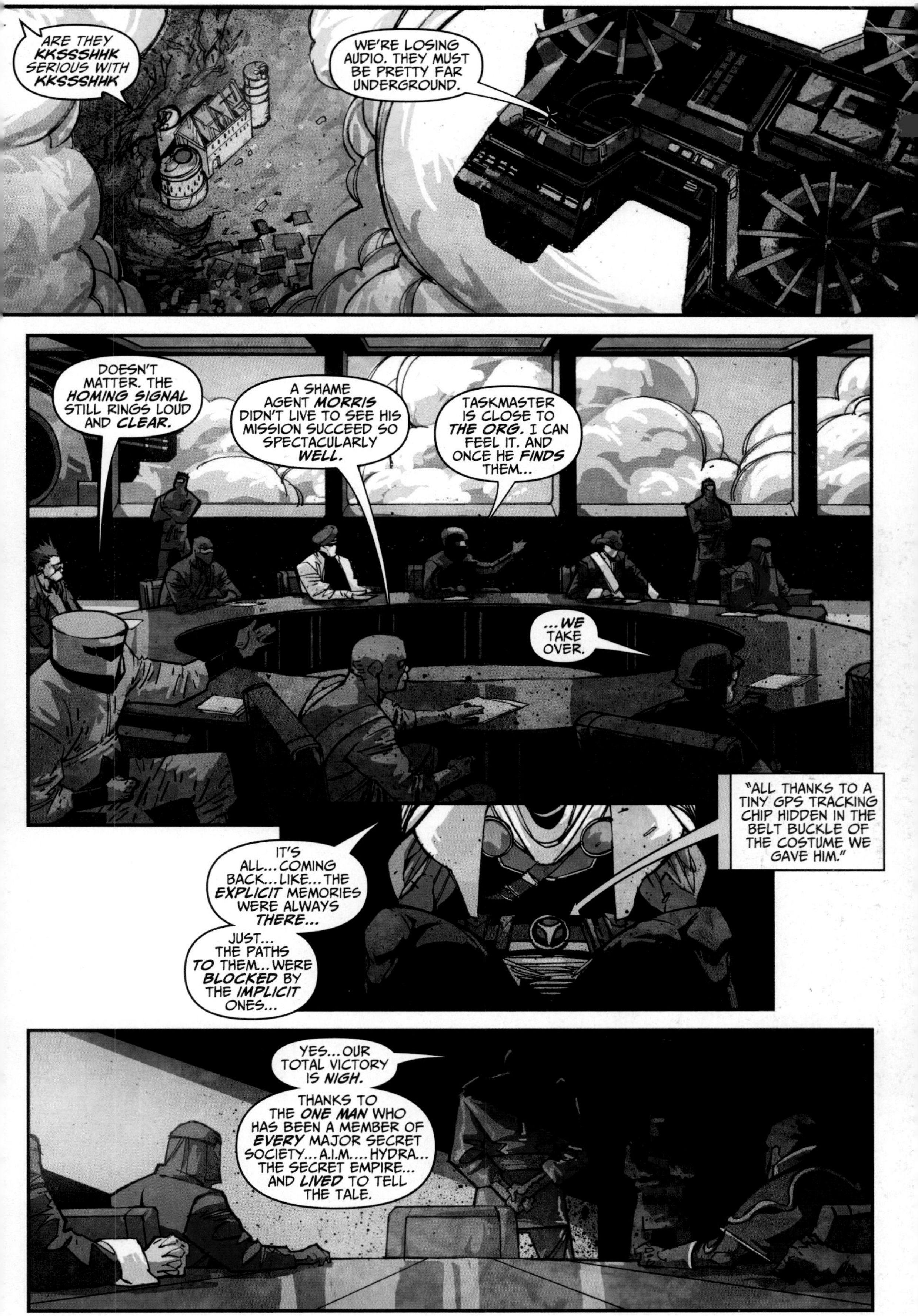
ARE THEY KKSSSHHK SERIOUS WITH KKSSSHHK
WE'RE LOSING AUDIO. THEY MUST BE PRETTY FAR UNDERGROUND.
DOESN'T MATTER. THE HOMING SIGNAL STILL RINGS LOUD AND CLEAR.
A SHAME AGENT MORRIS DIDN'T LIVE TO SEE HIS MISSION SUCCEED SO SPECTACULARLY WELL.
TASKMASTER IS CLOSE TO THE ORG. I CAN FEEL IT. AND ONCE HE FINDS THEM...
...WE TAKE OVER.
"ALL THANKS TO A TINY GPS TRACKING CHIP HIDDEN IN THE BELT BUCKLE OF THE COSTUME WE GAVE HIM."
IT'S ALL...COMING BACK...LIKE...THE EXPLICIT MEMORIES WERE ALWAYS THERE...
JUST... THE PATHS TO THEM...WERE BLOCKED BY THE IMPLICIT ONES...
YES...OUR TOTAL VICTORY IS NIGH.
THANKS TO THE ONE MAN WHO HAS BEEN A MEMBER OF EVERY MAJOR SECRET SOCIETY...A.I.M....HYDRA... THE SECRET EMPIRE... AND LIVED TO TELL THE TALE.

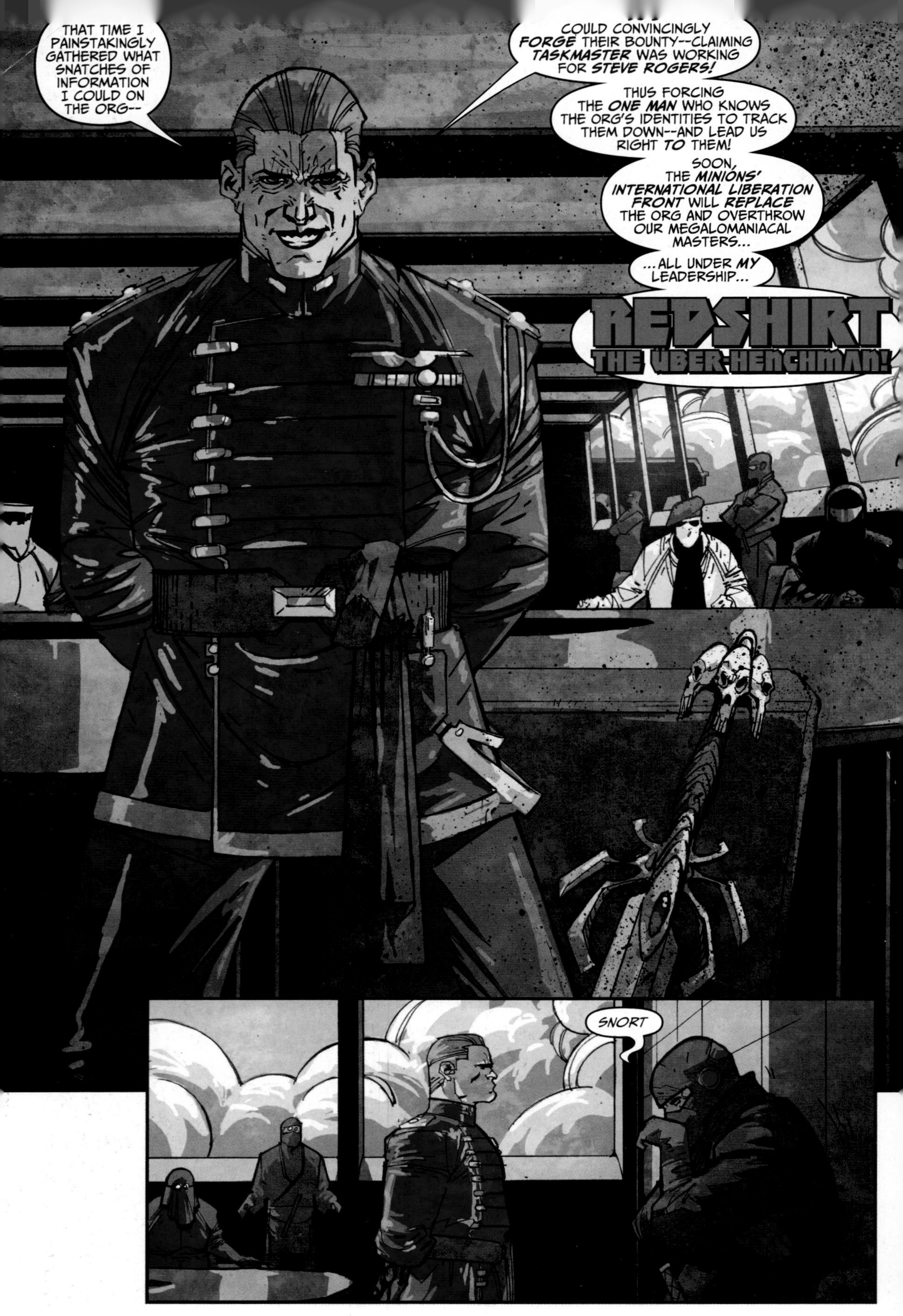
THAT TIME I PAINSTAKINGLY GATHERED WHAT SNATCHES OF INFORMATION I COULD ON THE ORG--
COULD CONVINCINGLY FORGE THEIR BOUNTY--CLAIMING TASKMASTER WAS WORKING FOR STEVE ROGERS!
THUS FORCING THE ONE MAN WHO KNOWS THE ORG'S IDENTITIES TO TRACK THEM DOWN--AND LEAD US RIGHT TO THEM!
SOON, THE MINIONS' INTERNATIONAL LIBERATION FRONT WILL REPLACE THE ORG AND OVERTHROW OUR MEGALOMANIACAL MASTERS...
...ALL UNDER MY LEADERSHIP...
REDSHIRT
THE ÜBER-HENCHMAN!
SNORT

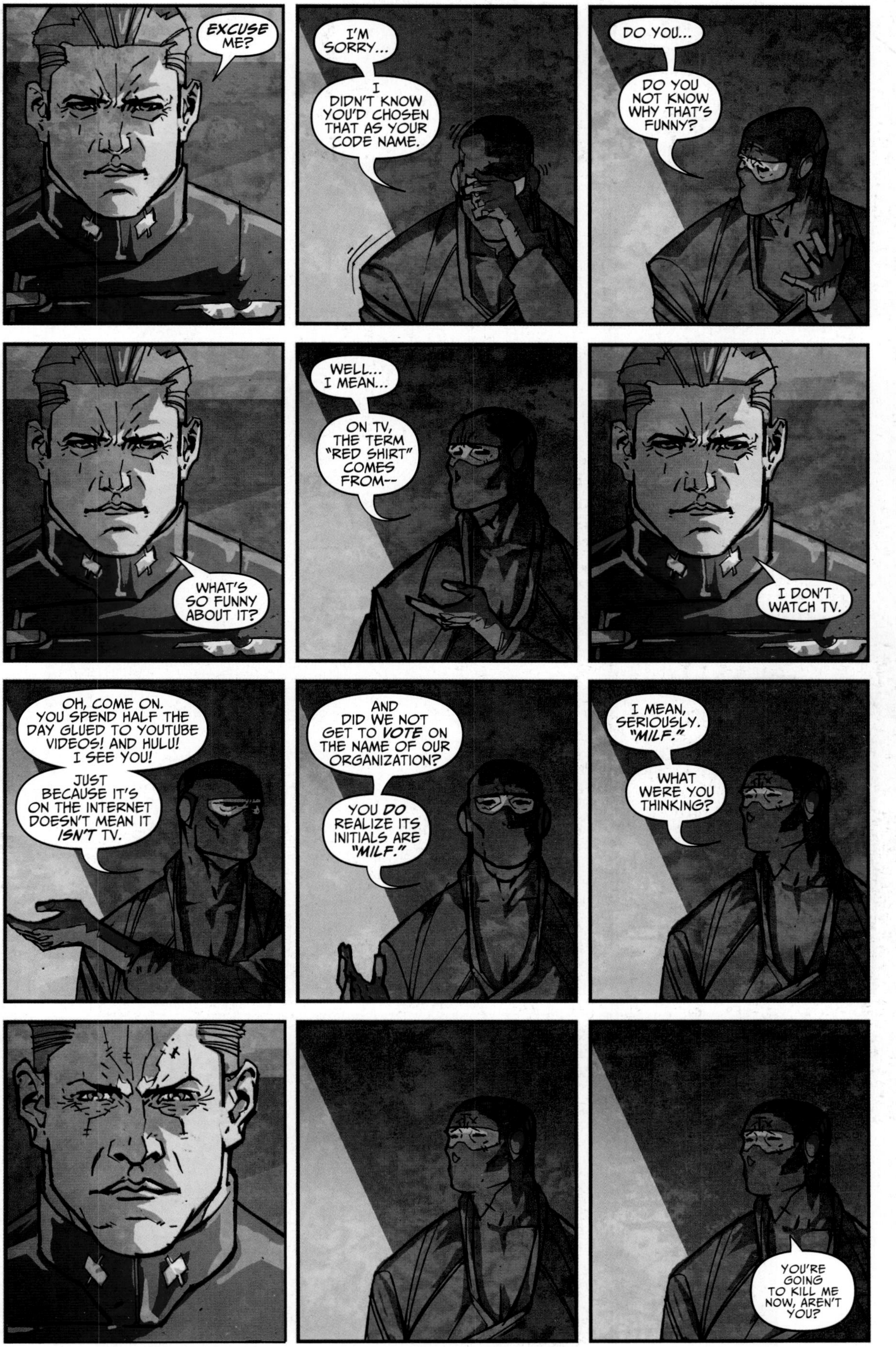
EXCUSE ME?
I'M SORRY...
I DIDN'T KNOW YOU'D CHOSEN THAT AS YOUR CODE NAME.
DO YOU...
DO YOU NOT KNOW WHY THAT'S FUNNY?
WHAT'S SO FUNNY ABOUT IT?
WELL... I MEAN...
ON TV, THE TERM "RED SHIRT" COMES FROM--
I DON'T WATCH TV.
OH, COME ON. YOU SPEND HALF THE DAY GLUED TO YOUTUBE VIDEOS! AND HULU! I SEE YOU!
JUST BECAUSE IT'S ON THE INTERNET DOESN'T MEAN IT ISN'T TV.
AND DID WE NOT GET TO VOTE ON THE NAME OF OUR ORGANIZATION?
YOU DO REALIZE ITS INITIALS ARE "MILF."
I MEAN, SERIOUSLY. "MILF."
WHAT WERE YOU THINKING?
YOU'RE GOING TO KILL ME NOW, AREN'T YOU?

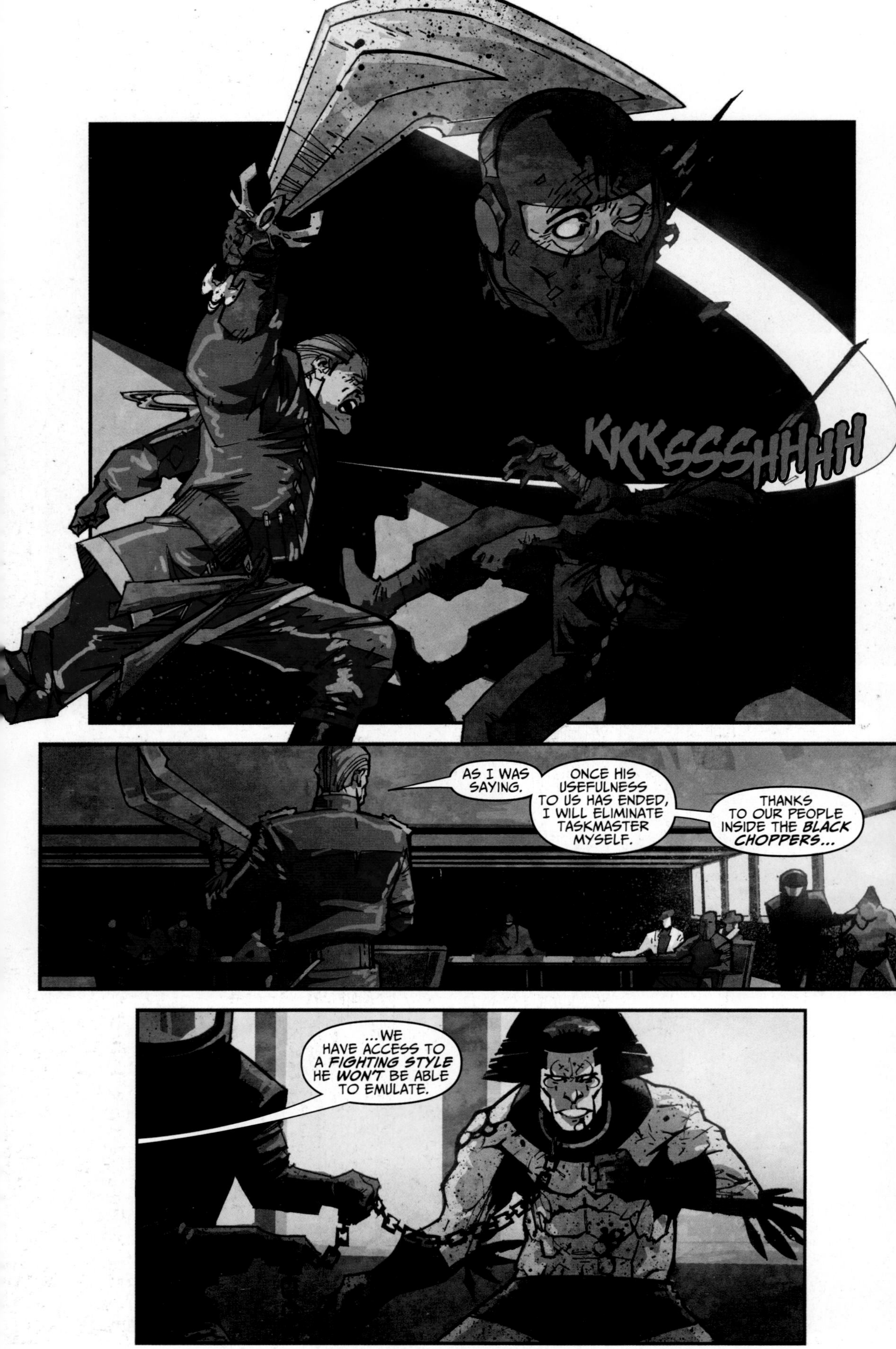
KKKSSSHHHH
AS I WAS SAYING.
ONCE HIS USEFULNESS TO US HAS ENDED, I WILL ELIMINATE TASKMASTER MYSELF.
THANKS TO OUR PEOPLE INSIDE THE *BLACK CHOPPERS*...
...WE HAVE ACCESS TO A *FIGHTING STYLE* HE *WON'T* BE ABLE TO EMULATE.

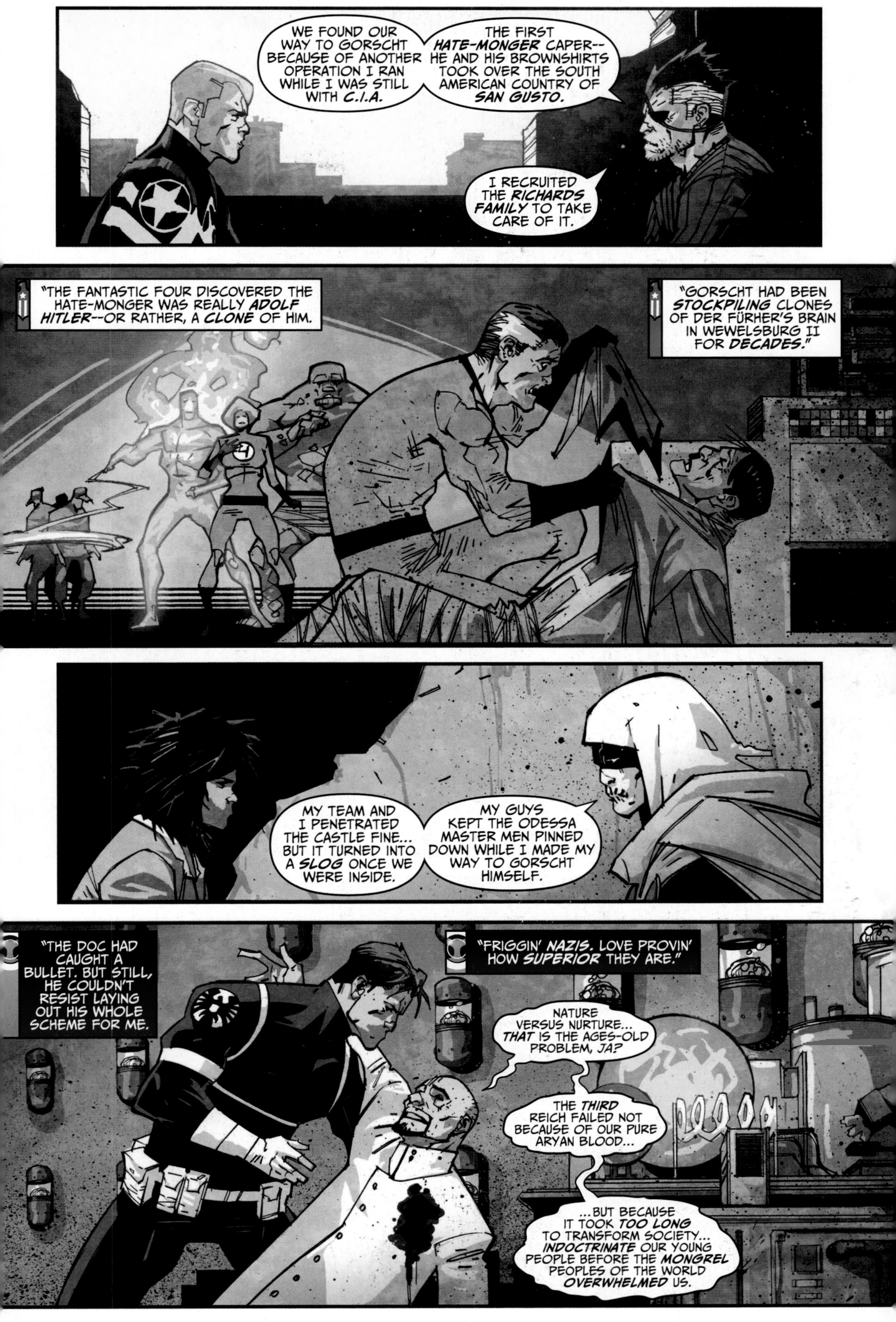
WE FOUND OUR WAY TO GORSCHT BECAUSE OF ANOTHER OPERATION I RAN WHILE I WAS STILL WITH C.I.A.
THE FIRST HATE-MONGER CAPER-- HE AND HIS BROWNSHIRTS TOOK OVER THE SOUTH AMERICAN COUNTRY OF SAN GUSTO.
I RECRUITED THE RICHARDS FAMILY TO TAKE CARE OF IT.
"THE FANTASTIC FOUR DISCOVERED THE HATE-MONGER WAS REALLY ADOLF HITLER--OR RATHER, A CLONE OF HIM.
"GORSCHT HAD BEEN STOCKPILING CLONES OF DER FÜRHER'S BRAIN IN WEWELSBURG II FOR DECADES."
MY TEAM AND I PENETRATED THE CASTLE FINE... BUT IT TURNED INTO A SLOG ONCE WE WERE INSIDE.
MY GUYS KEPT THE ODESSA MASTER MEN PINNED DOWN WHILE I MADE MY WAY TO GORSCHT HIMSELF.
"THE DOC HAD CAUGHT A BULLET. BUT STILL, HE COULDN'T RESIST LAYING OUT HIS WHOLE SCHEME FOR ME.
"FRIGGIN' NAZIS. LOVE PROVIN' HOW SUPERIOR THEY ARE."
NATURE VERSUS NURTURE... THAT IS THE AGES-OLD PROBLEM, JA?
THE THIRD REICH FAILED NOT BECAUSE OF OUR PURE ARYAN BLOOD...
...BUT BECAUSE IT TOOK TOO LONG TO TRANSFORM SOCIETY... INDOCTRINATE OUR YOUNG PEOPLE BEFORE THE MONGREL PEOPLES OF THE WORLD OVERWHELMED US.

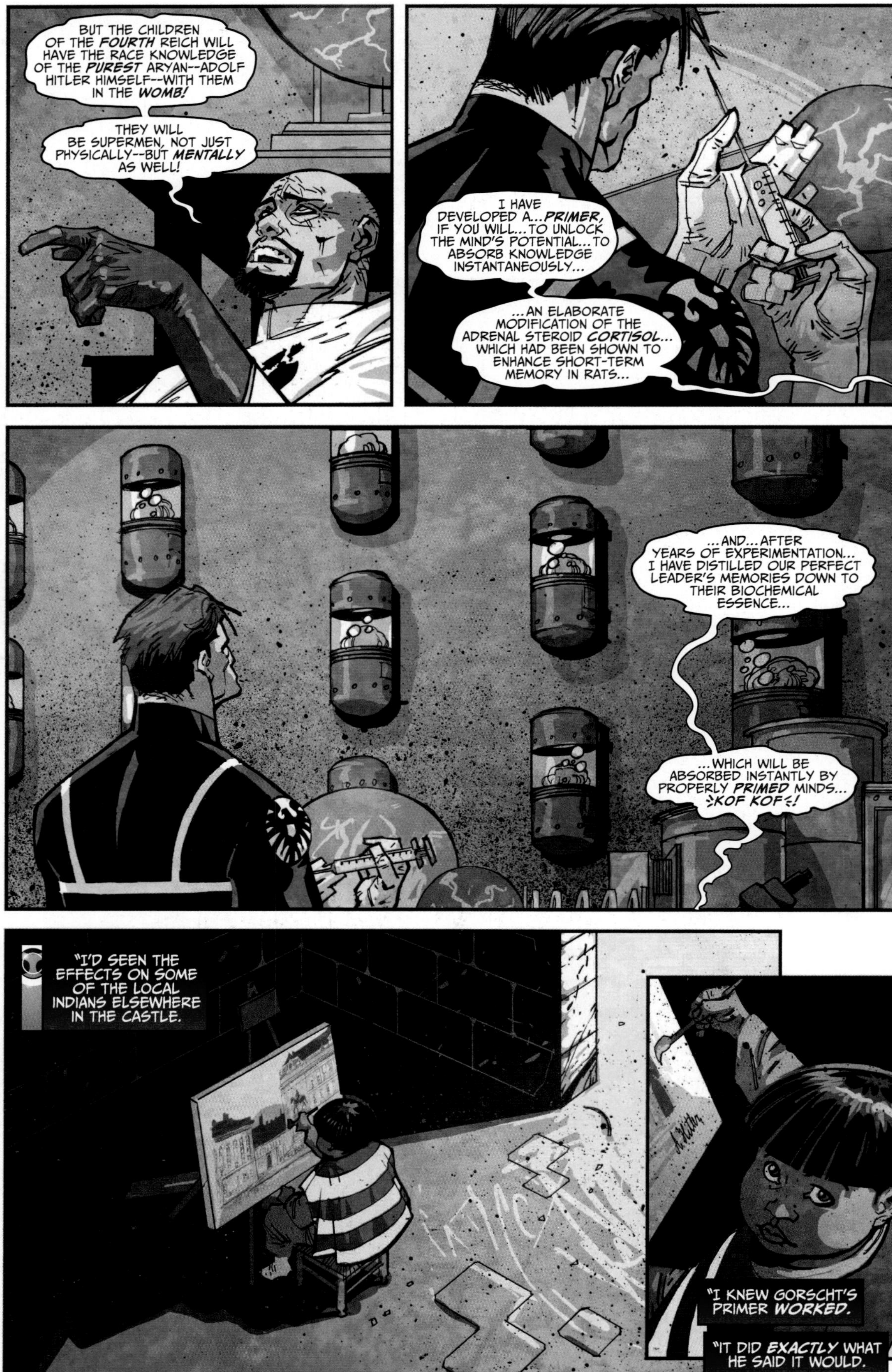
BUT THE CHILDREN OF THE *FOURTH* REICH WILL HAVE THE RACE KNOWLEDGE OF THE *PUREST* ARYAN--ADOLF HITLER HIMSELF--WITH THEM IN THE *WOMB!*
THEY WILL BE SUPERMEN, NOT JUST PHYSICALLY--BUT *MENTALLY* AS WELL!
I HAVE DEVELOPED A...*PRIMER*, IF YOU WILL...TO UNLOCK THE MIND'S POTENTIAL...TO ABSORB KNOWLEDGE INSTANTANEOUSLY...
...AN ELABORATE MODIFICATION OF THE ADRENAL STEROID *CORTISOL*... WHICH HAD BEEN SHOWN TO ENHANCE SHORT-TERM MEMORY IN RATS...
...AND...AFTER YEARS OF EXPERIMENTATION... I HAVE DISTILLED OUR PERFECT LEADER'S MEMORIES DOWN TO THEIR BIOCHEMICAL ESSENCE...
...WHICH WILL BE ABSORBED INSTANTLY BY PROPERLY *PRIMED* MINDS... *KOF KOF*!
"I'D SEEN THE EFFECTS ON SOME OF THE LOCAL INDIANS ELSEWHERE IN THE CASTLE.
"I KNEW GORSCHT'S PRIMER *WORKED.*
"IT DID *EXACTLY* WHAT HE SAID IT WOULD.

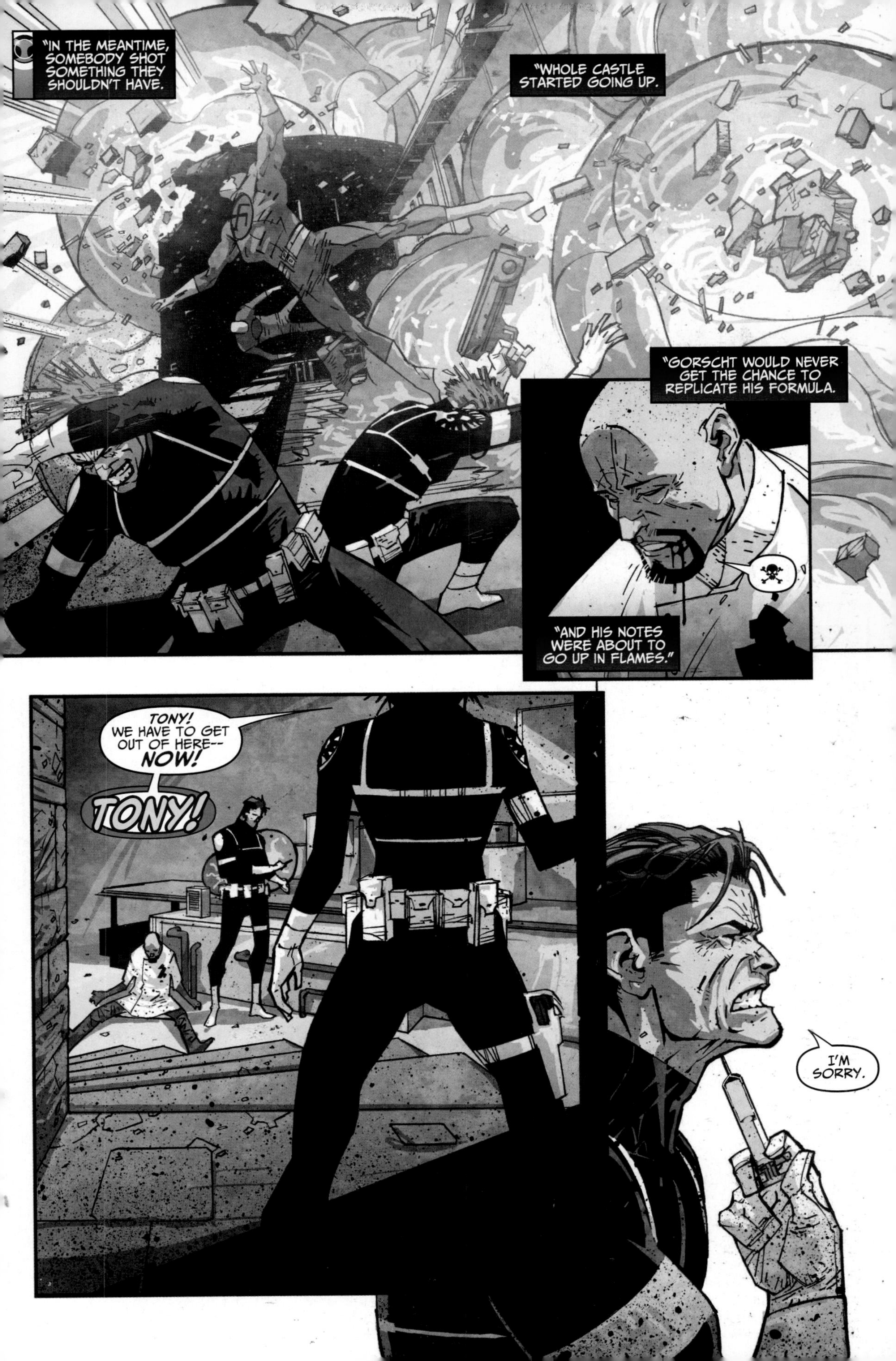
"IN THE MEANTIME, SOMEBODY SHOT SOMETHING THEY SHOULDN'T HAVE.
"WHOLE CASTLE STARTED GOING UP.
"GORSCHT WOULD NEVER GET THE CHANCE TO REPLICATE HIS FORMULA.
"AND HIS NOTES WERE ABOUT TO GO UP IN FLAMES."
TONY! WE HAVE TO GET OUT OF HERE-- NOW!
TONY!
I'M SORRY.

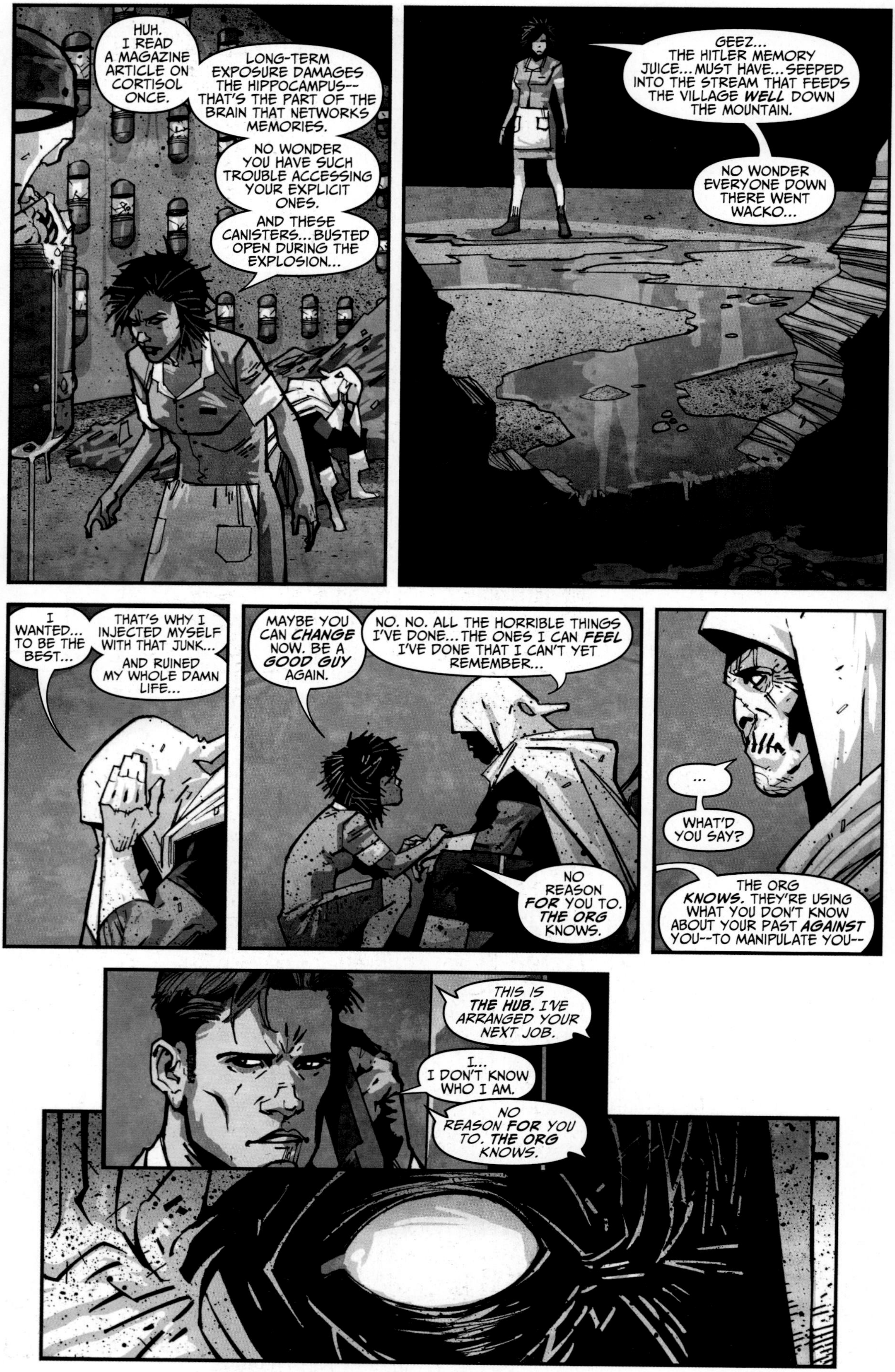
HUH. I READ A MAGAZINE ARTICLE ON CORTISOL ONCE.
LONG-TERM EXPOSURE DAMAGES THE HIPPOCAMPUS--THAT'S THE PART OF THE BRAIN THAT NETWORKS MEMORIES.
NO WONDER YOU HAVE SUCH TROUBLE ACCESSING YOUR EXPLICIT ONES.
AND THESE CANISTERS...BUSTED OPEN DURING THE EXPLOSION...
GEEZ... THE HITLER MEMORY JUICE...MUST HAVE...SEEPED INTO THE STREAM THAT FEEDS THE VILLAGE **WELL** DOWN THE MOUNTAIN.
NO WONDER EVERYONE DOWN THERE WENT WACKO...
I WANTED... TO BE THE BEST...
THAT'S WHY I INJECTED MYSELF WITH THAT JUNK...
AND RUINED MY WHOLE DAMN LIFE...
MAYBE YOU CAN **CHANGE** NOW. BE A **GOOD GUY** AGAIN.
NO. NO. ALL THE HORRIBLE THINGS I'VE DONE...THE ONES I CAN **FEEL** I'VE DONE THAT I CAN'T YET REMEMBER...
NO REASON **FOR** YOU TO. **THE ORG** KNOWS.
...
WHAT'D YOU SAY?
THE ORG **KNOWS.** THEY'RE USING WHAT YOU DON'T KNOW ABOUT YOUR PAST **AGAINST** YOU--TO MANIPULATE YOU--
THIS IS **THE HUB.** I'VE ARRANGED YOUR NEXT JOB.
I... I DON'T KNOW WHO I AM.
NO REASON **FOR** YOU TO. **THE ORG** KNOWS.

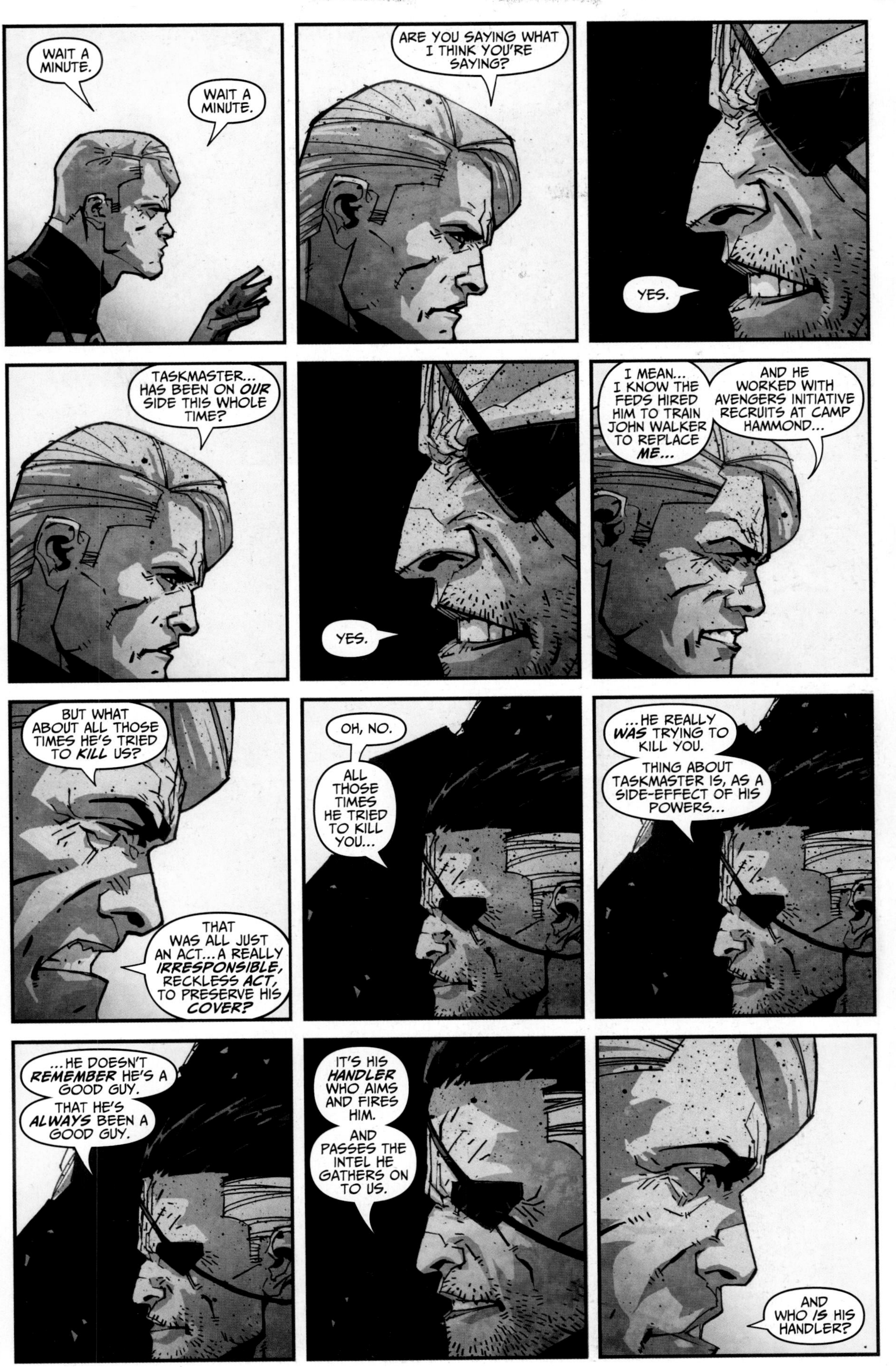

WAIT A MINUTE.
WAIT A MINUTE.
ARE YOU SAYING WHAT I THINK YOU'RE SAYING?
YES.
TASKMASTER... HAS BEEN ON *OUR* SIDE THIS WHOLE TIME?
YES.
I MEAN... I KNOW THE FEDS HIRED HIM TO TRAIN JOHN WALKER TO REPLACE *ME...*
AND HE WORKED WITH AVENGERS INITIATIVE RECRUITS AT CAMP HAMMOND...
BUT WHAT ABOUT ALL THOSE TIMES HE'S TRIED TO *KILL* US?
THAT WAS ALL JUST AN ACT... A REALLY *IRRESPONSIBLE,* RECKLESS *ACT,* TO PRESERVE HIS *COVER?*
OH, NO.
ALL THOSE TIMES HE TRIED TO KILL YOU...
...HE REALLY *WAS* TRYING TO KILL YOU.
THING ABOUT TASKMASTER IS, AS A SIDE-EFFECT OF HIS POWERS...
...HE DOESN'T *REMEMBER* HE'S A GOOD GUY.
THAT HE'S *ALWAYS* BEEN A GOOD GUY.
IT'S HIS *HANDLER* WHO AIMS AND FIRES HIM.
AND PASSES THE INTEL HE GATHERS ON TO US.
AND WHO *IS* HIS HANDLER?

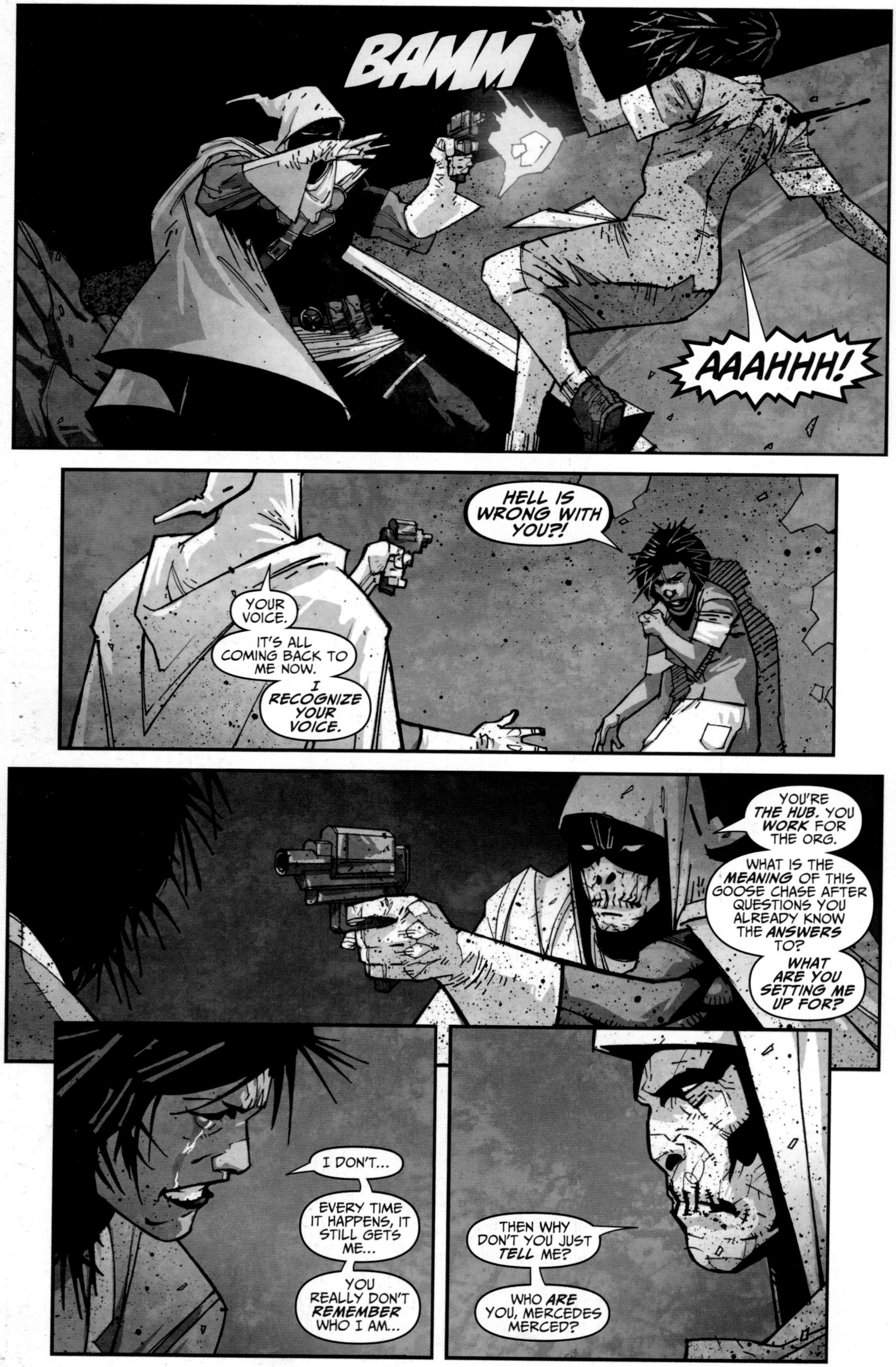
BAMM
AAAHHH!
HELL IS WRONG WITH YOU?!
YOUR VOICE.
IT'S ALL COMING BACK TO ME NOW.
I RECOGNIZE YOUR VOICE.
YOU'RE THE HUB. YOU WORK FOR THE ORG.
WHAT IS THE MEANING OF THIS GOOSE CHASE AFTER QUESTIONS YOU ALREADY KNOW THE ANSWERS TO?
WHAT ARE YOU SETTING ME UP FOR?
I DON'T...
EVERY TIME IT HAPPENS, IT STILL GETS ME...
YOU REALLY DON'T REMEMBER WHO I AM...
THEN WHY DON'T YOU JUST TELL ME?
WHO ARE YOU, MERCEDES MERCED?

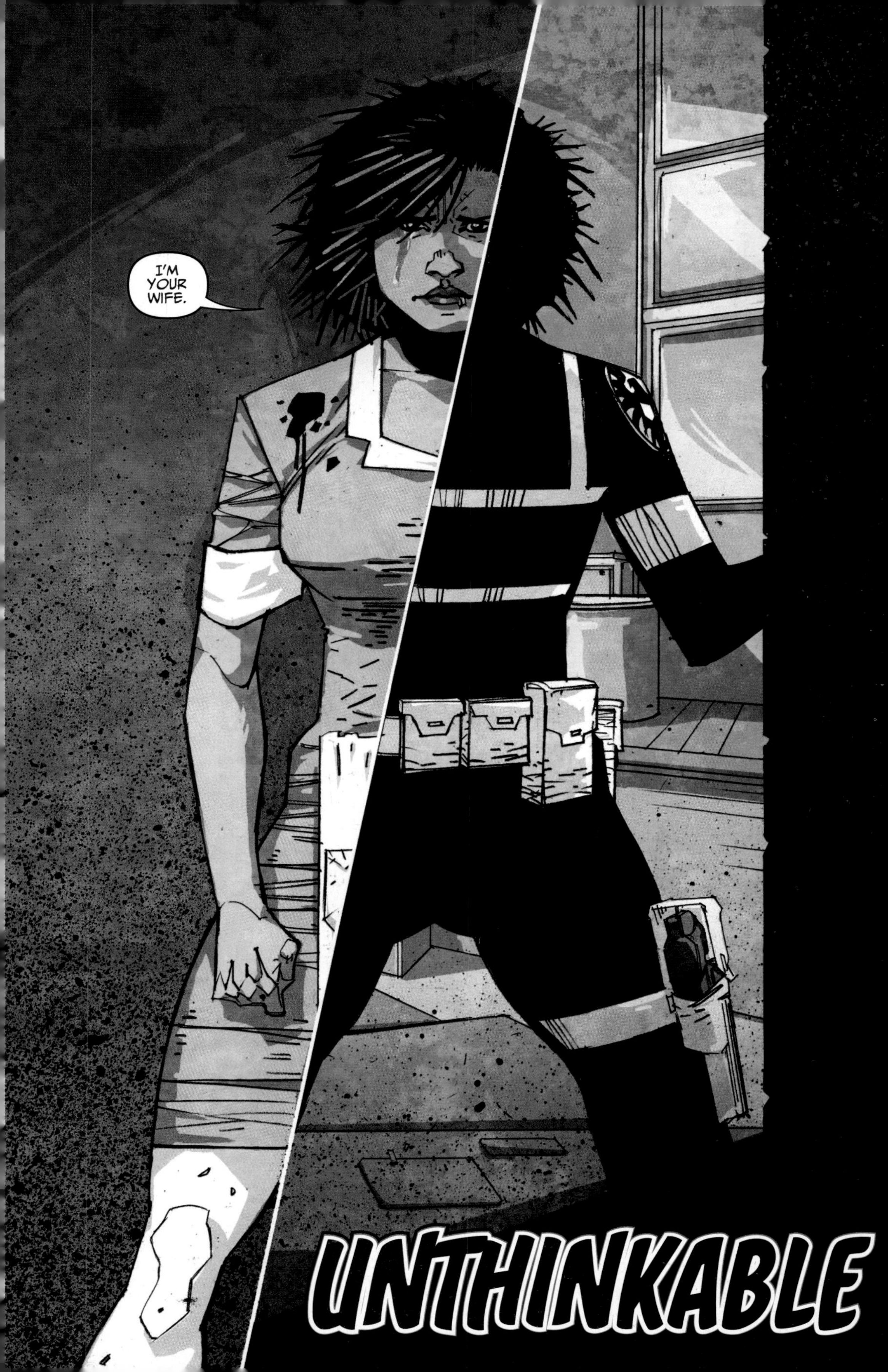
I'M YOUR WIFE.
UNTHINKABLE

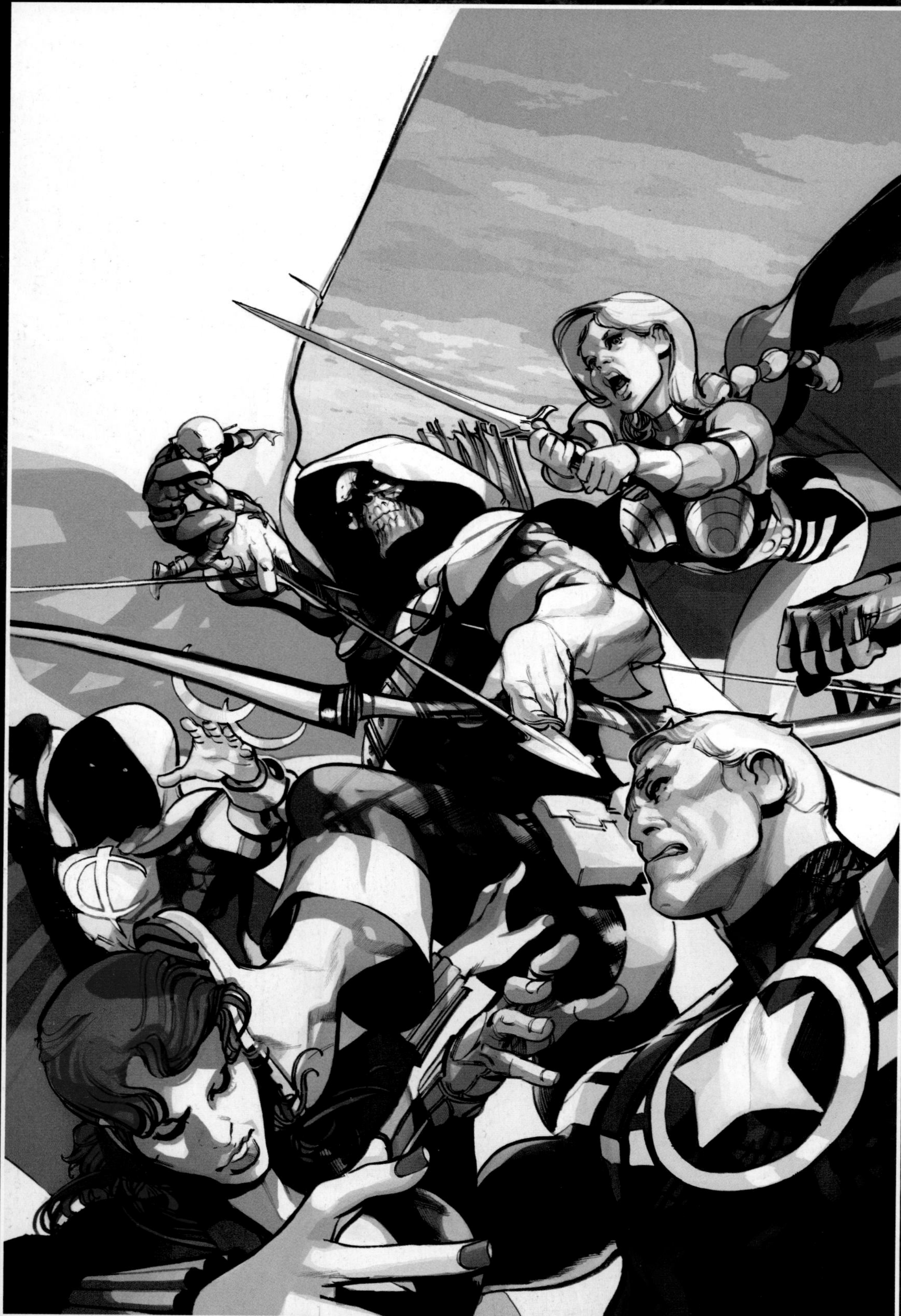

› FOUR ‹

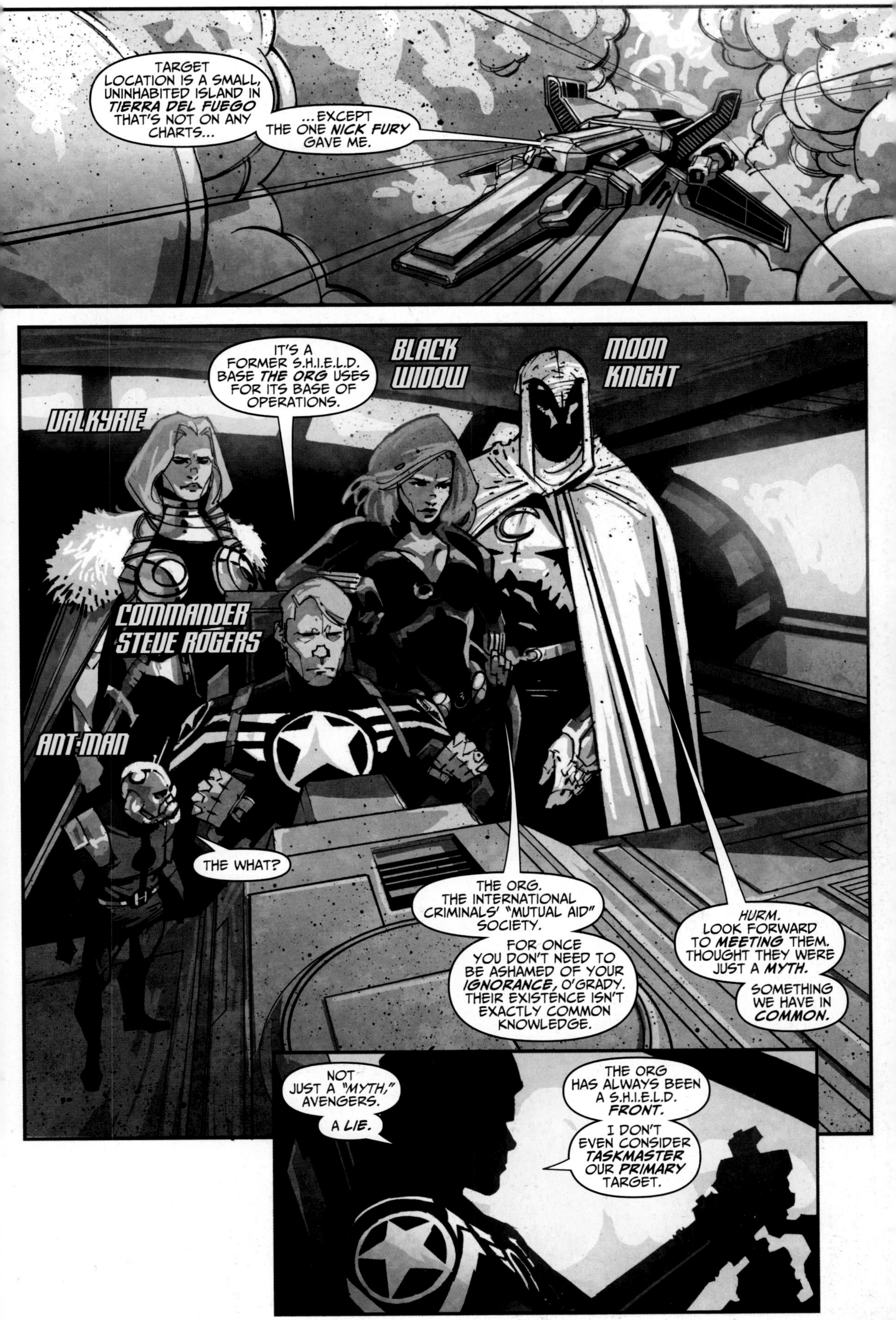
TARGET LOCATION IS A SMALL, UNINHABITED ISLAND IN TIERRA DEL FUEGO THAT'S NOT ON ANY CHARTS...
...EXCEPT THE ONE NICK FURY GAVE ME.
IT'S A FORMER S.H.I.E.L.D. BASE THE ORG USES FOR ITS BASE OF OPERATIONS.
BLACK WIDOW
MOON KNIGHT
VALKYRIE
COMMANDER STEVE ROGERS
ANT-MAN
THE WHAT?
THE ORG. THE INTERNATIONAL CRIMINALS' "MUTUAL AID" SOCIETY.
FOR ONCE YOU DON'T NEED TO BE ASHAMED OF YOUR IGNORANCE, O'GRADY. THEIR EXISTENCE ISN'T EXACTLY COMMON KNOWLEDGE.
HURM. LOOK FORWARD TO MEETING THEM. THOUGHT THEY WERE JUST A MYTH.
SOMETHING WE HAVE IN COMMON.
NOT JUST A "MYTH," AVENGERS.
A LIE.
THE ORG HAS ALWAYS BEEN A S.H.I.E.L.D. FRONT.
I DON'T EVEN CONSIDER TASKMASTER OUR PRIMARY TARGET.

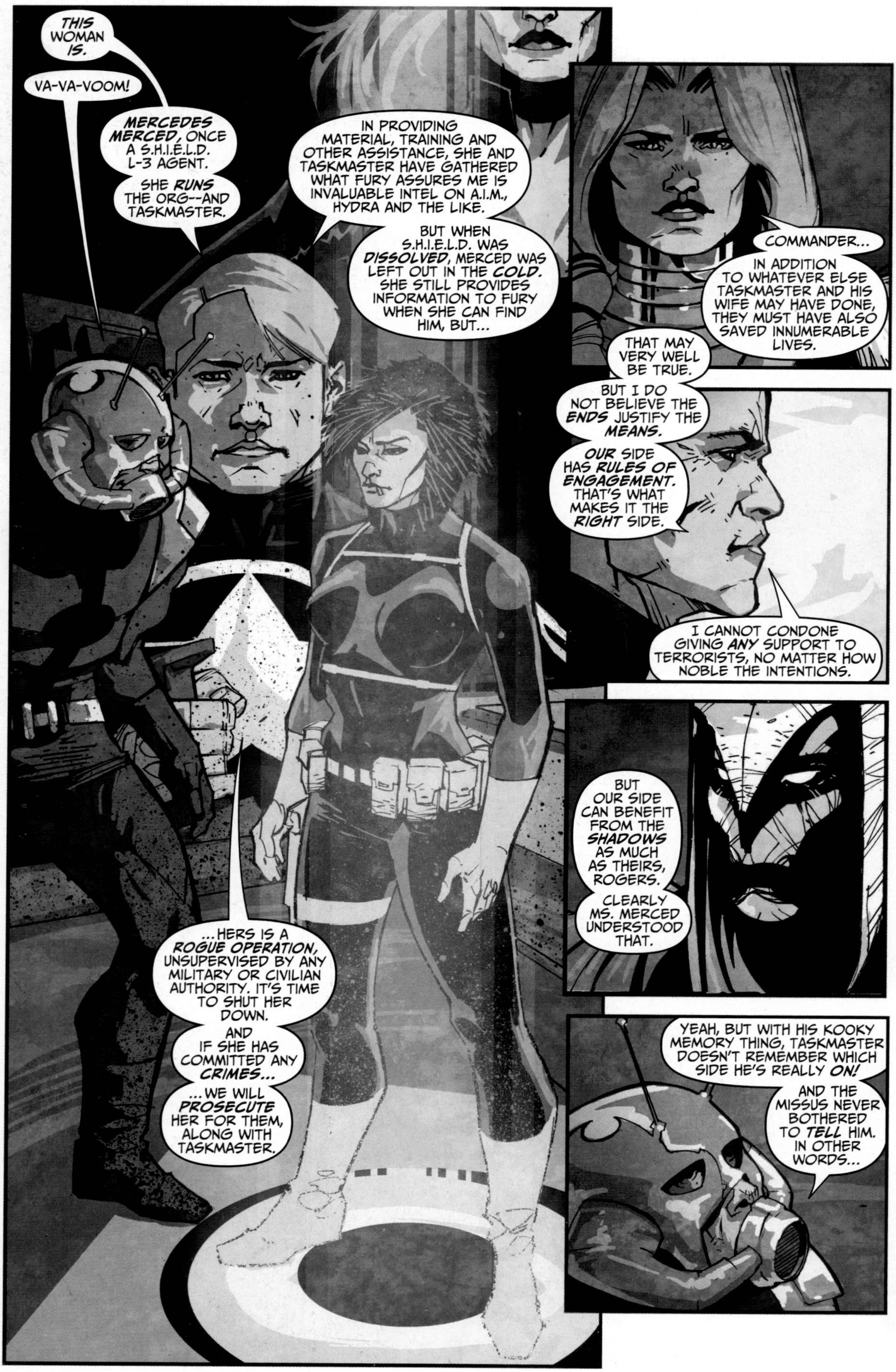
THIS WOMAN IS.
VA-VA-VOOM!
MERCEDES MERCED, ONCE A S.H.I.E.L.D. L-3 AGENT.
SHE RUNS THE ORG--AND TASKMASTER.
IN PROVIDING MATERIAL, TRAINING AND OTHER ASSISTANCE, SHE AND TASKMASTER HAVE GATHERED WHAT FURY ASSURES ME IS INVALUABLE INTEL ON A.I.M., HYDRA AND THE LIKE.
BUT WHEN S.H.I.E.L.D. WAS DISSOLVED, MERCED WAS LEFT OUT IN THE COLD. SHE STILL PROVIDES INFORMATION TO FURY WHEN SHE CAN FIND HIM, BUT...
...HERS IS A ROGUE OPERATION, UNSUPERVISED BY ANY MILITARY OR CIVILIAN AUTHORITY. IT'S TIME TO SHUT HER DOWN.
AND IF SHE HAS COMMITTED ANY CRIMES...
...WE WILL PROSECUTE HER FOR THEM, ALONG WITH TASKMASTER.
COMMANDER...
IN ADDITION TO WHATEVER ELSE TASKMASTER AND HIS WIFE MAY HAVE DONE, THEY MUST HAVE ALSO SAVED INNUMERABLE LIVES.
THAT MAY VERY WELL BE TRUE.
BUT I DO NOT BELIEVE THE ENDS JUSTIFY THE MEANS.
OUR SIDE HAS RULES OF ENGAGEMENT. THAT'S WHAT MAKES IT THE RIGHT SIDE.
I CANNOT CONDONE GIVING ANY SUPPORT TO TERRORISTS, NO MATTER HOW NOBLE THE INTENTIONS.
BUT OUR SIDE CAN BENEFIT FROM THE SHADOWS AS MUCH AS THEIRS, ROGERS.
CLEARLY MS. MERCED UNDERSTOOD THAT.
YEAH, BUT WITH HIS KOOKY MEMORY THING, TASKMASTER DOESN'T REMEMBER WHICH SIDE HE'S REALLY ON!
AND THE MISSUS NEVER BOTHERED TO TELL HIM. IN OTHER WORDS...

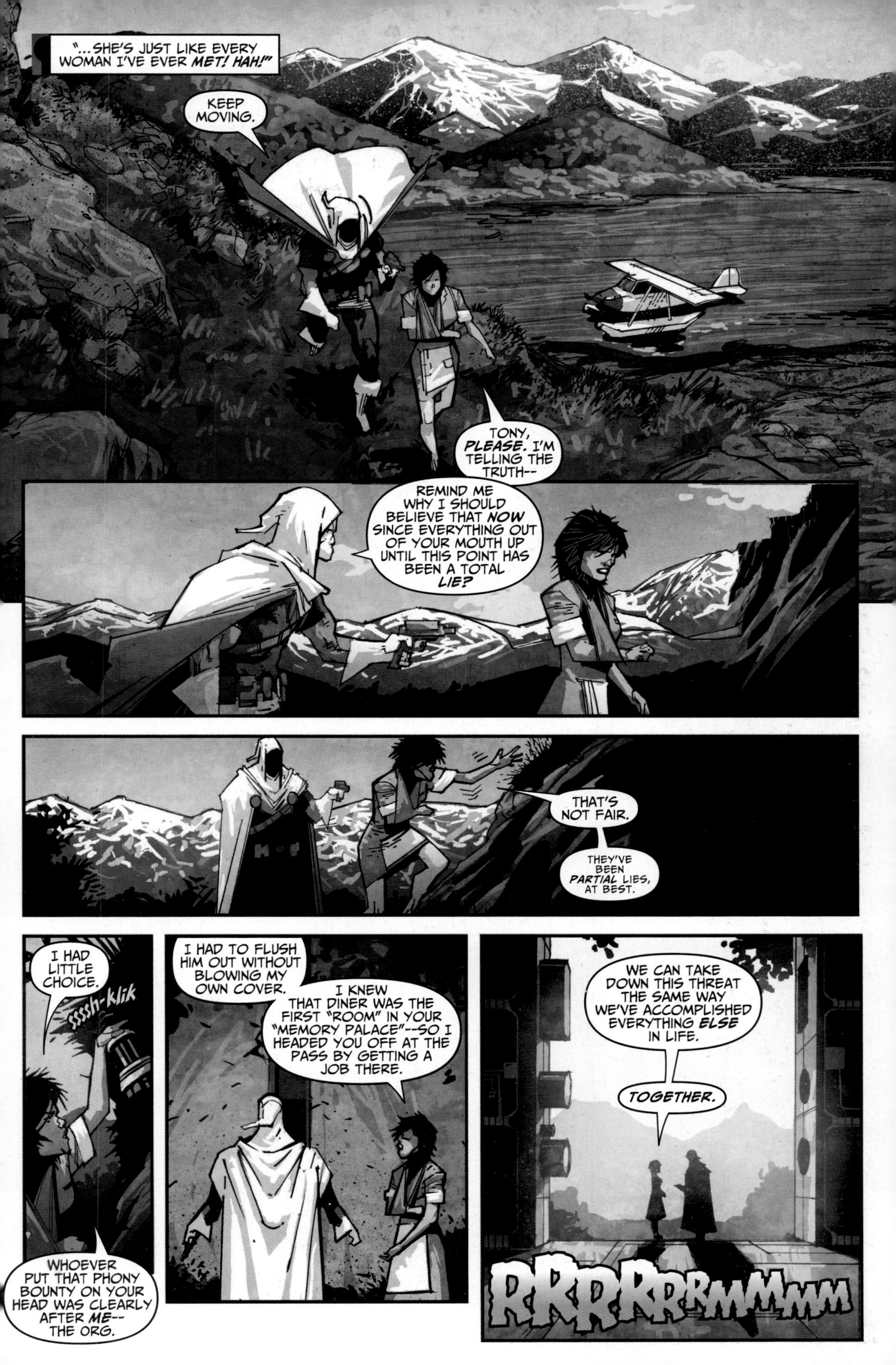
"...SHE'S JUST LIKE EVERY WOMAN I'VE EVER MET! HAH!"
KEEP MOVING.
TONY, PLEASE. I'M TELLING THE TRUTH--
REMIND ME WHY I SHOULD BELIEVE THAT NOW SINCE EVERYTHING OUT OF YOUR MOUTH UP UNTIL THIS POINT HAS BEEN A TOTAL LIE?
THAT'S NOT FAIR.
THEY'VE BEEN PARTIAL LIES, AT BEST.
I HAD LITTLE CHOICE.
SSSSH-KLIK
WHOEVER PUT THAT PHONY BOUNTY ON YOUR HEAD WAS CLEARLY AFTER ME-- THE ORG.
I HAD TO FLUSH HIM OUT WITHOUT BLOWING MY OWN COVER.
I KNEW THAT DINER WAS THE FIRST "ROOM" IN YOUR "MEMORY PALACE"--SO I HEADED YOU OFF AT THE PASS BY GETTING A JOB THERE.
WE CAN TAKE DOWN THIS THREAT THE SAME WAY WE'VE ACCOMPLISHED EVERYTHING ELSE IN LIFE.
TOGETHER.
RRRRRRRMMMMM

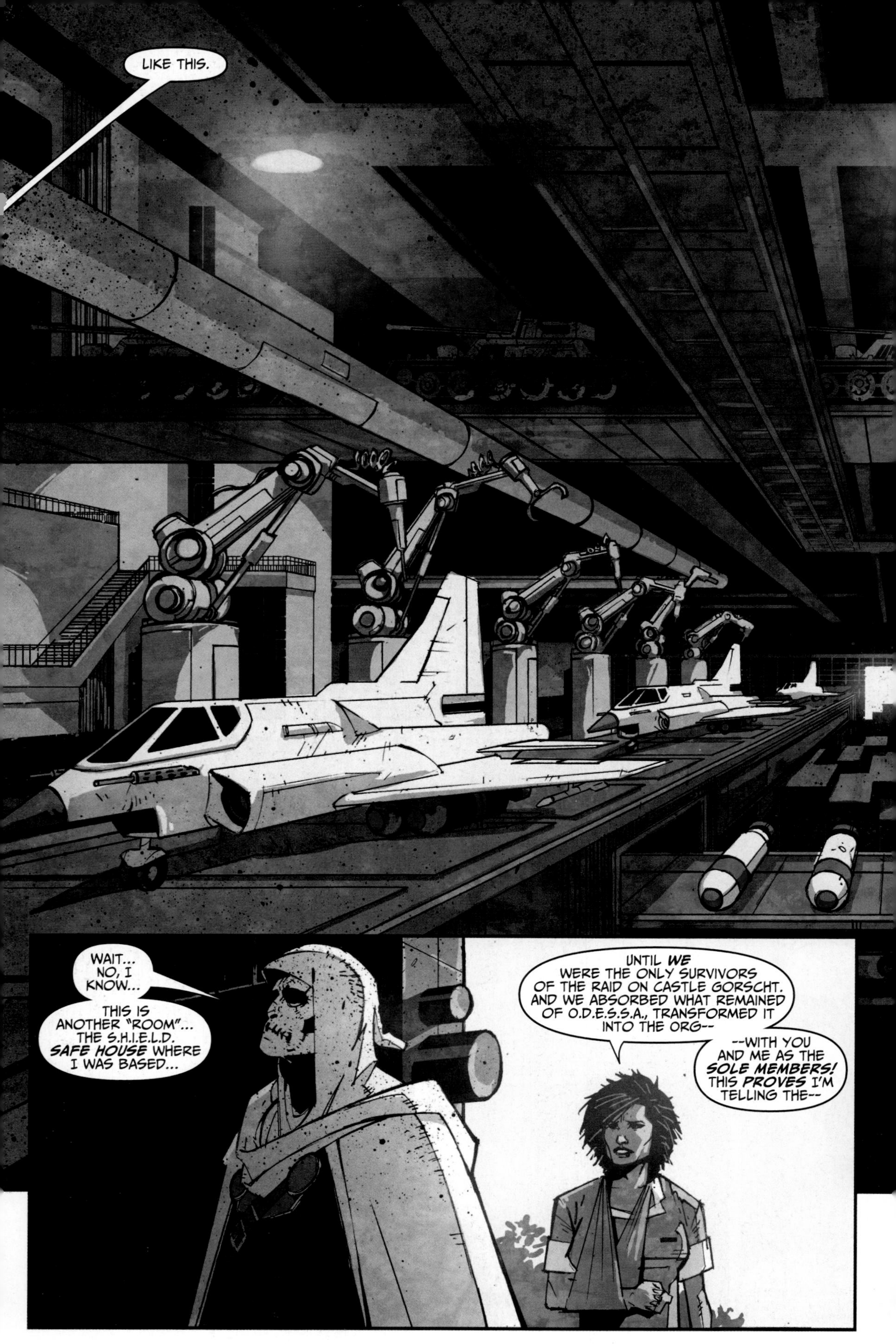
LIKE THIS.
WAIT... NO, I KNOW...
THIS IS ANOTHER "ROOM"... THE S.H.I.E.L.D. SAFE HOUSE WHERE I WAS BASED...
UNTIL WE WERE THE ONLY SURVIVORS OF THE RAID ON CASTLE GORSCHT. AND WE ABSORBED WHAT REMAINED OF O.D.E.S.S.A., TRANSFORMED IT INTO THE ORG--
--WITH YOU AND ME AS THE SOLE MEMBERS! THIS PROVES I'M TELLING THE--

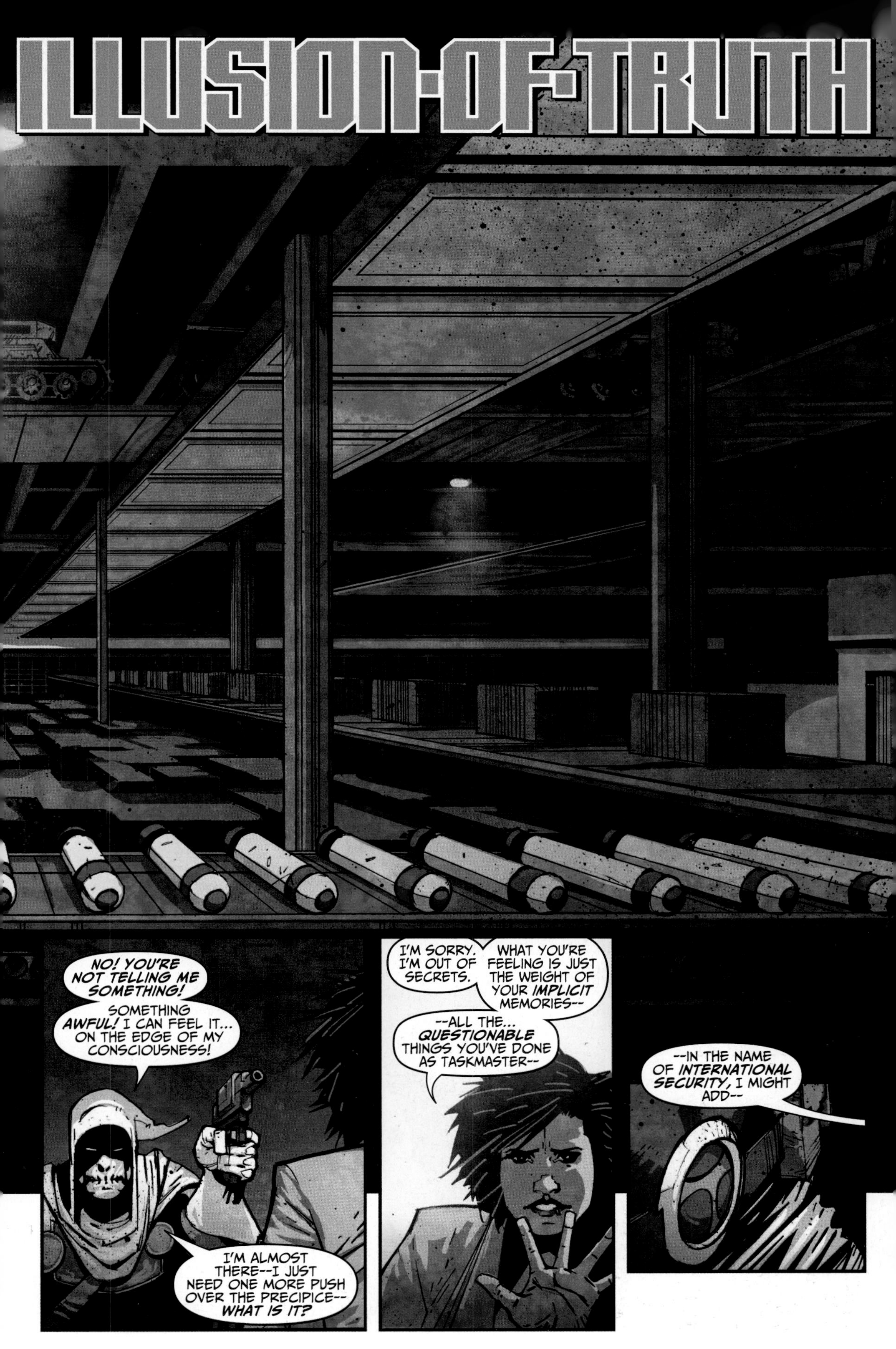
ILLUSION-OF-TRUTH
NO! YOU'RE NOT TELLING ME SOMETHING!
SOMETHING AWFUL! I CAN FEEL IT... ON THE EDGE OF MY CONSCIOUSNESS!
I'M ALMOST THERE--I JUST NEED ONE MORE PUSH OVER THE PRECIPICE-- WHAT IS IT?
I'M SORRY. I'M OUT OF SECRETS.
WHAT YOU'RE FEELING IS JUST THE WEIGHT OF YOUR IMPLICIT MEMORIES--
--ALL THE... QUESTIONABLE THINGS YOU'VE DONE AS TASKMASTER--
--IN THE NAME OF INTERNATIONAL SECURITY, I MIGHT ADD--

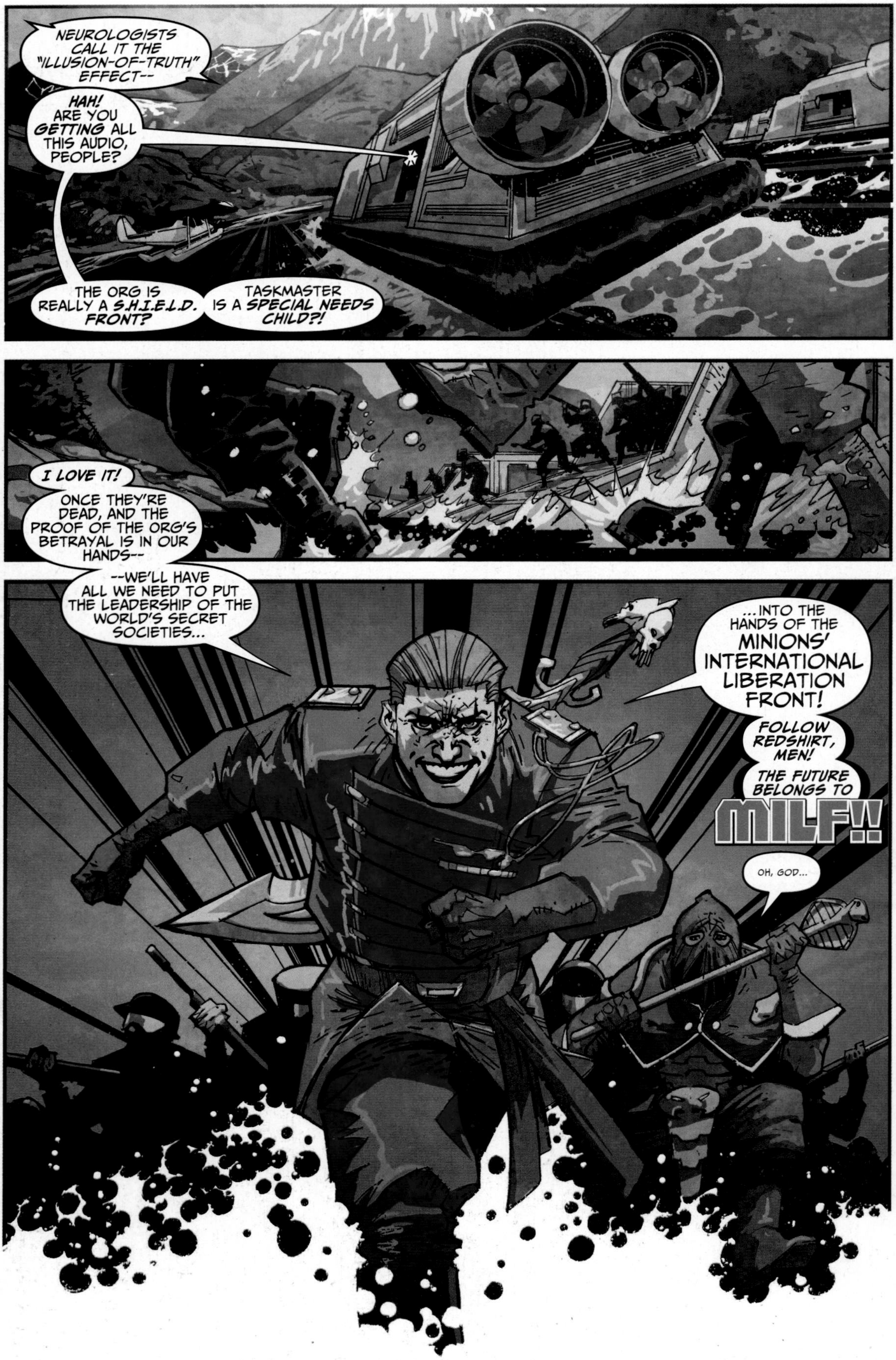
NEUROLOGISTS CALL IT THE "ILLUSION-OF-TRUTH" EFFECT--
HAH! ARE YOU GETTING ALL THIS AUDIO, PEOPLE?
THE ORG IS REALLY A S.H.I.E.L.D. FRONT?
TASKMASTER IS A SPECIAL NEEDS CHILD?!
I LOVE IT!
ONCE THEY'RE DEAD, AND THE PROOF OF THE ORG'S BETRAYAL IS IN OUR HANDS--
--WE'LL HAVE ALL WE NEED TO PUT THE LEADERSHIP OF THE WORLD'S SECRET SOCIETIES...
...INTO THE HANDS OF THE MINIONS' INTERNATIONAL LIBERATION FRONT!
FOLLOW REDSHIRT, MEN!
THE FUTURE BELONGS TO
MILF!!
OH, GOD...

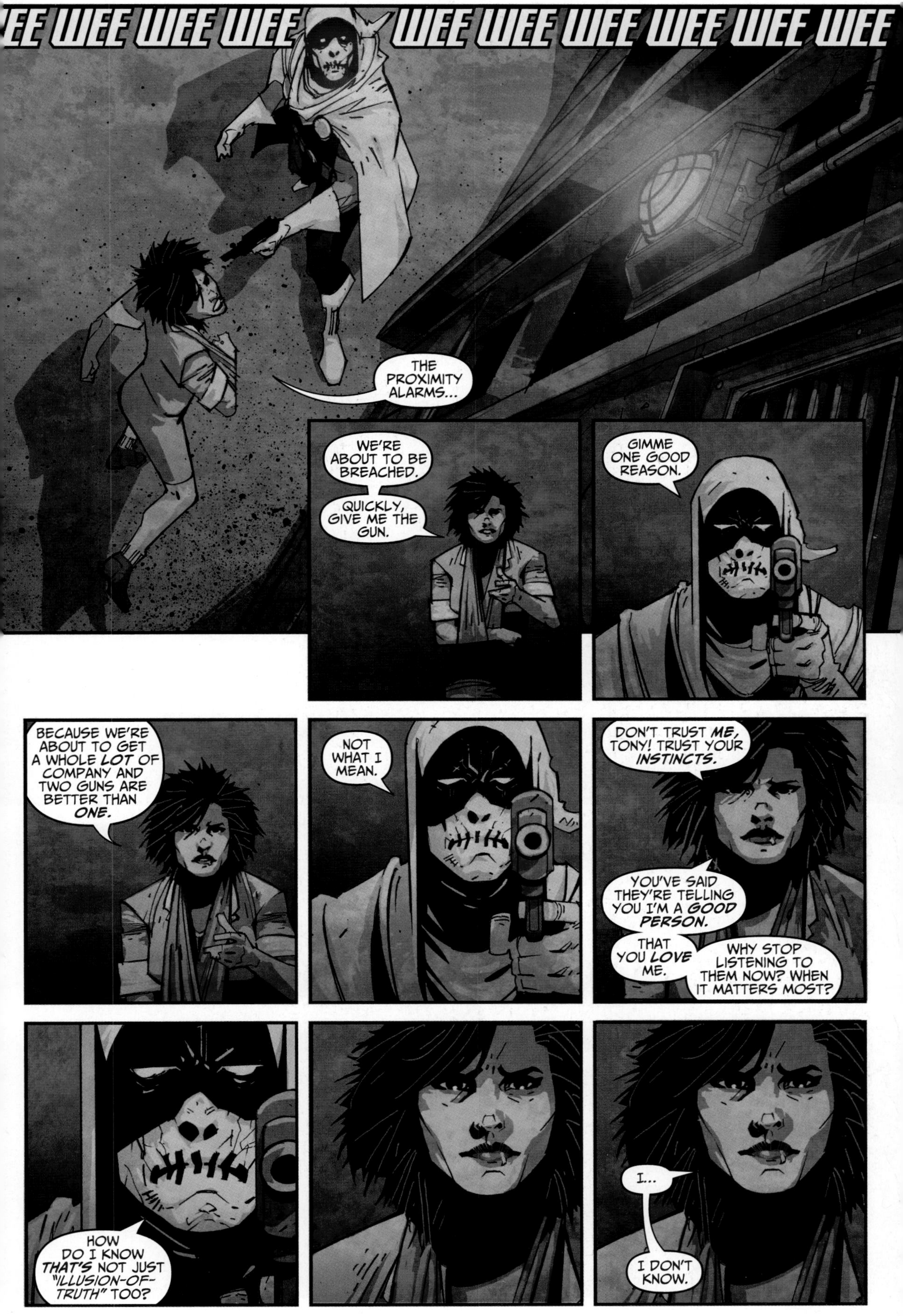
EE WEE WEE WEE WEE WEE WEE WEE WEE WEE
THE PROXIMITY ALARMS...
WE'RE ABOUT TO BE BREACHED.
QUICKLY, GIVE ME THE GUN.
GIMME ONE GOOD REASON.
BECAUSE WE'RE ABOUT TO GET A WHOLE LOT OF COMPANY AND TWO GUNS ARE BETTER THAN ONE.
NOT WHAT I MEAN.
DON'T TRUST ME, TONY! TRUST YOUR INSTINCTS.
YOU'VE SAID THEY'RE TELLING YOU I'M A GOOD PERSON.
THAT YOU LOVE ME.
WHY STOP LISTENING TO THEM NOW? WHEN IT MATTERS MOST?
HOW DO I KNOW THAT'S NOT JUST "ILLUSION-OF-TRUTH" TOO?
I...
I DON'T KNOW.

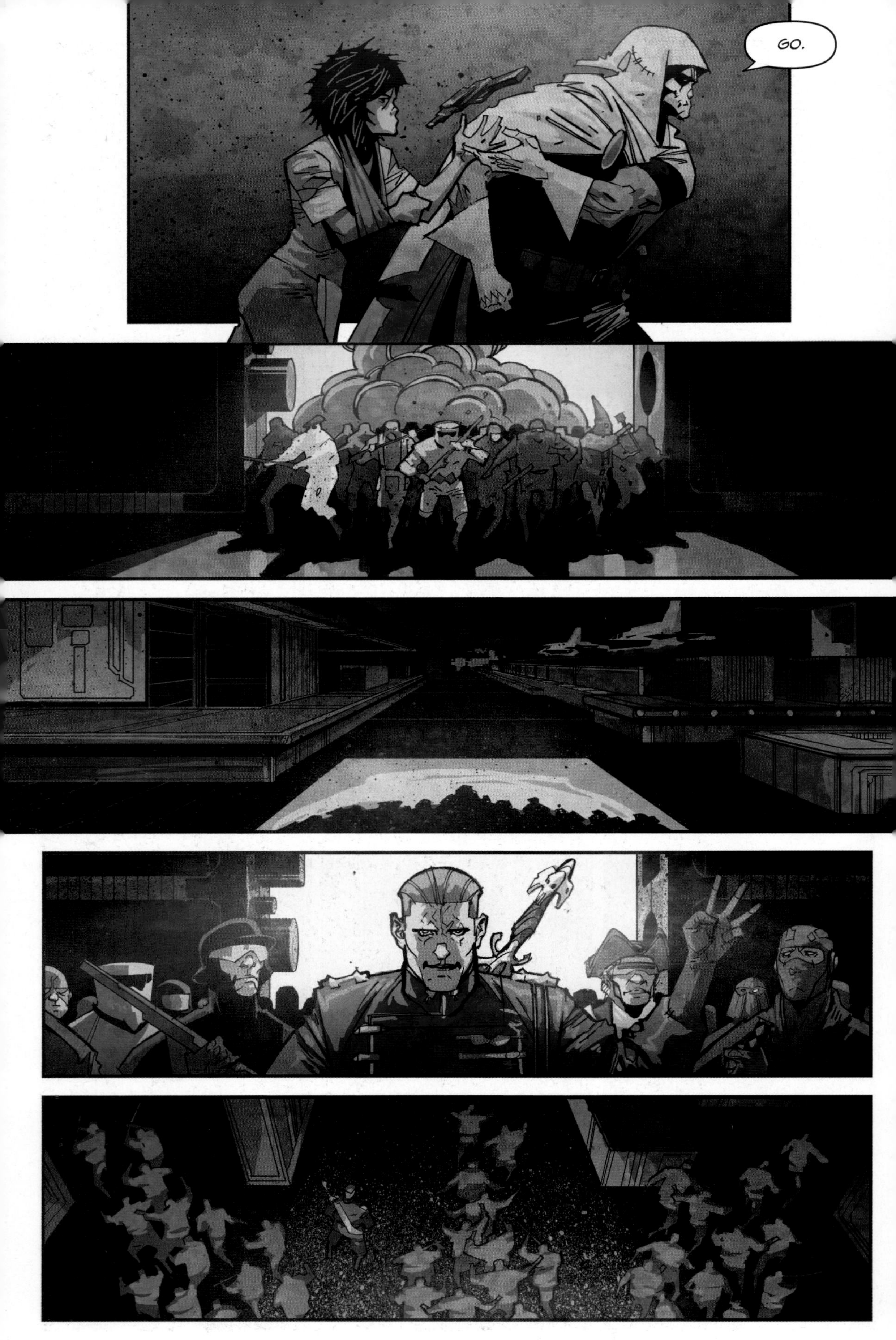
GO.

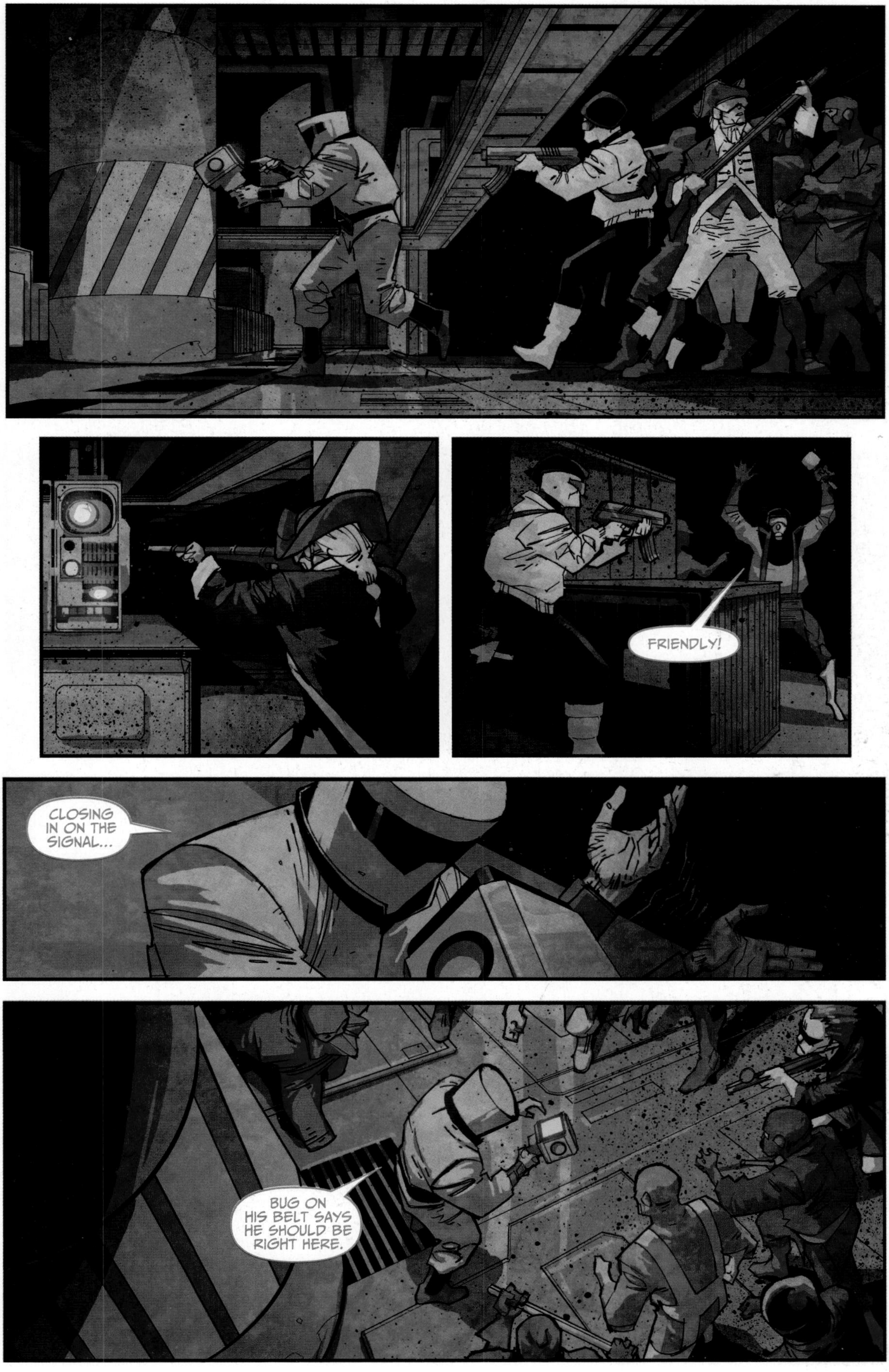
FRIENDLY!
CLOSING IN ON THE SIGNAL...
BUG ON HIS BELT SAYS HE SHOULD BE RIGHT HERE.

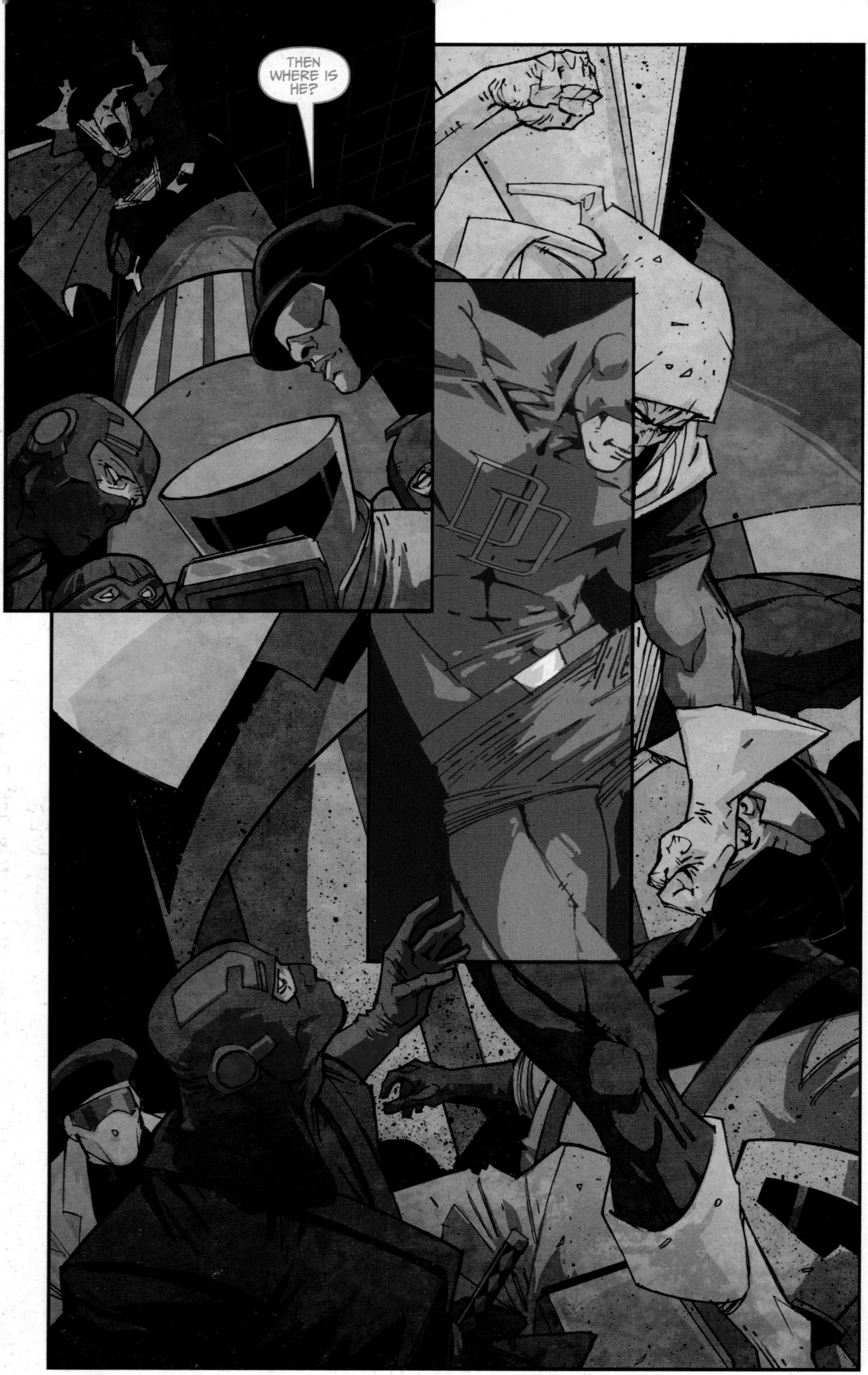
THEN WHERE IS HE?

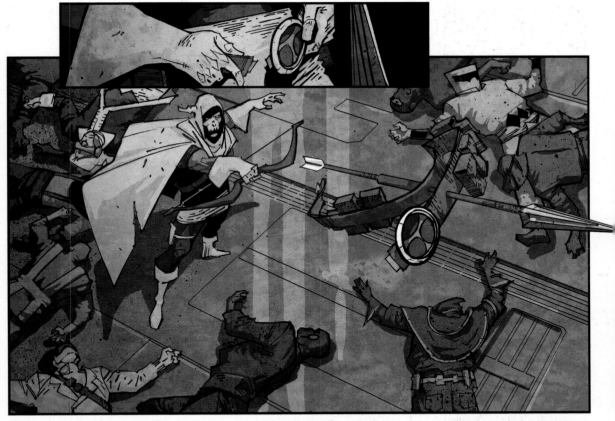

TUNK

WAIT!

HE'S HAULING ASS, OVER--

AW, CRA--

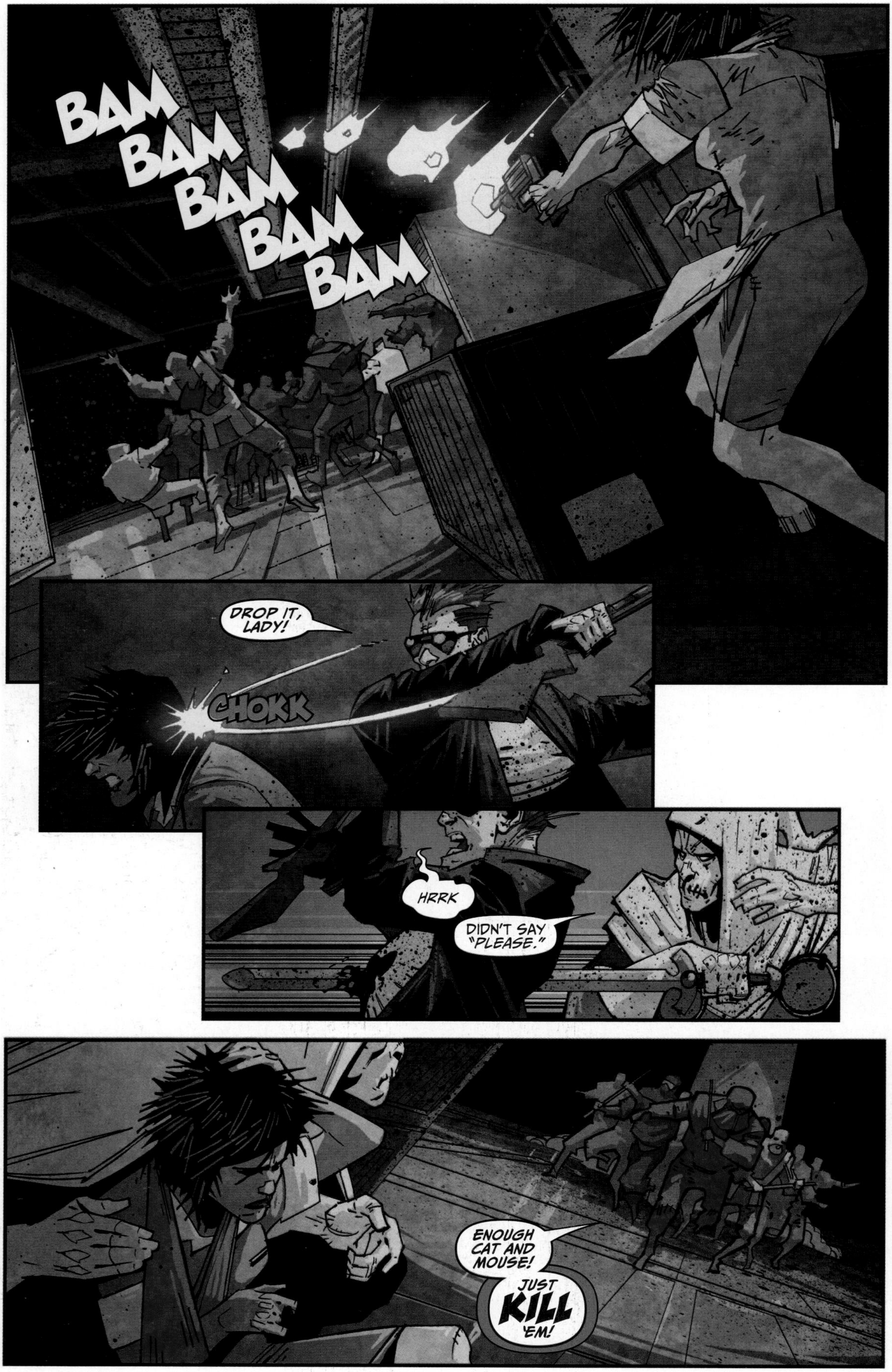
BAM
BAM
BAM
BAM
BAM
DROP IT, LADY!
CHOKK
HRRK
DIDN'T SAY "PLEASE."
ENOUGH CAT AND MOUSE!
JUST KILL 'EM!

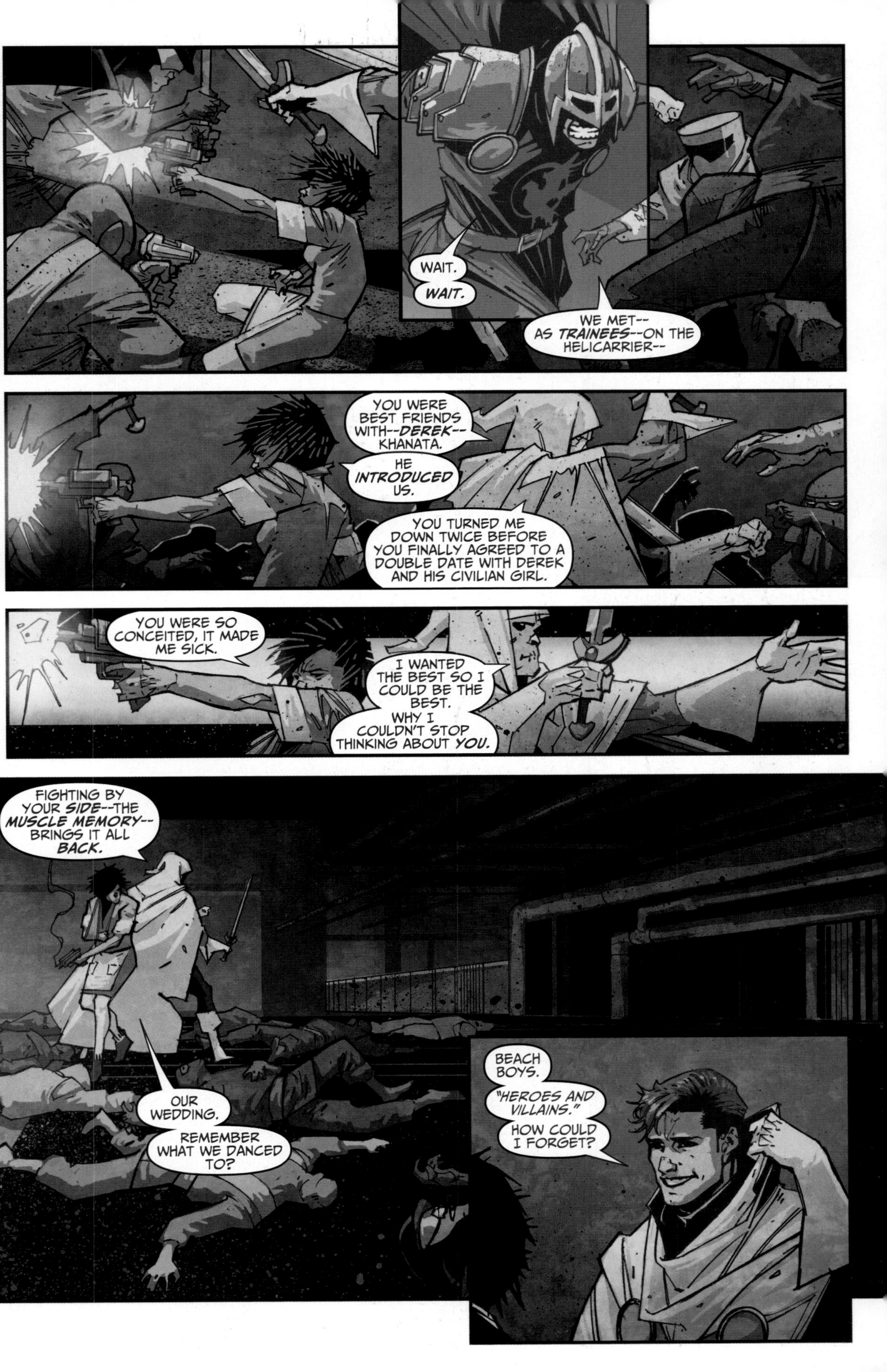
WAIT. WAIT.
WE MET-- AS TRAINEES--ON THE HELICARRIER--
YOU WERE BEST FRIENDS WITH--DEREK-- KHANATA.
HE INTRODUCED US.
YOU TURNED ME DOWN TWICE BEFORE YOU FINALLY AGREED TO A DOUBLE DATE WITH DEREK AND HIS CIVILIAN GIRL.
YOU WERE SO CONCEITED, IT MADE ME SICK.
I WANTED THE BEST SO I COULD BE THE BEST.
WHY I COULDN'T STOP THINKING ABOUT YOU.
FIGHTING BY YOUR SIDE--THE MUSCLE MEMORY-- BRINGS IT ALL BACK.
OUR WEDDING.
REMEMBER WHAT WE DANCED TO?
BEACH BOYS.
"HEROES AND VILLAINS."
HOW COULD I FORGET?

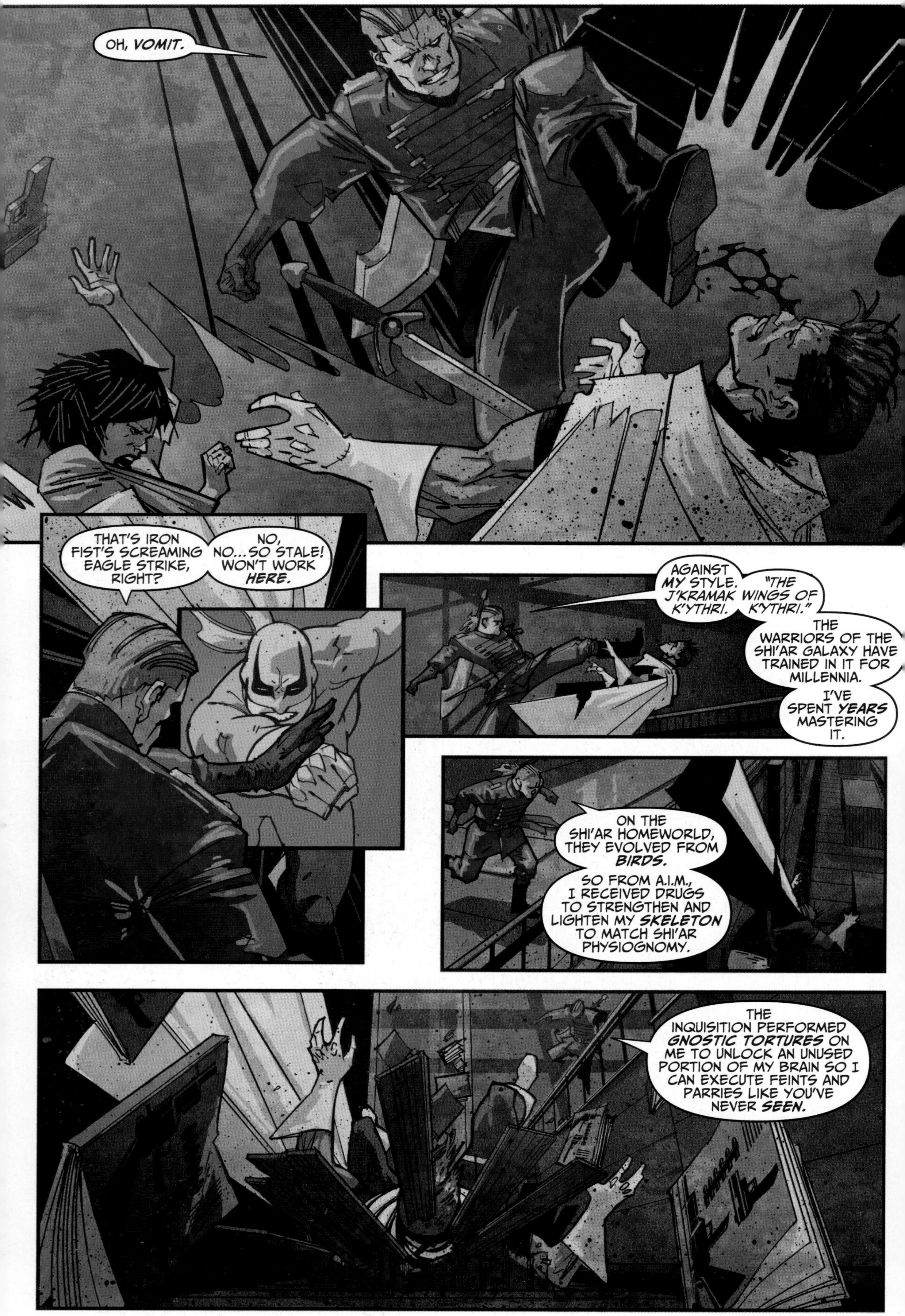
OH, VOMIT.
THAT'S IRON FIST'S SCREAMING EAGLE STRIKE, RIGHT?
NO, NO...SO STALE! WON'T WORK HERE.
AGAINST MY STYLE. J'KRAMAK K'YTHRI.
"THE WINGS OF K'YTHRI."
THE WARRIORS OF THE SHI'AR GALAXY HAVE TRAINED IN IT FOR MILLENNIA.
I'VE SPENT YEARS MASTERING IT.
ON THE SHI'AR HOMEWORLD, THEY EVOLVED FROM BIRDS.
SO FROM A.I.M., I RECEIVED DRUGS TO STRENGTHEN AND LIGHTEN MY SKELETON TO MATCH SHI'AR PHYSIOGNOMY.
THE INQUISITION PERFORMED GNOSTIC TORTURES ON ME TO UNLOCK AN UNUSED PORTION OF MY BRAIN SO I CAN EXECUTE FEINTS AND PARRIES LIKE YOU'VE NEVER SEEN.

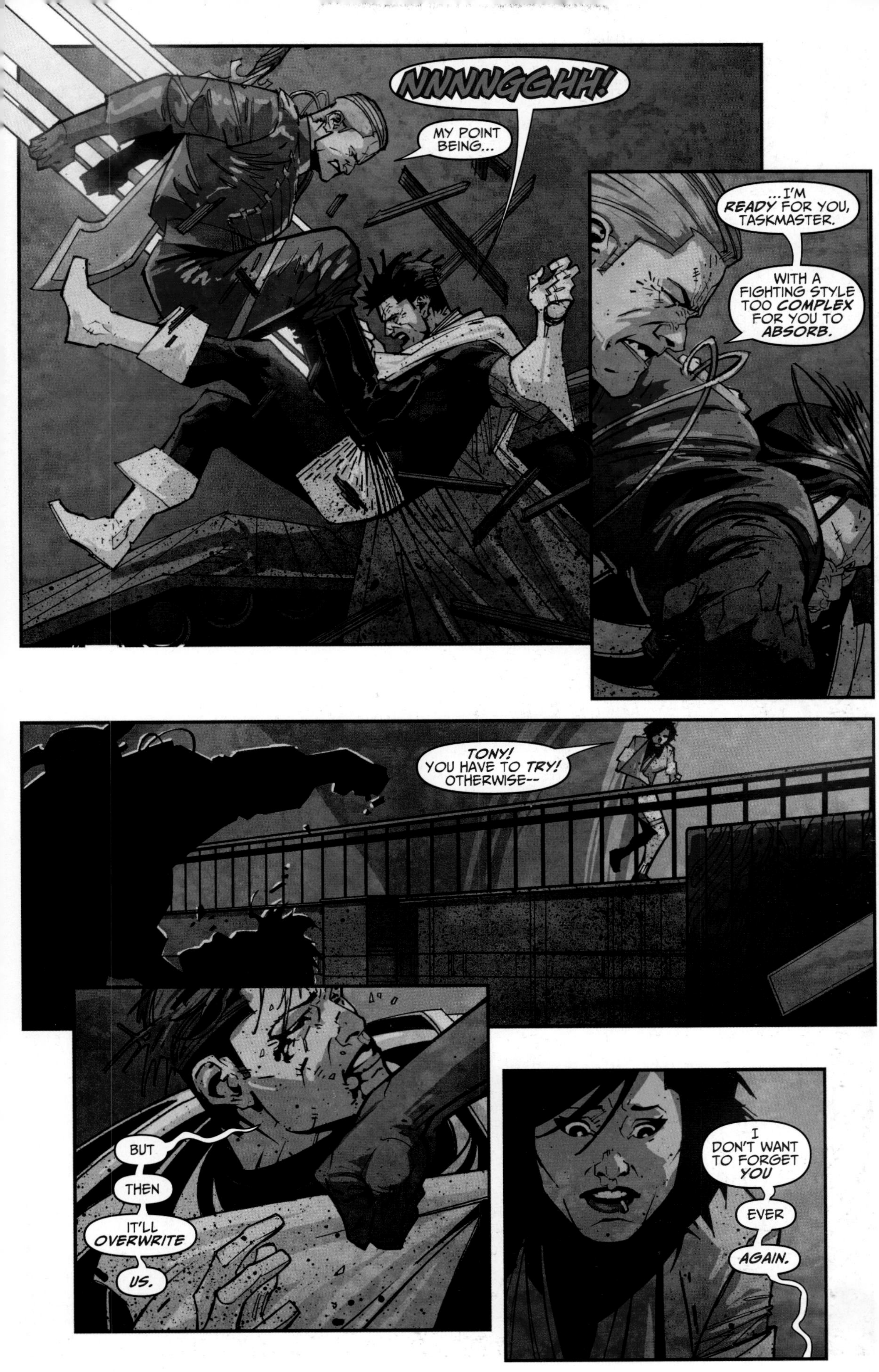
NNNNGGHH!
MY POINT BEING...
...I'M READY FOR YOU, TASKMASTER.
WITH A FIGHTING STYLE TOO COMPLEX FOR YOU TO ABSORB.
TONY! YOU HAVE TO TRY! OTHERWISE--
BUT
THEN
IT'LL OVERWRITE
US.
I DON'T WANT TO FORGET YOU
EVER
AGAIN.

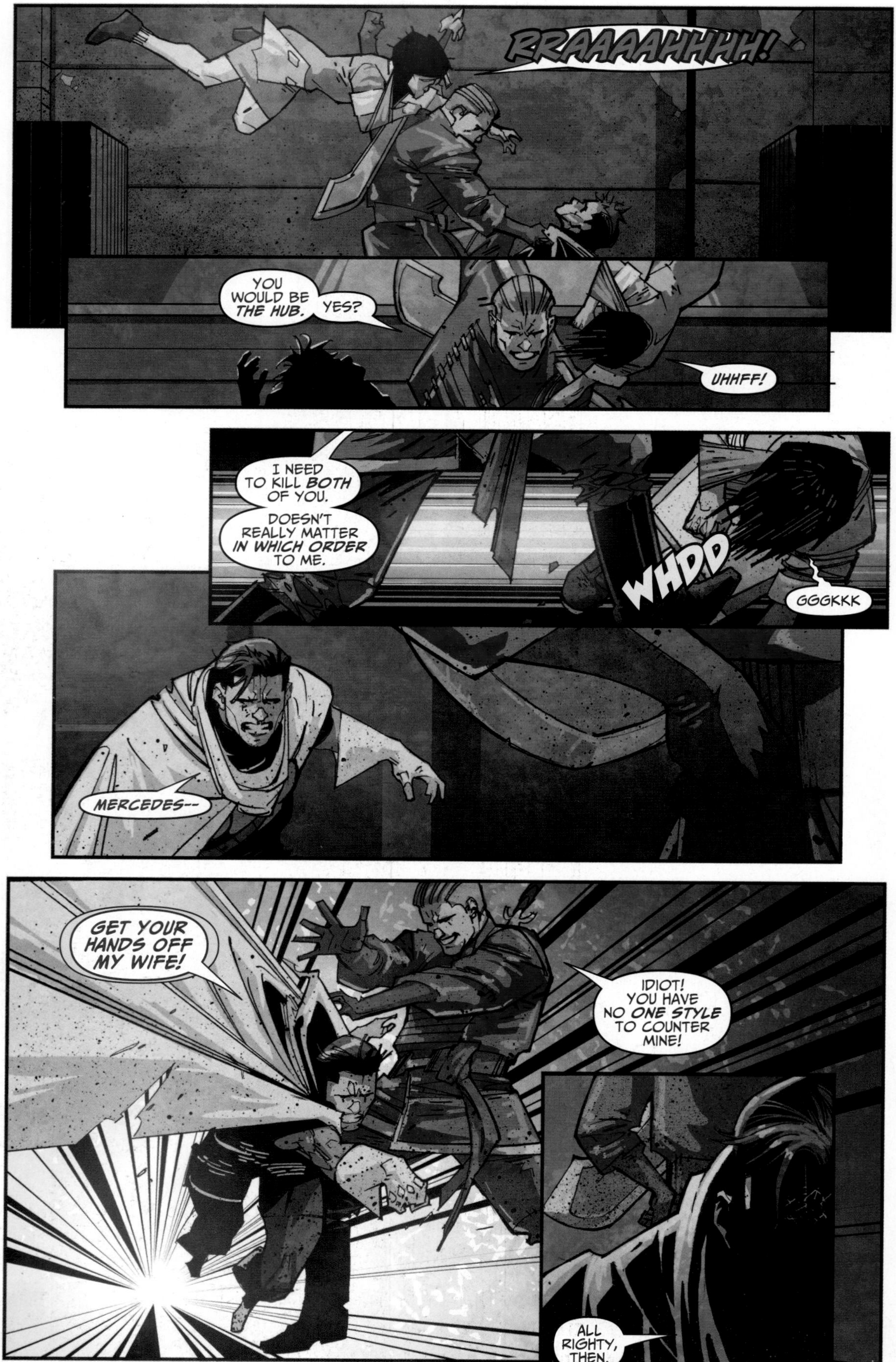
RRAAAAHHHH!
YOU WOULD BE THE HUB.
YES?
UHHFF!
I NEED TO KILL BOTH OF YOU.
DOESN'T REALLY MATTER IN WHICH ORDER TO ME.
WHDD
GGGKKK
MERCEDES--
GET YOUR HANDS OFF MY WIFE!
IDIOT! YOU HAVE NO ONE STYLE TO COUNTER MINE!
ALL RIGHTY, THEN.

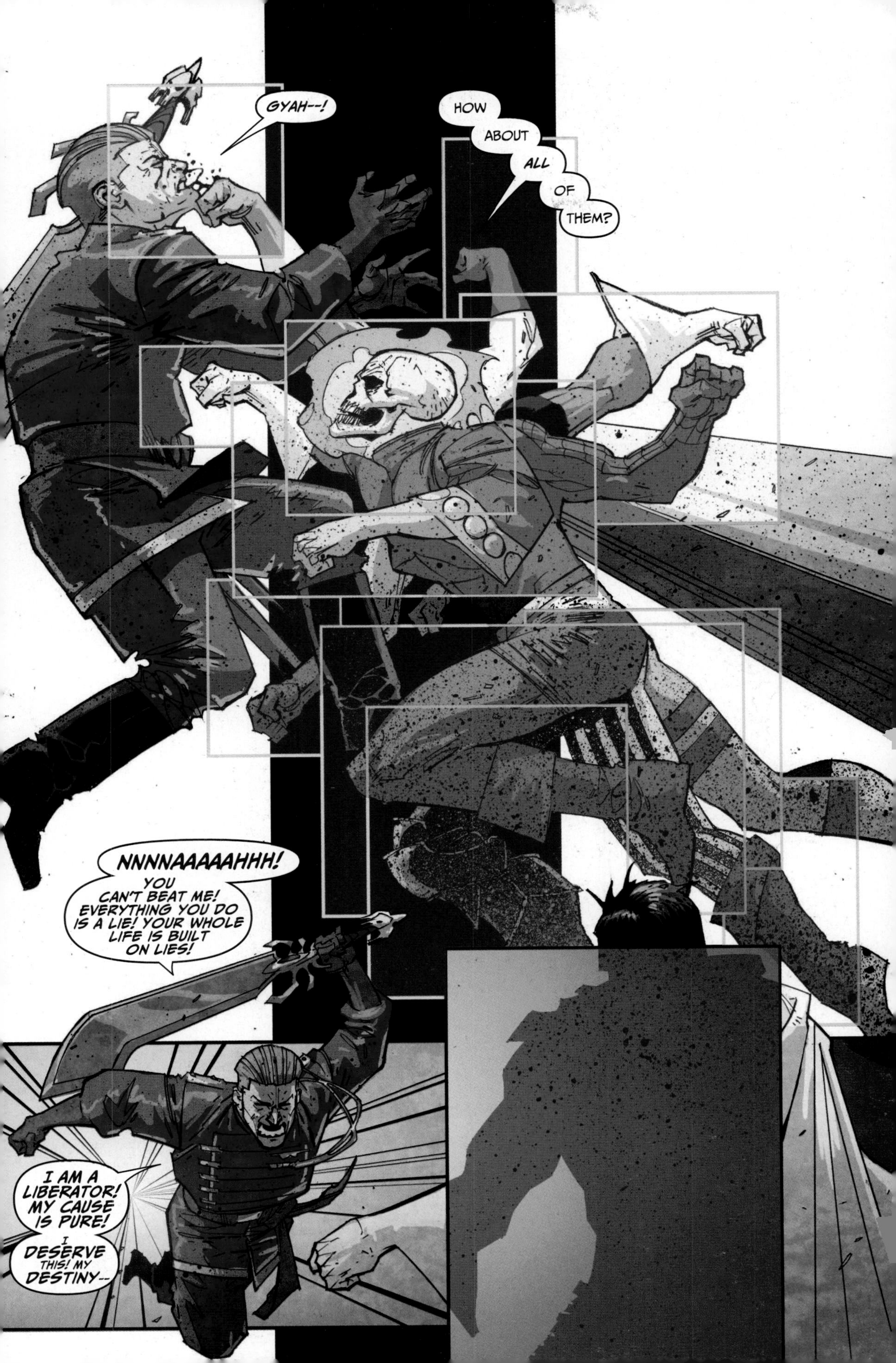
GYAH--!
HOW ABOUT ALL OF THEM?
NNNNAAAAAHHH! YOU CAN'T BEAT ME! EVERYTHING YOU DO IS A LIE! YOUR WHOLE LIFE IS BUILT ON LIES!
I AM A LIBERATOR! MY CAUSE IS PURE!
I DESERVE THIS! MY DESTINY--

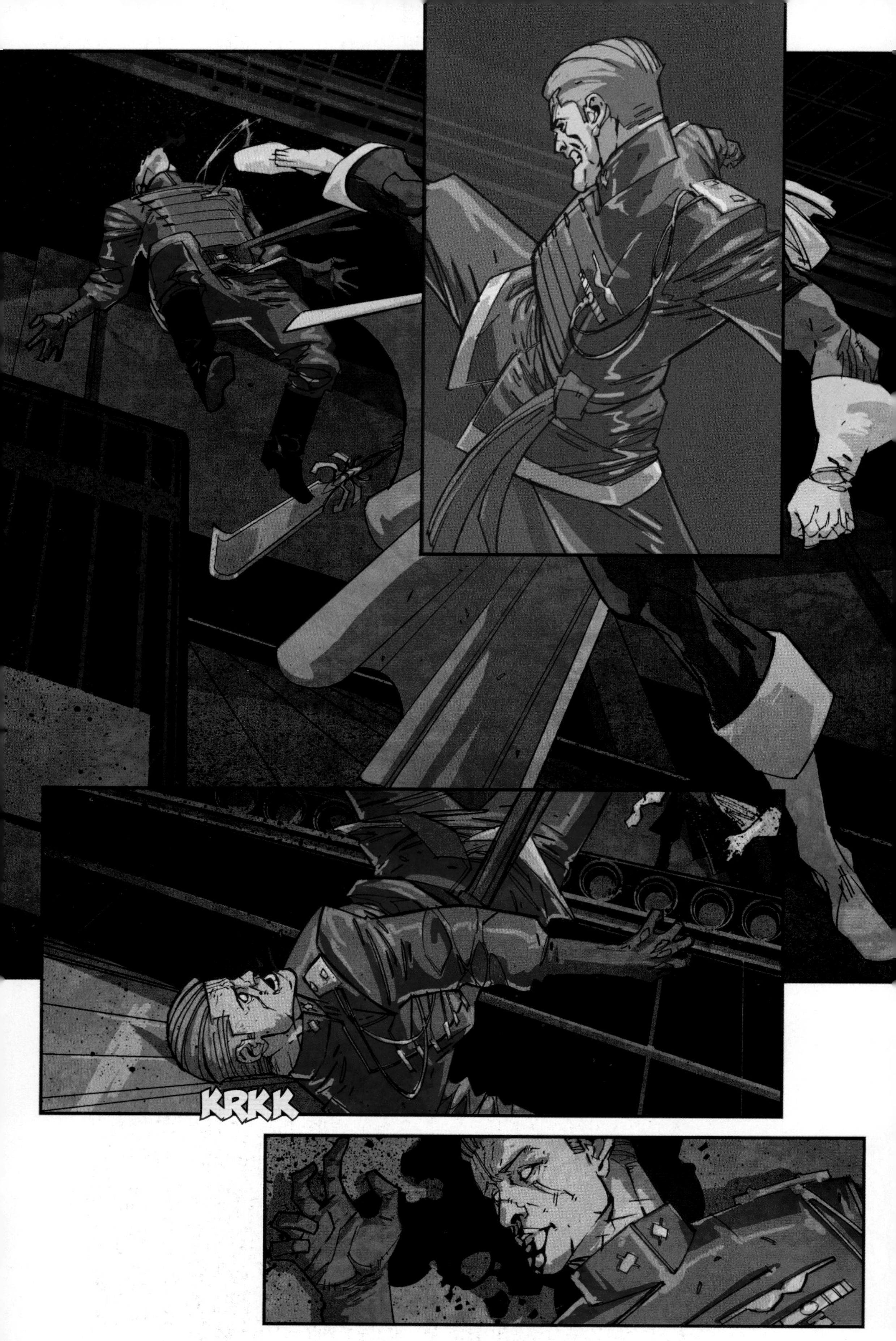
KRKK

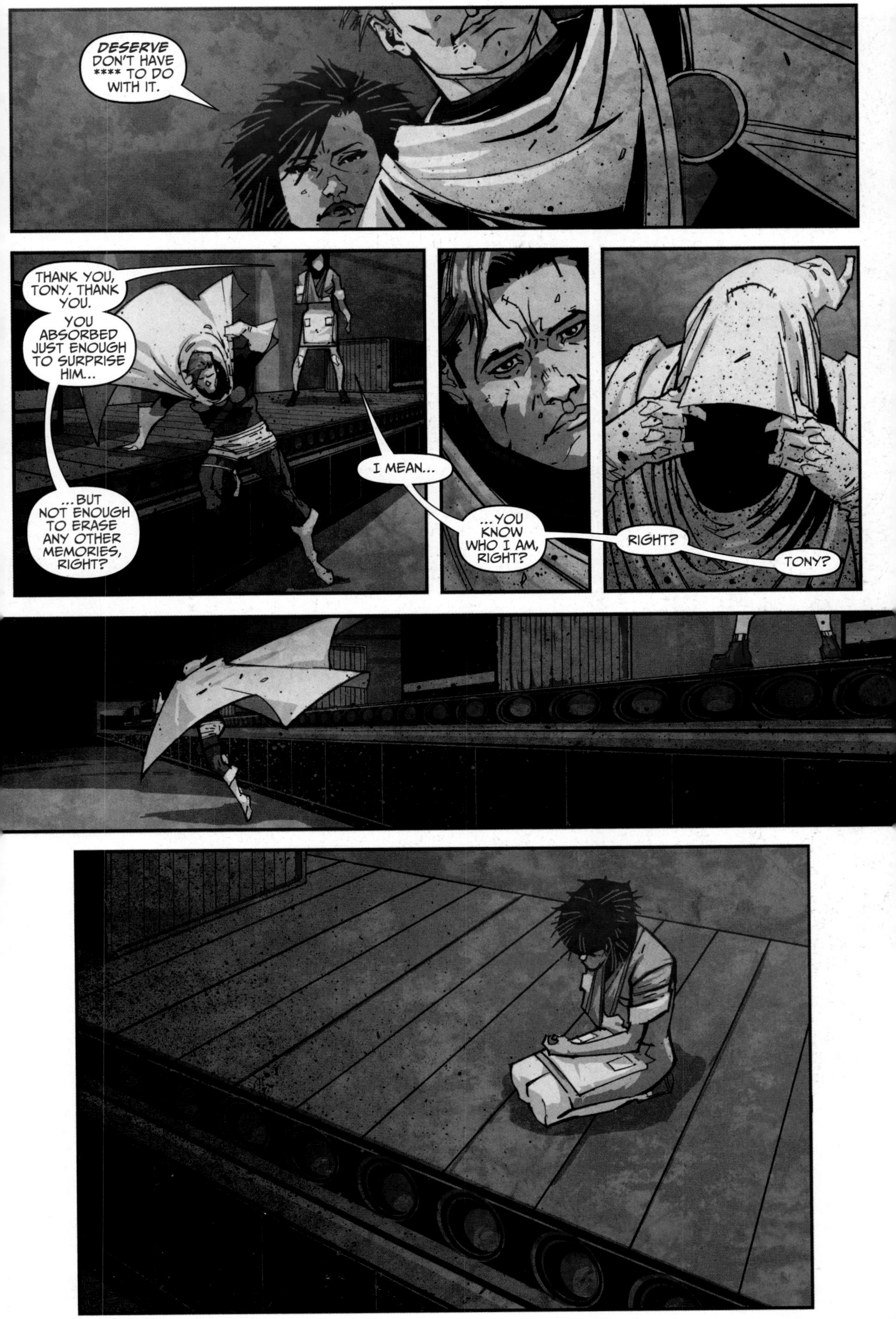
DESERVE DON'T HAVE **** TO DO WITH IT.
THANK YOU, TONY. THANK YOU.
YOU ABSORBED JUST ENOUGH TO SURPRISE HIM...
...BUT NOT ENOUGH TO ERASE ANY OTHER MEMORIES, RIGHT?
I MEAN...
...YOU KNOW WHO I AM, RIGHT?
RIGHT?
TONY?

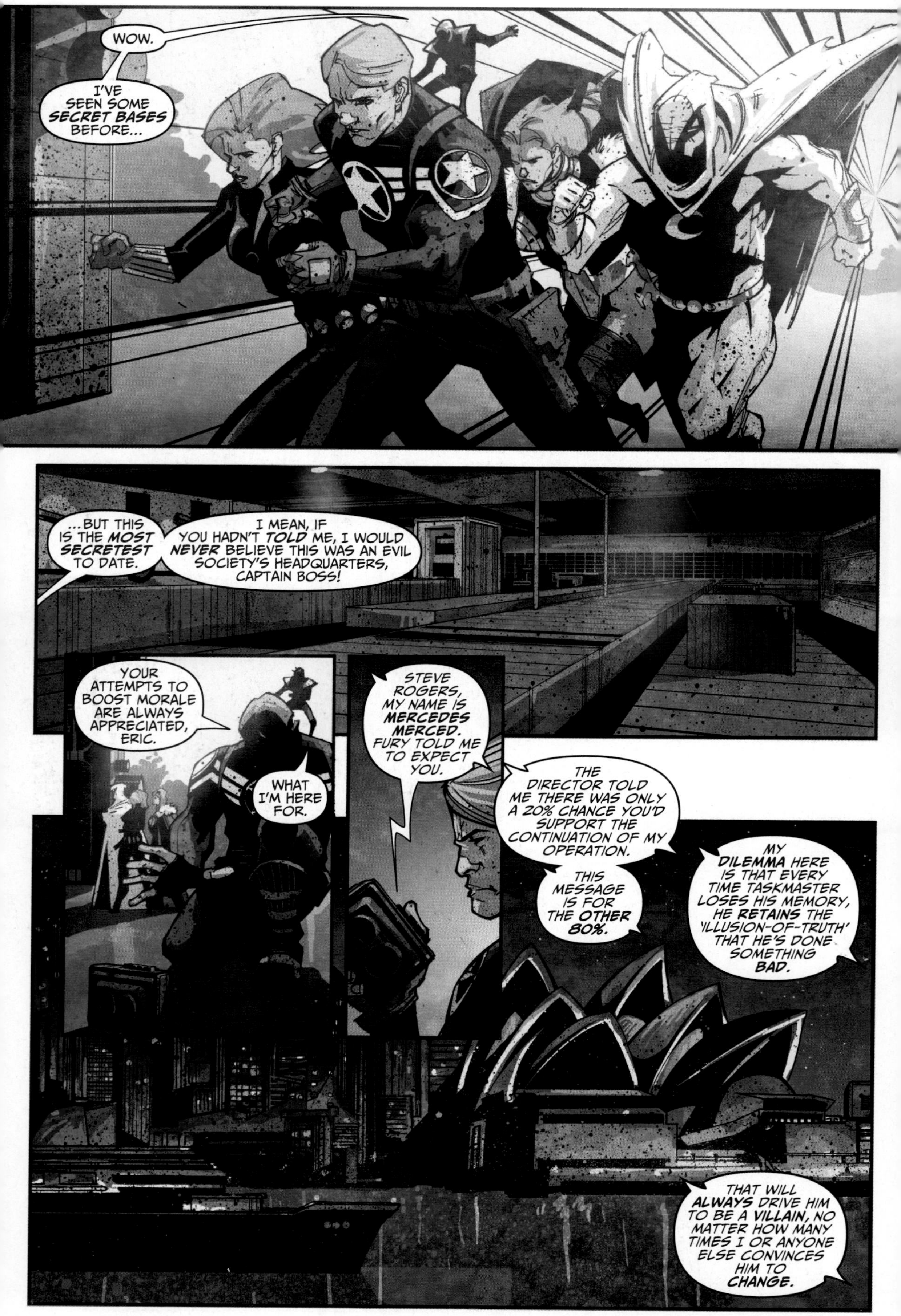
WOW.
I'VE SEEN SOME SECRET BASES BEFORE...
...BUT THIS IS THE MOST SECRETEST TO DATE.
I MEAN, IF YOU HADN'T TOLD ME, I WOULD NEVER BELIEVE THIS WAS AN EVIL SOCIETY'S HEADQUARTERS, CAPTAIN BOSS!
YOUR ATTEMPTS TO BOOST MORALE ARE ALWAYS APPRECIATED, ERIC.
WHAT I'M HERE FOR.
STEVE ROGERS, MY NAME IS MERCEDES MERCED. FURY TOLD ME TO EXPECT YOU.
THE DIRECTOR TOLD ME THERE WAS ONLY A 20% CHANCE YOU'D SUPPORT THE CONTINUATION OF MY OPERATION.
THIS MESSAGE IS FOR THE OTHER 80%.
MY DILEMMA HERE IS THAT EVERY TIME TASKMASTER LOSES HIS MEMORY, HE RETAINS THE 'ILLUSION-OF-TRUTH' THAT HE'S DONE SOMETHING BAD.
THAT WILL ALWAYS DRIVE HIM TO BE A VILLAIN, NO MATTER HOW MANY TIMES I OR ANYONE ELSE CONVINCES HIM TO CHANGE.

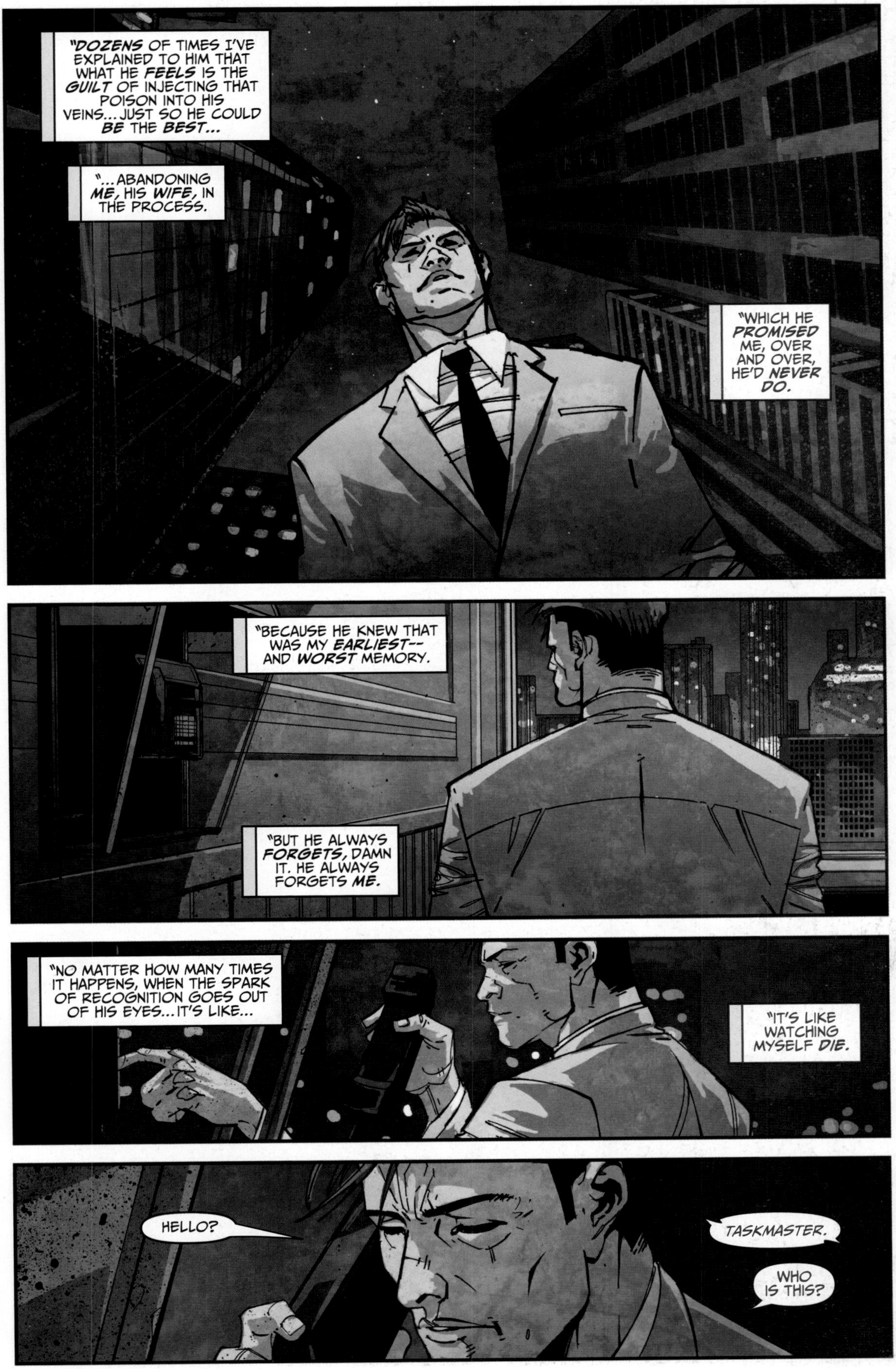
"DOZENS OF TIMES I'VE EXPLAINED TO HIM THAT WHAT HE FEELS IS THE GUILT OF INJECTING THAT POISON INTO HIS VEINS... JUST SO HE COULD BE THE BEST...
"...ABANDONING ME, HIS WIFE, IN THE PROCESS.
"WHICH HE PROMISED ME, OVER AND OVER, HE'D NEVER DO.
"BECAUSE HE KNEW THAT WAS MY EARLIEST-- AND WORST MEMORY.
"BUT HE ALWAYS FORGETS, DAMN IT. HE ALWAYS FORGETS ME.
"NO MATTER HOW MANY TIMES IT HAPPENS, WHEN THE SPARK OF RECOGNITION GOES OUT OF HIS EYES... IT'S LIKE...
"IT'S LIKE WATCHING MYSELF DIE.
HELLO?
TASKMASTER.
WHO IS THIS?

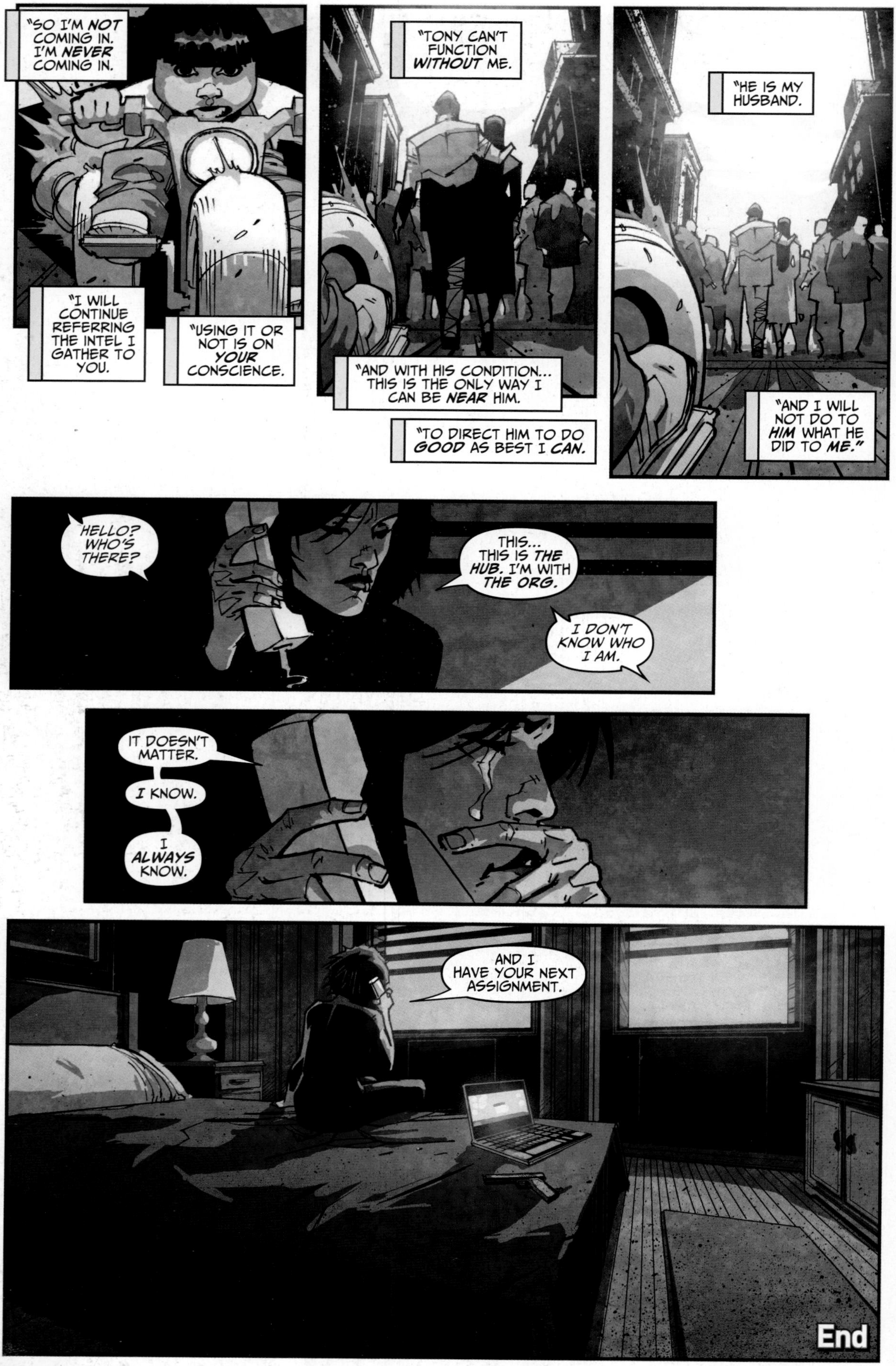
"SO I'M NOT COMING IN. I'M NEVER COMING IN.
"I WILL CONTINUE REFERRING THE INTEL I GATHER TO YOU.
"USING IT OR NOT IS ON YOUR CONSCIENCE.
"TONY CAN'T FUNCTION WITHOUT ME.
"AND WITH HIS CONDITION... THIS IS THE ONLY WAY I CAN BE NEAR HIM.
"TO DIRECT HIM TO DO GOOD AS BEST I CAN.
"HE IS MY HUSBAND.
"AND I WILL NOT DO TO HIM WHAT HE DID TO ME."
HELLO? WHO'S THERE?
THIS... THIS IS THE HUB. I'M WITH THE ORG.
I DON'T KNOW WHO I AM.
IT DOESN'T MATTER.
I KNOW.
I ALWAYS KNOW.
AND I HAVE YOUR NEXT ASSIGNMENT.
End

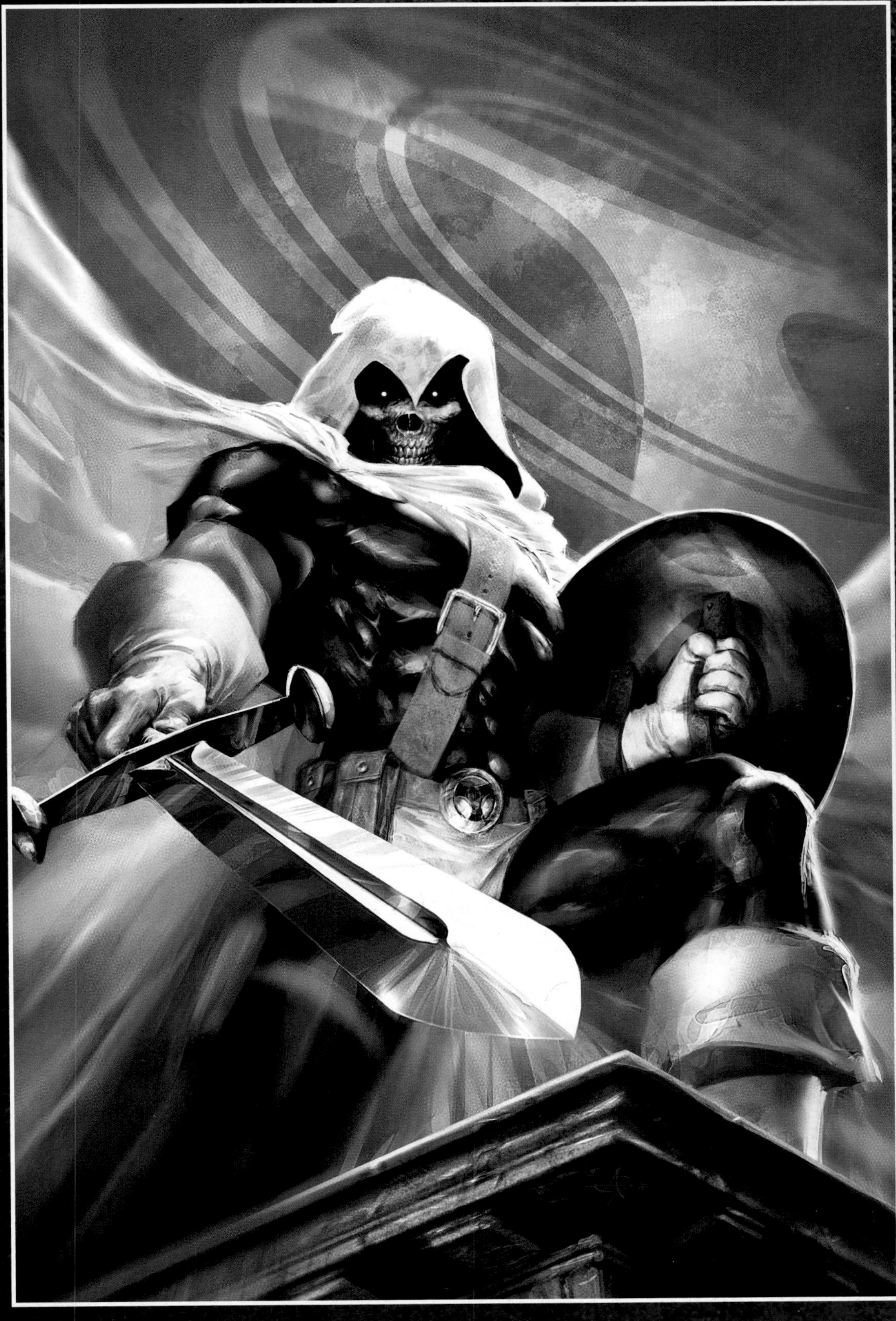

UNUSED COVER FOR ISSUE #1 BY **ALEX GARNER**

TASKMASTER'S
TALENT POOL

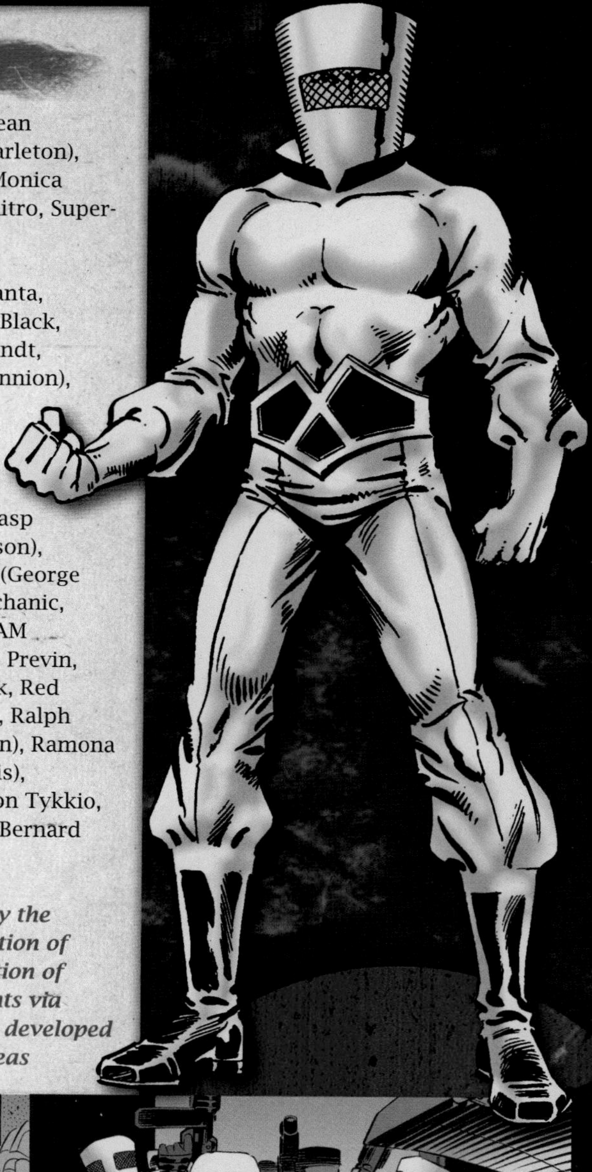

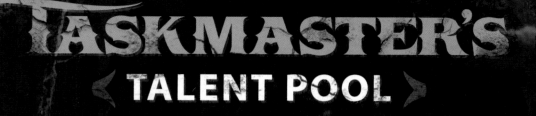

A.I.M.

CURRENT MEMBERS: Njeri Damphousse, Sean Madigan, Mark Macross, MODOK (George Tarleton), Evelyn Necker, Peggy Park, Hyun Rahman, Monica Rappacini, Abu-Jamal Rodriguez, Betty Sumitro, Super-Adaptoid

FORMER MEMBERS: Paul Allen, Theron Atlanta, B'Tumba, Baron Samedi, Clete Billups, Julia Black, Timothy Black, Brace, Lars Branco, Ellen Brandt, Solemne Brannex, Cache, Chain (Thomas Bannion), Delia Childress, George Clinton, Brice Courtland, Cyborg, Commander Cypher, Harry Daze, Destructor (Kerwin Korman), Clytemnestra Erwin, Fixer (Paul Ebersol), Janet Galloway, David Garrett, Lyle Getz, Grasp (Herb Bannion), Grizzly, Harness (Erika Benson), James Hendrickson, Highwayman, Lifeform (George Prufrock), Carl Lombardi, Chet Madden, Mechanic, Mentallo (Marvin Flumm), Mindstorm, MODAM (Olinka Barankova), Maxwell Mordius, Drake Previn, Protocide (Clinton McIntyre), Jethro Prufrock, Red Skull (Johann Shmidt), Count Bornag Royale, Ralph Ryder, Arthur Shaman, Sonic (Daniel Bannion), Ramona Starr, Karl Steiner, Strikeback (Anthony Davis), Stryke, Timekeeper, Valdemar Tykkio, Yorgon Tykkio, Victorius (Victor Conrad), Kseniya Vladitch, Bernard Worrell, Stanley Zane

A.I.M. (Advanced Idea Mechanics), formerly the scientific division of Hydra, is an organization of brilliant scientists dedicated to the acquisition of power and the overthrow of all governments via technological means. Over the years it has developed various splinter groups: AID (Advanced Ideas in Destruction), RAID (Radically Advanced Ideas in Destruction), and AGM (Advanced Genocide Mechanics), each with its own purpose.

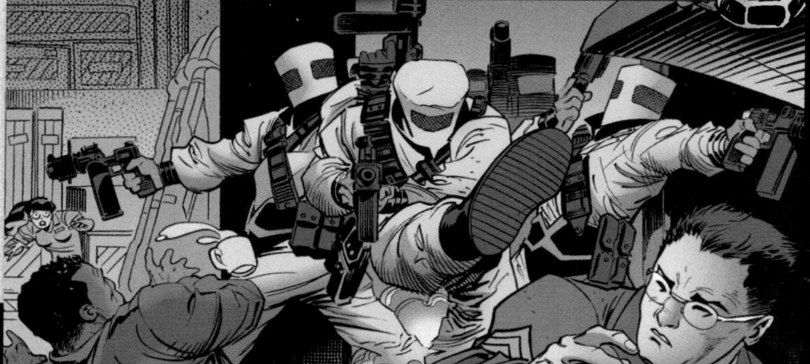

FIRST APPEARANCE:
Strange Tales #146 (1966)

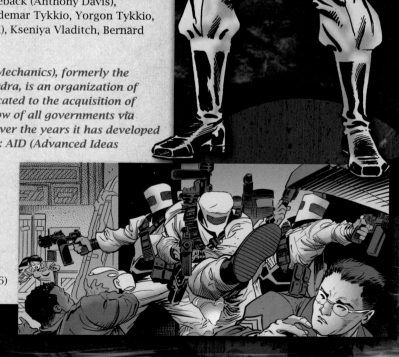

HYDRA

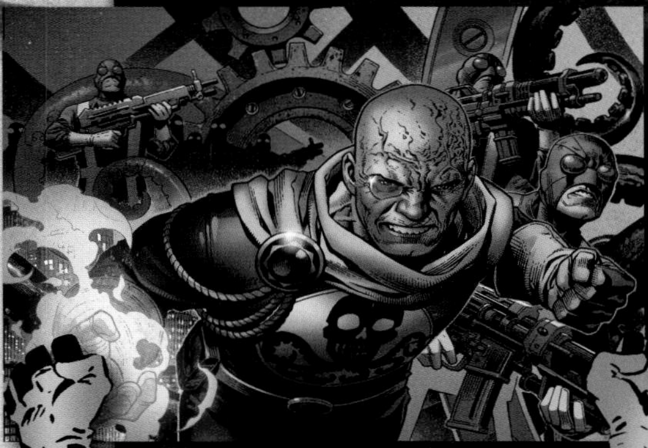

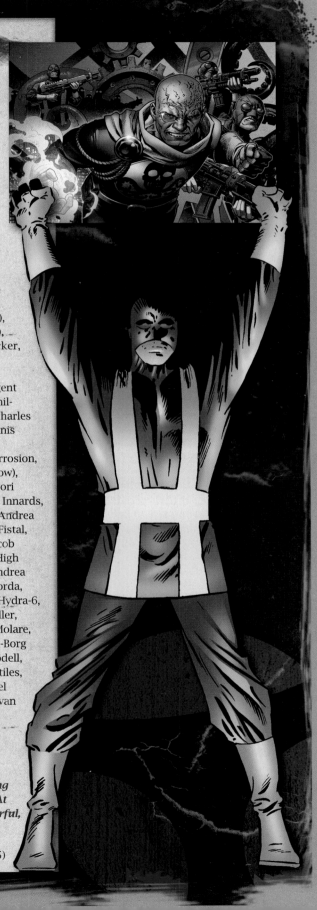

CURRENT MEMBERS:
LEADERS: Hive, Edgar Lascombe, Kraken, Gorgon (Tomi Shishido), Madame Hydra (Ophelia Sarkissian), Gerald Richter, Wolfgang von Strucker

OTHER AGENTS: Kalee Batrei, Bowman, Connely, Dreadnoughts, Horst Eisele, Vincente Fortunato, Garotte (Tyrannus Cordin), Hammer, Militant, Cassandra Romulus, Erik Saltz, Scylla, Tactical Force, Arthur Woodman

FORMER MEMBERS:
LEADERS: Elsie Carson, Deltite, Richard Fisk, Grim Reaper (Eric Williams), Imperial Hydra (Arnold Brown), Kingpin (Wilson Fisk), Madame Hydra (Valentina Allegra de Fontaine), Mother of Pearl, Number 72, Red Skull (Johann Shmidt), Sensational Hydra, Silvermane (Silvio Manfredi), Space Phantom, Otto Vermis, Elsbeth von Strucker, Werner von Strucker, Yellow Claw

OTHER AGENTS: Absorbing Man (Carl Creel), Agent H (Laura Brown), Agent U (Robert Rickard), Annihil-Agent 47, Answer (Aaron Nicholson), Assassin, Charles Atkins, Batroc, Blackwing (Joseph Manfredi), Dennis Bowden, Bull's-Eye, Catalyst, Chameleon (Dmitri Kravinoff), Commander Kraken, Cool Million, Corrosion, Crippler (Carl Striklan), Crossbones (Brock Rumlow), Crown, Dakini, William Darvin, Deadmaker (Gregori Anatolovich), Dismember, D.O.A. (Gregory Belial, Innards, Malpractice, Pyre, Rotwrap), Kitty Drake, Fenris (Andrea & Andreas von Strucker), William Fields, George Fistal, Fixer (Norbert Ebersol), Fox (Reynard Slinker), Jacob Fury, Guillotine (Nicos Pelletier), Lance Halstan, High Zero, Jackhammer, el Jaguar (Ramon de Rico), Andrea Janson, Knockabout (Jarno Sprague), Vladimir Korda, Rudolf Kranz, Karl Kraus, Jared Kurtz, Madame Hydra-6, Mammoth, Man-Killer (Katrina Van Horn), Mankiller, Mentallo (Marvin Flumm), Mindstorm, Antwoin Molare, Simon Mycroft, Number 16, Dmitri Petrovich, Psi-Borg (Fionna Wyman), Ralph Sanzetti, Sathan, Mac Scodell, Silver Fox, Spider-Woman (Jessica Drew), Molly Stiles, System Crash (Bitmap, Infomorph, Killobyte, Steel Collar, Technospike, Wirehead), Ron Takimoto, Ivan Trefkov, Simon Valk, Violence (Violet Pinkerton), Warlord (Huang Zhu), Weasel, Whale, James Winderfield, Nancy Winderfield, Wolfen

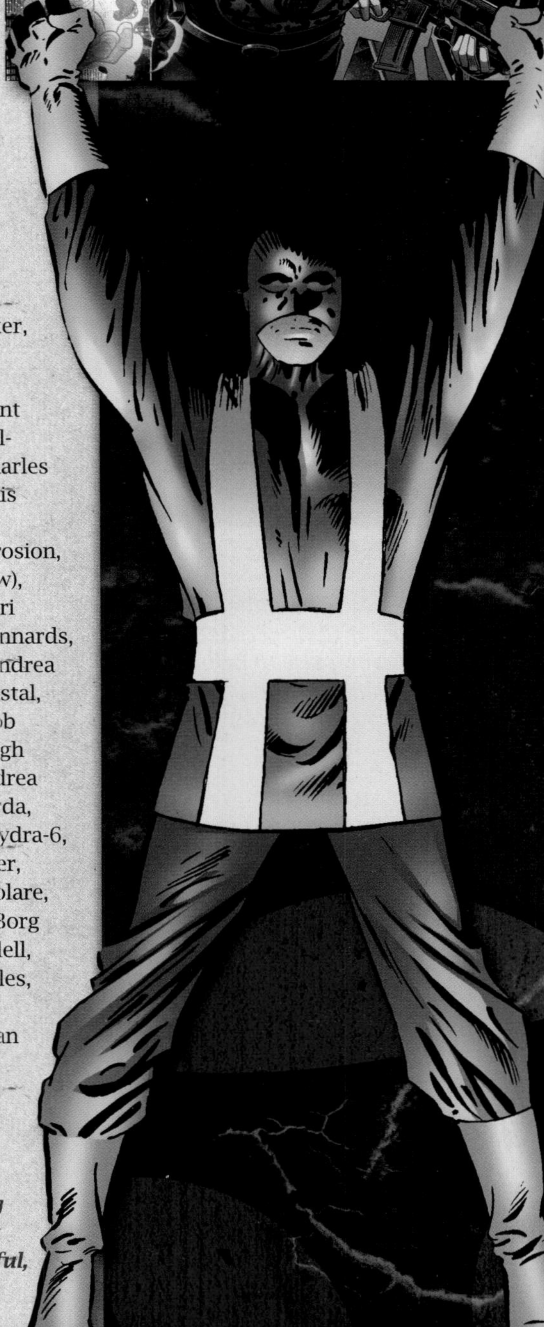

Hydra is a worldwide subversive organization dedicated to global domination by overthrowing all governments to create a new world order. At its height, Hydra was the most extensive, powerful, and dangerous such organization in history.

FIRST APPEARANCE: *Strange Tales* #135 (1965)

SECRET EMPIRE

CURRENT MEMBERS: Brute Force (Fieldstone, Fizgig, Hoarfrost, Hoopsnake, Ingot, Loblolly, Scarum, Watchfire), Calvin Burlingame, Richard Cholmondely, Thomas Gloucester, Mad Dog (Robert Baxter), Professor Power (Anthony Power), Shocktroopers, Matt Surman, William Taurey, Harcourt Vickers

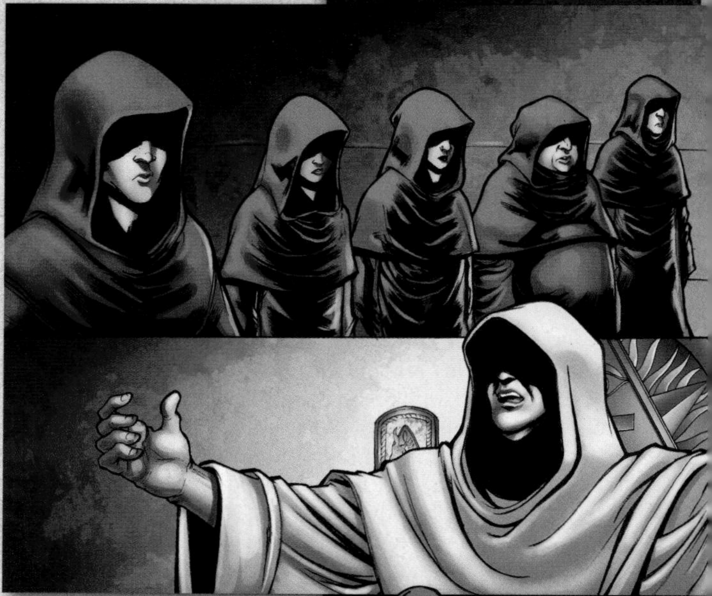

OTHER AGENTS: Boomerang/Outback (Fred Myers), Brotherhood of Evil Mutants (Blob, Mastermind/Jason Wyngarde, Unus), Baron (Helmut) Zemo, Cheer Chadwick, Hesperus Chadwick, Chainsaw, Charcoal (Charlie Burlingame), Lynn Church, Cloud, Dr. Faustus, Linda Donaldson, Mr. Farrell, Gargantua (Edward Cobert), Griffin (John Horton), Quentin Harderman, Harridan, Javelynn, Carl Maddicks, Midnight (Jeffrey Wilde), Moonstone (Lloyd Bloch), Mutant Force (Burner, Lifter, Peeper, Shocker/Randall Darby, Slither), Bo Ollsen, Pretorians, Quasimodo, Jay Sanford, Seekers (Chain, Grasp, Sonic), Seraph, Thunderball (Eliot Franklin), Trick Shot, Tumbler (John Robert Keane), Viper (Jordan Dixon), Viper, Martin Willis, Wyre, Zeitgeist (Larry Ekler)

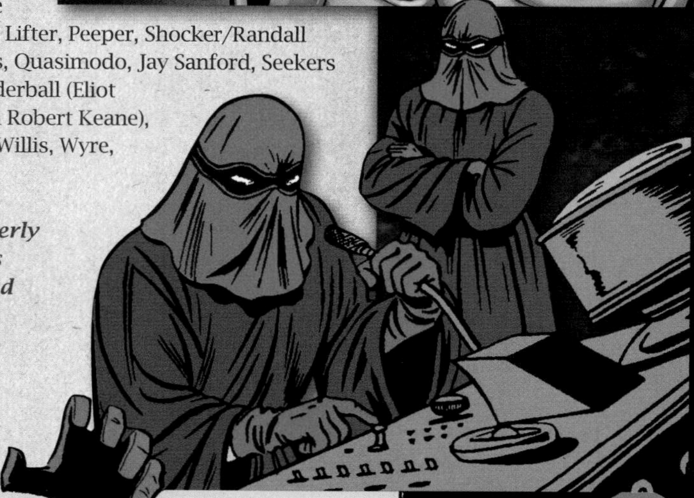

A subversive organization, formerly a subsidiary of Hydra created as a criminal enterprise to help fund Hydra, dedicated to conquering the U.S.A. via conspiracies and underground armies.

FIRST APPEARANCE: *Tales to Astonish* #81 (1966)

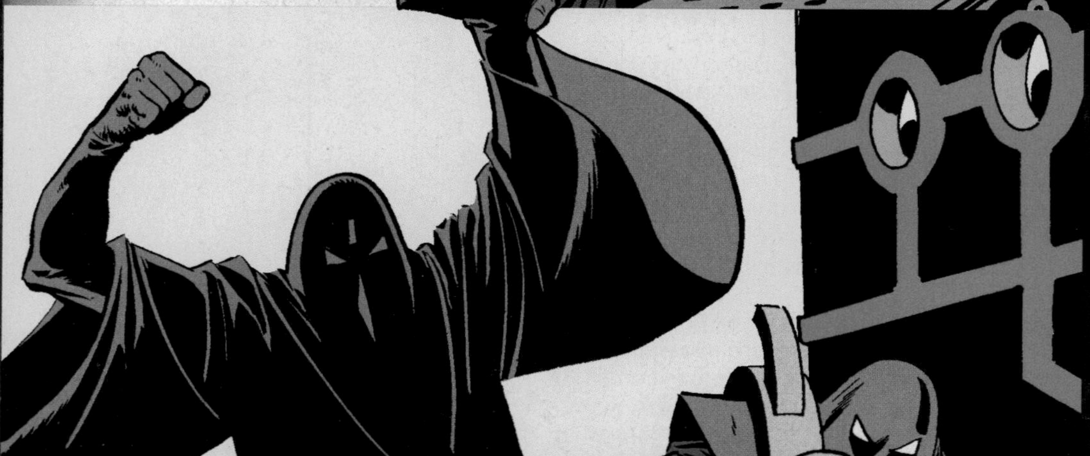

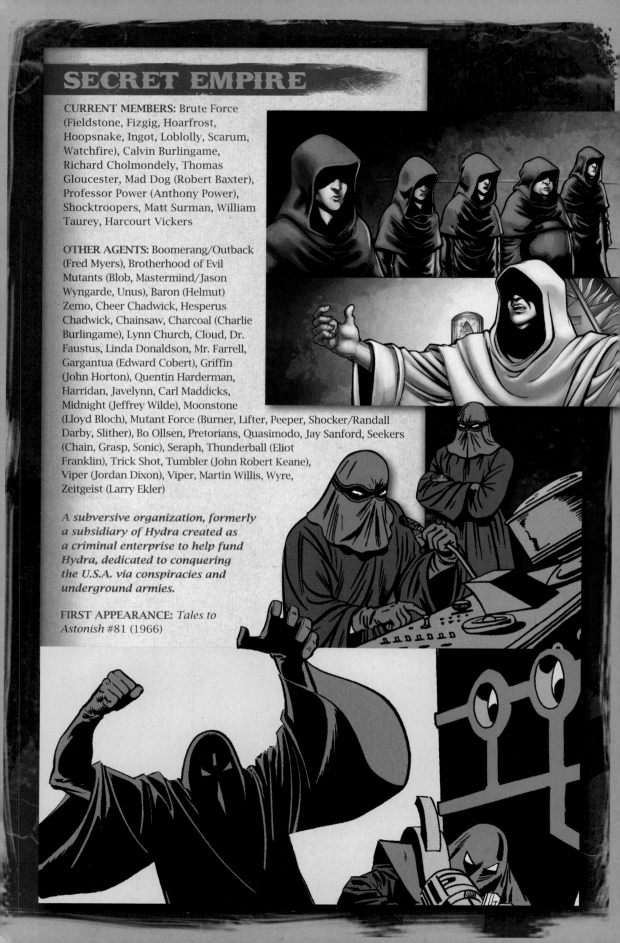

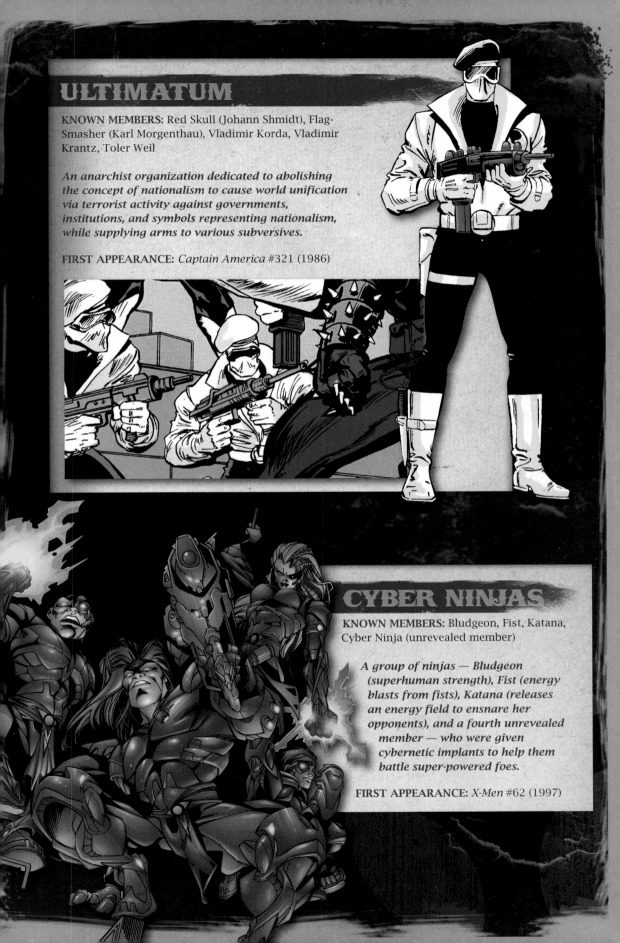

ULTIMATUM

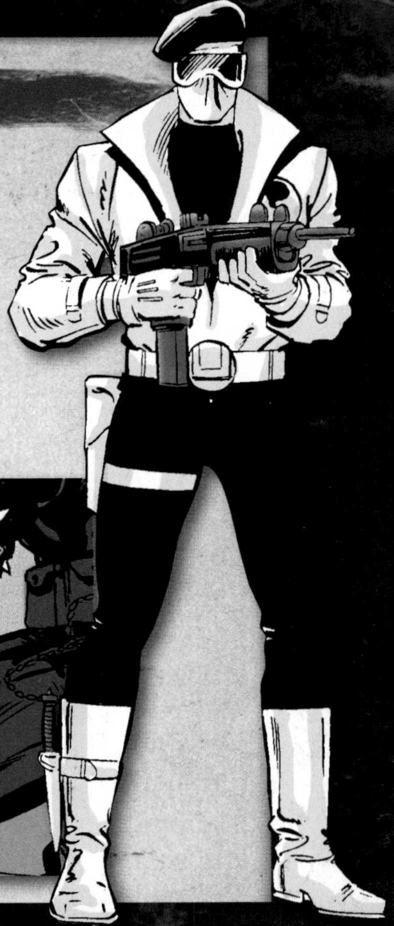

KNOWN MEMBERS: Red Skull (Johann Shmidt), Flag-Smasher (Karl Morgenthau), Vladimir Korda, Vladimir Krantz, Toler Weil

An anarchist organization dedicated to abolishing the concept of nationalism to cause world unification via terrorist activity against governments, institutions, and symbols representing nationalism, while supplying arms to various subversives.

FIRST APPEARANCE: *Captain America* #321 (1986)

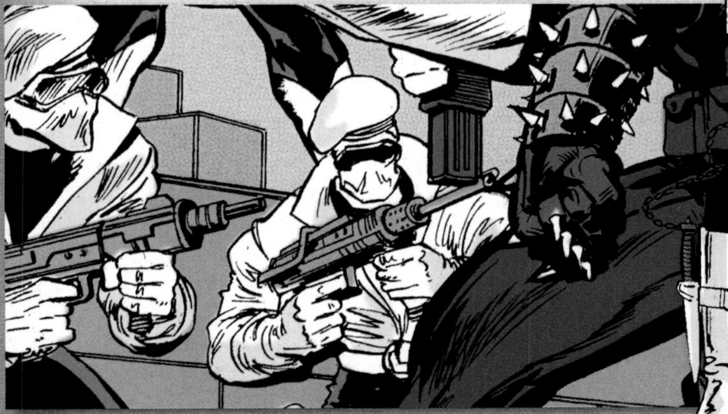

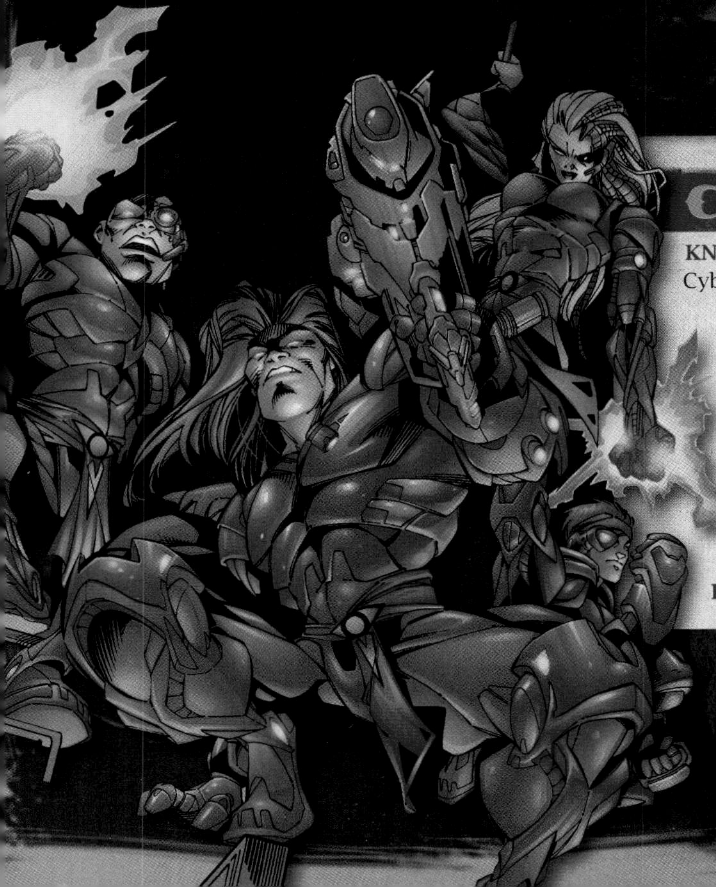

CYBER NINJAS

KNOWN MEMBERS: Bludgeon, Fist, Katana, Cyber Ninja (unrevealed member)

A group of ninjas — Bludgeon (superhuman strength), Fist (energy blasts from fists), Katana (releases an energy field to ensnare her opponents), and a fourth unrevealed member — who were given cybernetic implants to help them battle super-powered foes.

FIRST APPEARANCE: *X-Men* #62 (1997)

LORDS OF THE LIVING LIGHTNING

A doomsday cult of extremists formerly known as the Legion of the Living Lightning that sell hi-tech weapons to terrorists in hopes of triggering an apocalyptic war, allowing them to become the rulers of humanity.

FIRST APPEARANCE: *Tales to Astonish* #97 (1967)

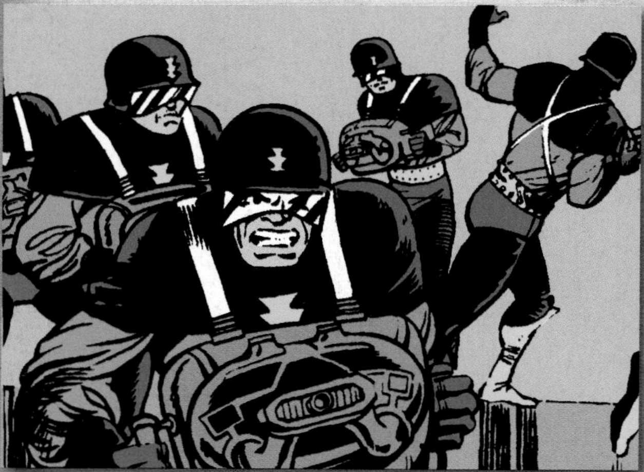

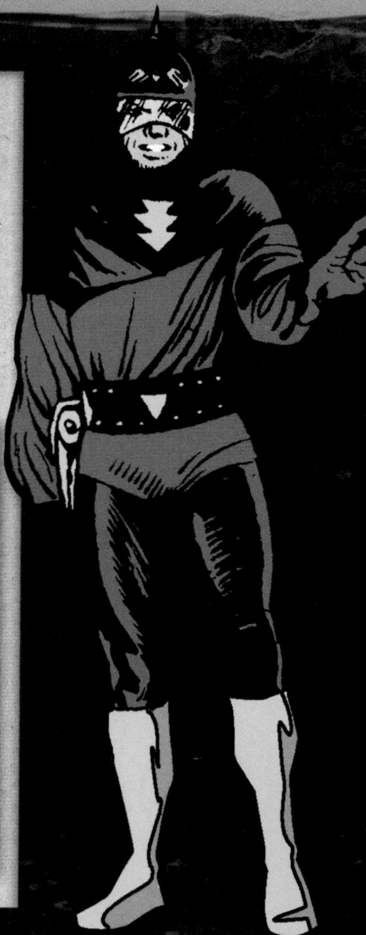

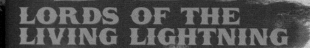

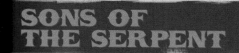

SONS OF THE SERPENT

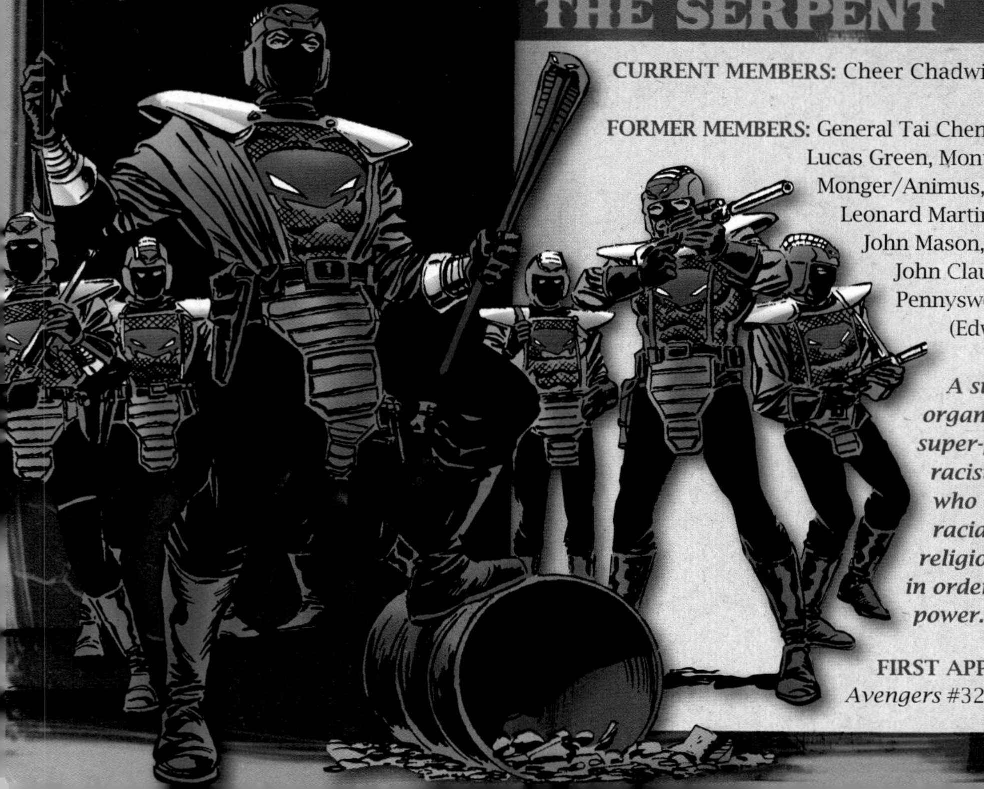

CURRENT MEMBERS: Cheer Chadwick, Dan Dunn

FORMER MEMBERS: General Tai Chen, Russell Daboia, Lucas Green, Montague Hale, Hate-Monger/Animus, Ajanii Jackson, Leonard Martin Kryzewski, John Mason, Number 16, John Claude "J.C." Pennysworth, Skinhead (Edward Cross)

A subversive organization of super-patriotic racist Americans who oppose all racial, ethnic, and religious minorities in order to gain power.

FIRST APPEARANCE: *Avengers* #32 (1966)

BLACK CHOPPERS

A motorcycle gang comprised solely of extraterrestrials doing the arcane bidding of some unknown conspiratorial organization.

FIRST APPEARANCE: *Taskmaster #1 (2010)*

TRENCHCOAT MAFIA

Internet-addicted youths linked through a single encrypted message board site that directs them to live out their first-person shooter fantasies.

FIRST APPEARANCE: *Taskmaster #1 (2010)*

MILITIAMEN

Fringe survivalist group seeking to remake the United States "as the Founding Fathers intended," i.e., with 18th-century-level technology and culture.

FIRST APPEARANCE: *Taskmaster* #1 (2010)

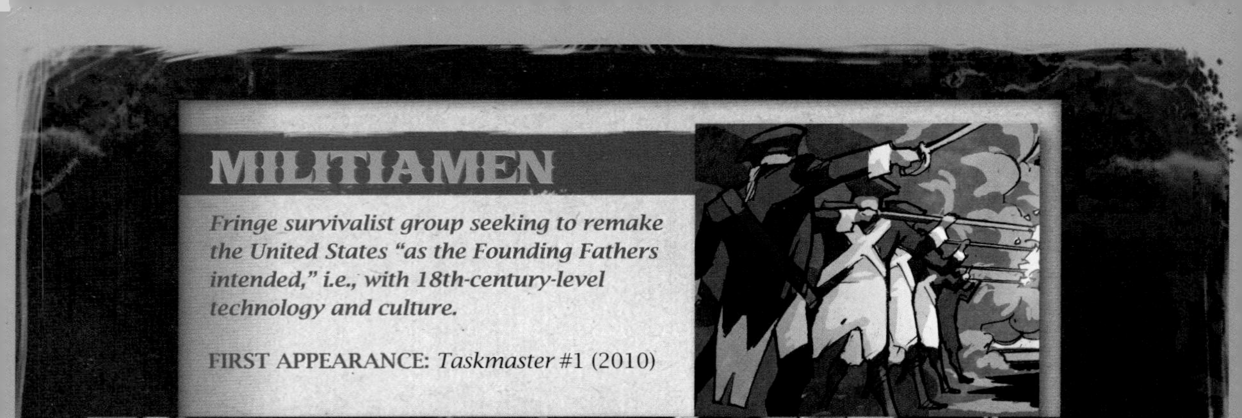

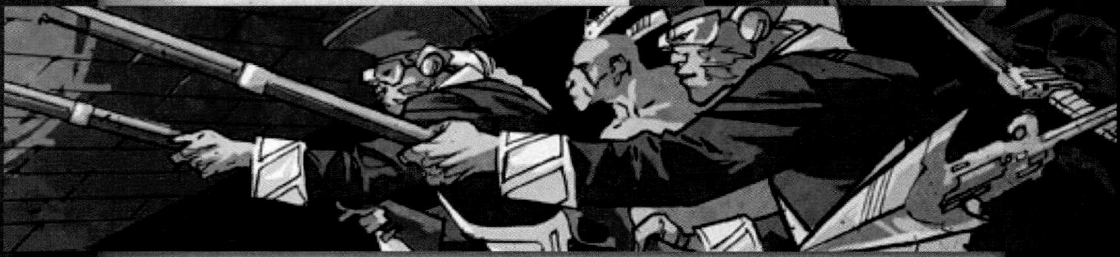

INQUISITION

Sadomasochistic fanatics who believe near-constant personal torture is necessary to "extract" deep philosophical truths about the universe.

FIRST APPEARANCE: *Taskmaster* #1 (2010)

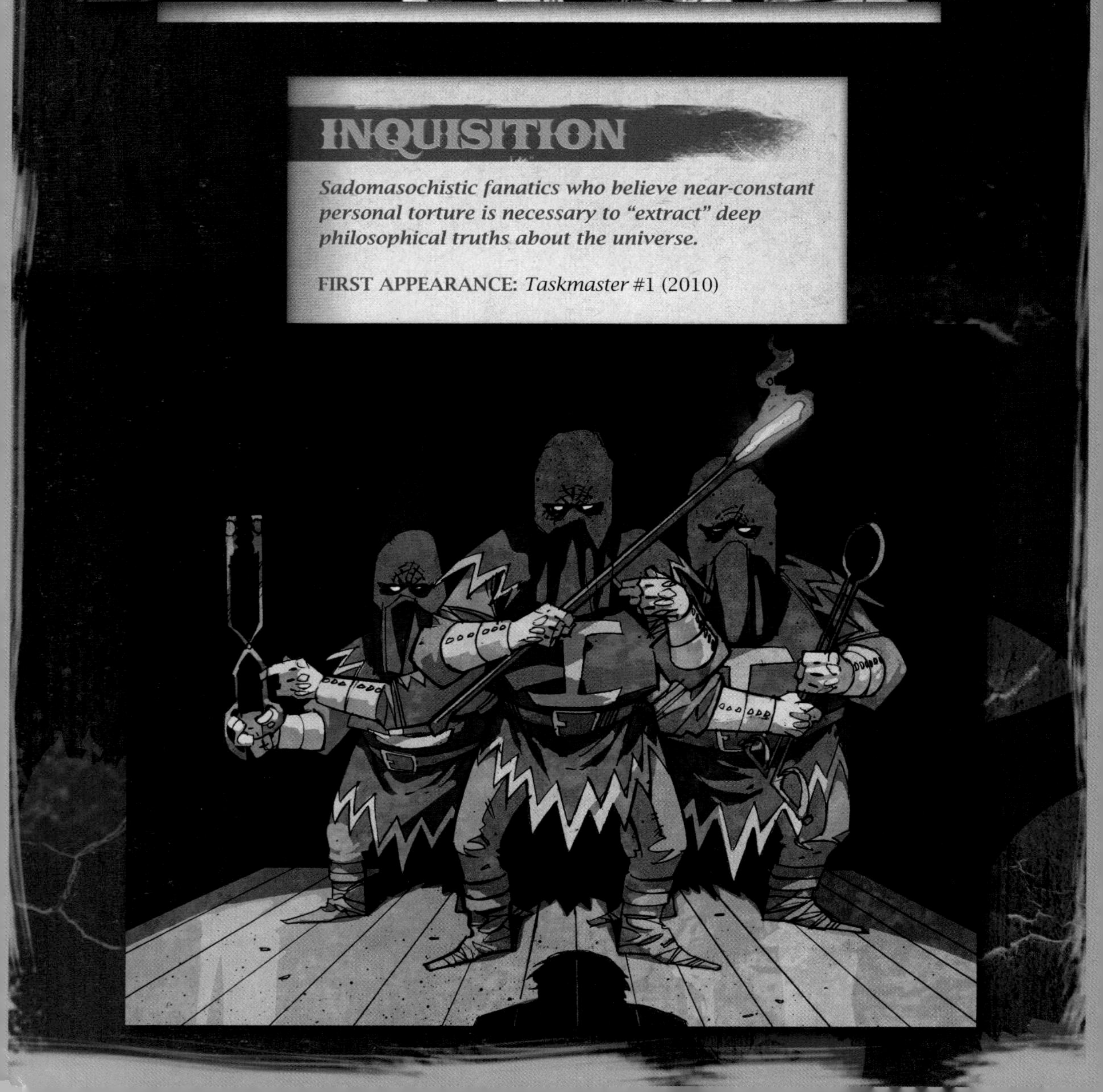

TASKMASTER'S STUDENTS

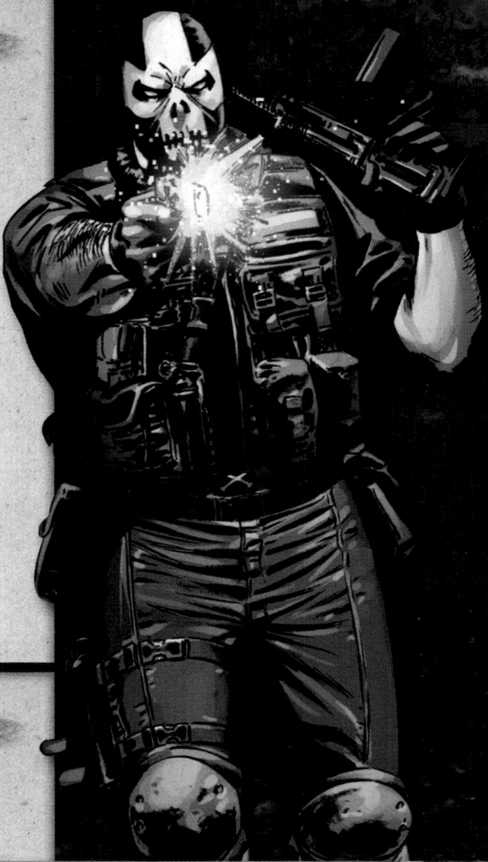

Red Skull (Johann Shmidt) — when Red Skull was in cloned body of Steve Rogers
USAgent
Diamondback (Rachel Leighton)
Blood Spider (Michael Bingham)
Death-shield (Timothy Karlskin)
Jagged Bow (Joe Emberlin)
Snapdragon (Sheoke Sanada)
Crossbones (Brock Rumlow) ▶
Cutthroat (Danny Leighton)
Deadpool
Agent X (Alex Heyden)
Anaconda (Blanche Sitznski)
Deadpool Interns (Deadair, Deadweight, Deadend)
Jolt (Kyi)
Mad Dog (Robert "Buzz" Baxter)
Spymaster (unrevealed)
Spymaster (Nathan Lemon)

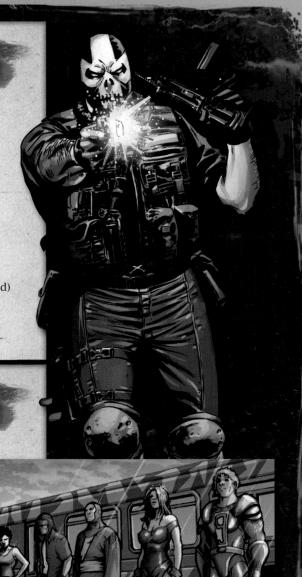

AVENGERS INITIATIVE TRAINEES

Annex
Ant-Man (O'Grady)
Butterball
Crusader (Z'Reg)
Dragon Lord (Tako Shamara)
Geiger (Delilah Dearborn)
Gorilla Girl
Komodo (Melati Kusama)
Melee
Prodigy (Ritchie Gilmore)
Proton (Geldoff)
Red 9
Scarlet Spiders (Michael, Van, Patrick)
Speedball (Earth-8101)
Stature (Cassie Lang)
3-D Man (Delroy Garrett)
Ultragirl

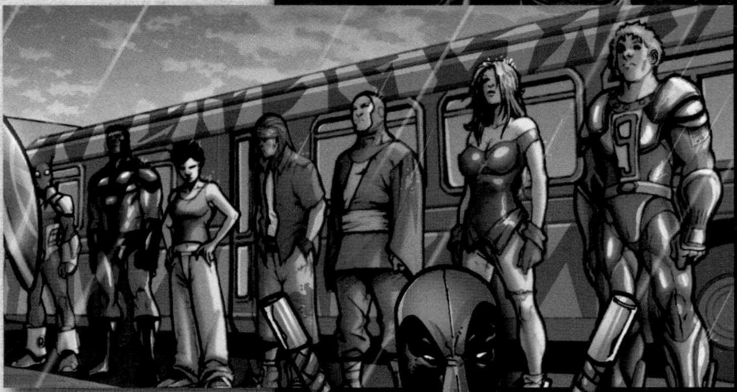

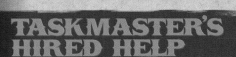

TASKMASTER'S HIRED HELP

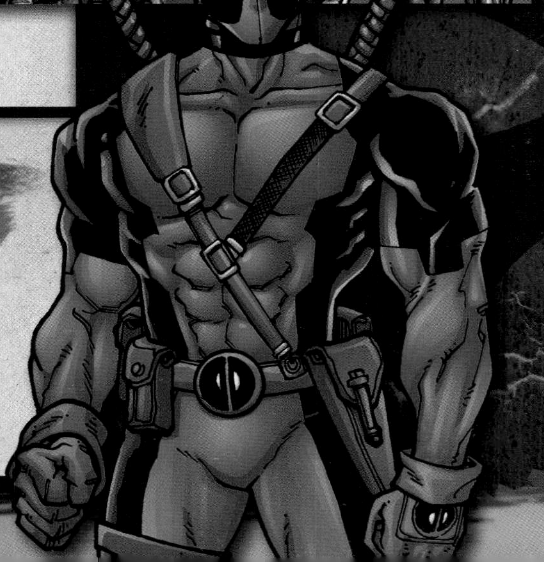

Albino (Augusta Seger)
Batroc's Brigade (Batroc, Machete, Zaran)
Oddball (Elton Healey)
Copycat
Constrictor
Deadpool ▶
Weasel

Text: **DAVID WILTFONG** • Design: **ARLENE SO**

ISSUE 1 PAGE 1 SCRIPT

Panel 1: Establishing shot of "AMBROSIA DINER," under the 7 train in Long Island City in Queens, New York.

It is at NIGHT — around two o'clock in the morning, in fact, so feel free to channel your inner Edward Hopper.

1. JUKEBOX (in diner):   I've been in this town so long that back in the city

2. MERCEDES (in diner):   Look. My friend.

3. MERCEDES ("):   I am as much a proponent of "The Customer's Always Right" as the *next* American wage slave...

Panel 2: Inside the diner, inside a side booth. From the POV of the man in the booth, we're angled up at the waitress, MERCEDES MERCED, a cute indie chick of Puerto Rican descent: dyed streaks in her hair, nose stud, the whole bit. She's holding a steaming pot of coffee and the name "MERCEDES" is visible on the nametag over her heart and she is smiling bemusedly down on us.

4. MERCEDES: ...but do you *have* to keep playing the *same song* over and over and *over* again?

5. MAN (OFF):   "Heroes & Villains." *Classic* peak-period Brian Wilson. All o' "Smile" revolves around it, baby.

6. MERCEDES: Yeah, that's great.

7. MERCEDES: But do you think Brian really *meant* human beings to listen to it *continuously* for *three hours?*

8. JUKEBOX FLOATER: I've been taken for lost and gone

Panel 3: PULL BACK - WIDE ANGLE of the interior of the diner. In the background, a MAN sits at a booth, his back to us. He is Taskmaster out of costume, whom we last glimpsed at the end of our ENTER THE HEROIC AGE story. Standing over him is Mercedes. Slumped in the foreground of our shot is the only other person here: what appears to be a drunk in front of a cup of coffee wearing a baseball cap — but we'll learn soon enough he's a HYDRA AGENT playing possum.

9. MAN: Oh. Sorry.

10. MAN: Didn't realize I was interferin' with the two a.m. Monday *"rush."*

11. MERCEDES: Well L, M, A *and* O.

12. MERCEDES: But can you cut *me* some slack? I'm on the home stretch of back-to-back shifts.

Panel 4: Angle on the booth — there is a miniature JUKEBOX set there. The man has four or five glittering stacks of QUARTERS there — US 25-cent pieces. According to the display, the juke is currently playing *"HEROES & VILLAINS — The Beach Boys."*

13. MERCEDES (RIGHT):   I'm hobbling around on stumps *and* now I also want to tear my ears off.

14. MAN (OFF LEFT):   Hmmm.

15. MAN (OFF LEFT):   What do *I* get in return if I *stop?*

Panel 5: Mercedes arches one eyebrow with a scoffing smile. From this angle we can see her "MERECEDES" nametag plainly.

16. MERCEDES: *Then* you *woke up.*

17. MAN (OFF LEFT):   Hold on. *Wait* for it... *Mercedes,* right?

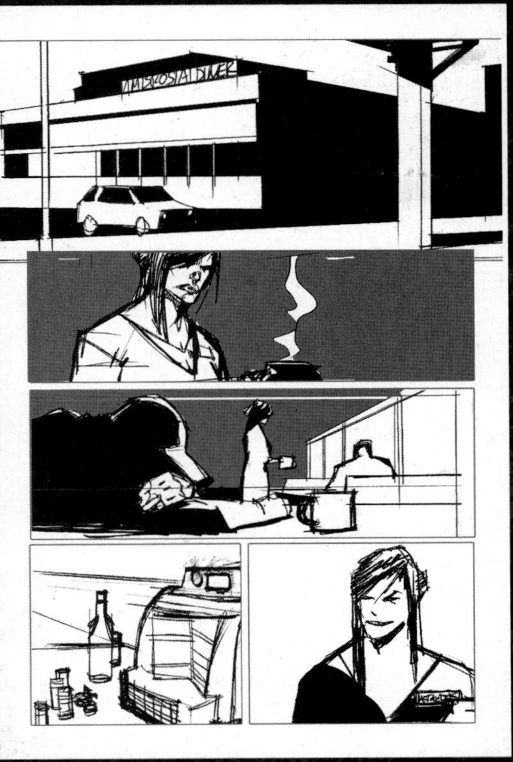

ISSUE 1 PAGE 1 SKETCH

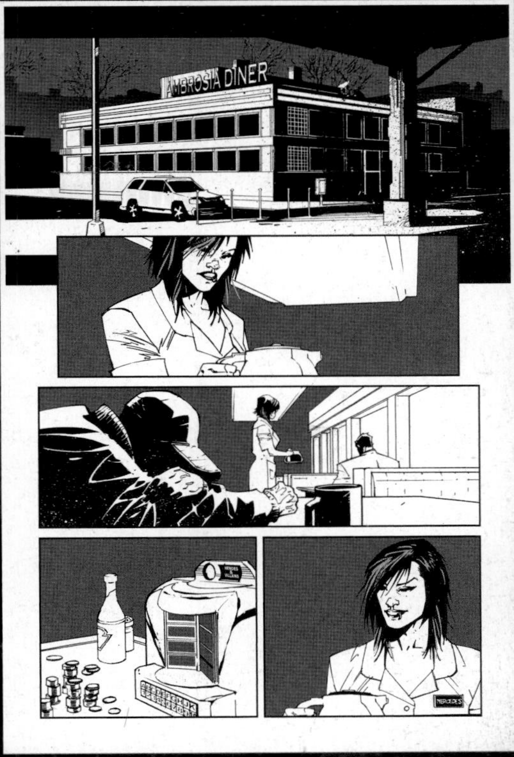
AMBROSIA DINER

ISSUE 1 PAGE 1 INKS

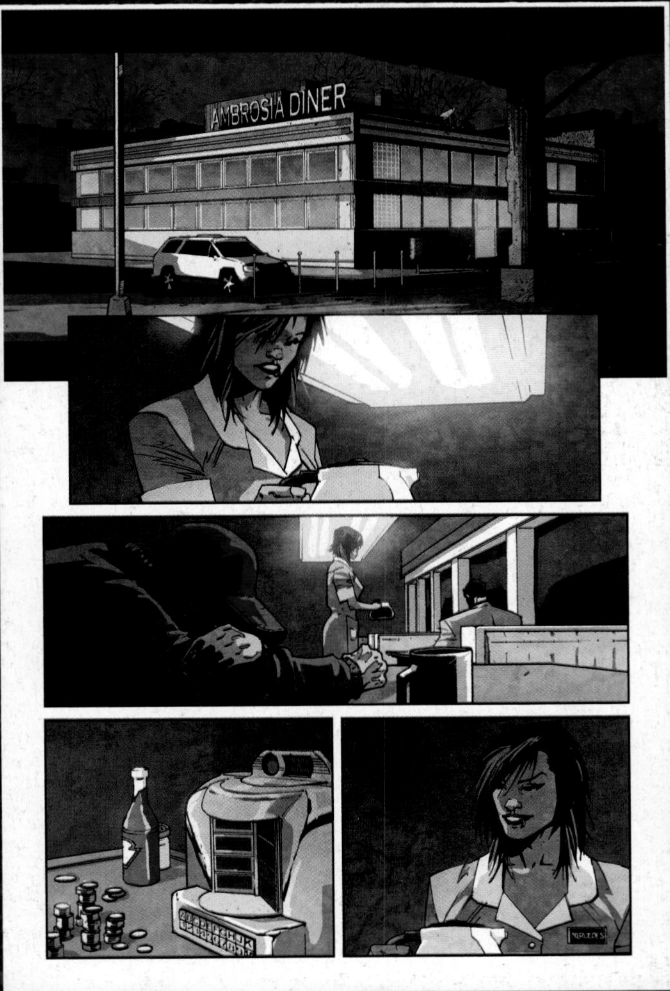
AMBROSIA DINER

ISSUE 1 PAGE 1
FINAL

ISSUE 1 PAGE 2

Panel 1: CROSSHAIRS POV: We're looking at the man through the window of the diner through the scope of a sniper rifle. The CROSSHAIRS of the scope block the man's face from view. Mercedes is sort of visible standing beside him.

1. MERCEDES (jagged):   It's what the nametag says.

2. MAN (jagged):   Y'see, Mercedes, if you *must* know, I am tryin' to *remember* somethin'.

3. MAN (jagged):   Somethin' *important.*

Panel 2: REVERSE ANGLE — An abandoned storefront with a gap over the door where its sign used to be. Papered over the glass storefront window is a big paper notice: **FOR RENT • CALL 347-555-9845**

4. JAGGED FLOATER: This here is what you'd call a *mnemonic technique.*

5. JAGGED FLOATER: "The Memory Palace."

Panel 3: ZOOM IN — SMALL PANEL — A small circle has been cut in one of the letters of the "For Rent" sign. We can barely see the glint on the lens of a NIGHT VISION MONOCULAR on the other side of the window.

7. JAGGED FLOATER: You build a palace in your *mind.*

8. JAGGED FLOATER: Each *room* represents somethin' you're trying to memorize.

Panel 4: BIG PANEL — INTERIOR, VACANT STOREFRONT — The only thing really in here are a trio of ADVANCED IDEA MECHANICS BEEKEEPERS. All are facing the storefront window (i.e., us). One holds the monocular to his eye. Another points a PARABOLIC MICROPHONE at us. The other stands behind the others, checking his watch.

Here's AIM beekeeper reference. It's hard to tell from this, but through the mesh of the helmet you can vaguely see their eyes, eyebrows and the bridge of their noses. http://www.marveldirectory.com/pictures/groupsandteams/aim.gif

9. MICROPHONE (jagged):   You *stock* that room with objects and associations that *trigger* the info you're lookin' for…

8. AIM #1:   Time check.

9. AIM #3:   Seven past two.

10. AIM #3:   Why don't we just kill the Judas now, while he's feeding his face—

Panel 5: CU — The AIM guy with the monocular turns around to face us.

11. AIM #1:   How about I just power up the *Suicide Ray* for you? Be quicker *and* easier.

12. AIM #1:   The Org said *quarter* past, dumbass. Same as all the bounty bids. *That's* when we attack. And not a *second* before.

Panel 6: Angle on duffle bag lying on the ground — detail on a PATCH, which is a SKULL with a HYPODERMIC NEEDLE and a BUBBLING TEST TUBE underneath instead of bones in a skull-and-crossbones. The legend over the patch reads: **"A.I.M. MURDERTECH"**. The legend under the patch reds: **"DEATH BY SCIENCE"**.

13. AIM #1 (OFF):   *Nobody* crosses The Org.

14. AIM #1 (OFF):   Not even *us.*

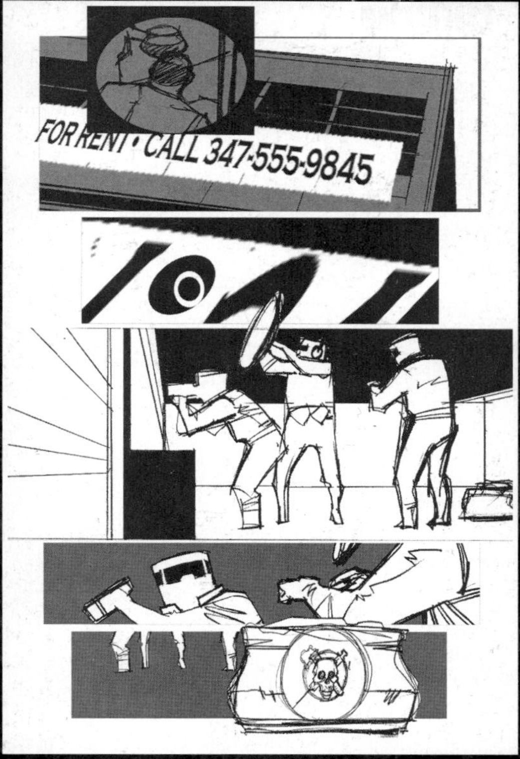
FOR RENT • CALL 347-555-9845

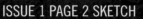

ISSUE 1 PAGE 2 SKETCH

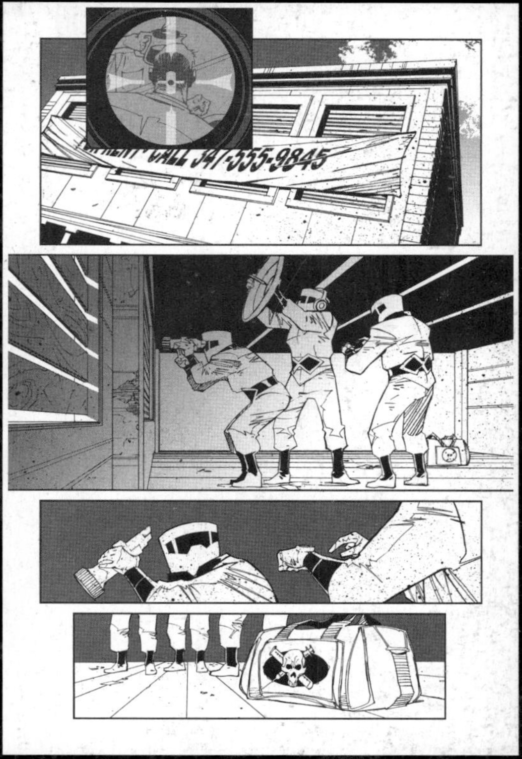
CALL 347-555-9845

ISSUE 1 PAGE 2 INKS

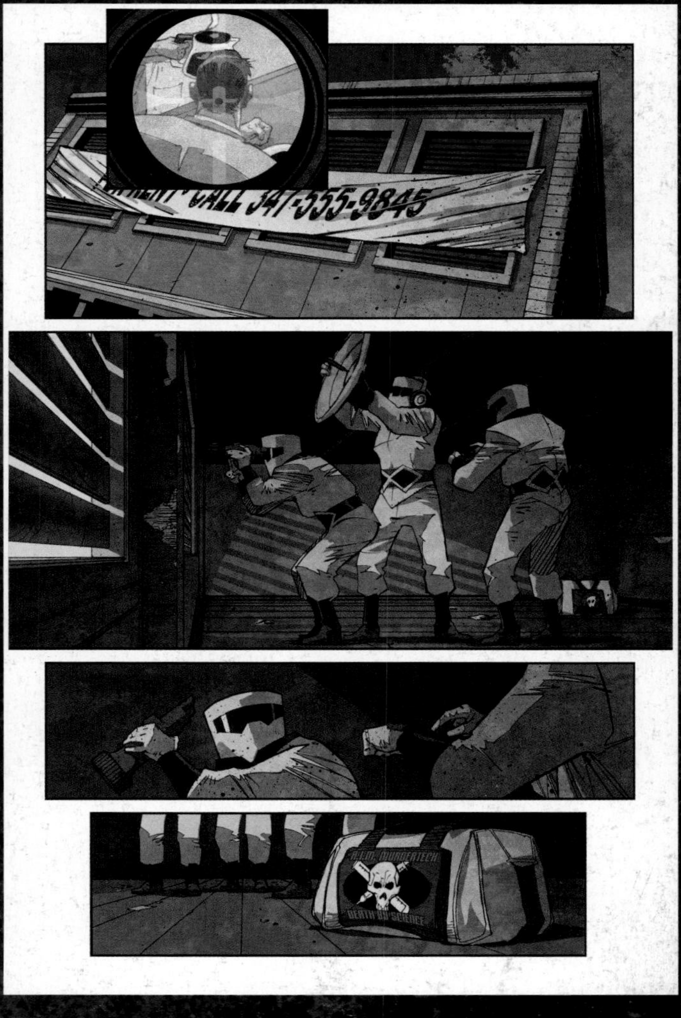
CALL 347-555-9845

ISSUE 1 PAGE 2
FINAL

ISSUE 1 PAGE 3

Panel 1: Back in diner, angle down on MAN'S table: He's eating a well-known diner dish in the States: Chicken Soulvaki, with fries.

1. MAN (OFF):   Works *best* if the rooms in your Memory Palace are places you've actually been.

2. MAN (OFF):   Like... last time I was here. I was eatin' Chicken Soulvaki... like I am now...

3. MAN (OFF):   ..."Heroes & Villains" was on the jukebox, like it is here...

Panel 2: FLASHBACK: LARGE PANEL: TASKMASTER'S POV: ELEKTRA leaps toward us, sai pointing directly at us!! As we're looking through Tasky's eyes, we can't see him, of course. Show hints around her that we're in this diner — completely trashed!

4. TASKMASTER'S VOICE: "...and there was a *woman.*"

Panel 3: REVERSE ANGLE: ANOTHER SNIPER POV: This one from ABOVE, a MAGNETING RESONANCE IMAGE actually through the wall — It's all grainy and gray made up of lines, like the sonogram of a fetus. As per before, Taskmaster's real face is disguised from us by the CROSSHAIRS over his face, and Mercedes still stands beside him.

5. MERCEDES (jagged):   There so often *is.*

6. MERCEDES (jagged):   Who was she?

7. MAN (jagged):   No. Wait. Quid pro quo here.

8. HYDRA AGENT (OFF):   Say ... where's *Morris?*

Panel 4: ELEVATED 7 TRACK — A trio of HYDRA AGENTS await on the elevated 7 track above the diner. One looks through the massive "LOBSTER EYE" scope mounted on a gigantic RAIL GUN SNIPER RIFLE.

9. HYDRA AGENT #1:   Can't believe he didn't come on this op. I mean he practically *worshipped* this guy--

10. HYDRA AGENT #2:   Who *didn't?* Man taught me to snap a neck *one-handed--*

11. HYDRA AGENT #3:   Can the *Memory Lane.* How long before The Org declares the opening of *Rat-Hunting Season?*

Panel 5: Angle down — Hydra agent's POV — he looks at his wristwatch, which shows it's ten past two o'clock. The gag here is the watch face is is the HYDRA SYMBOL.

12. HYDRA AGENT (OFF):   Five minutes, hard case.

13. HYDRA AGENT (OFF):   Hail freakin' Hydra.

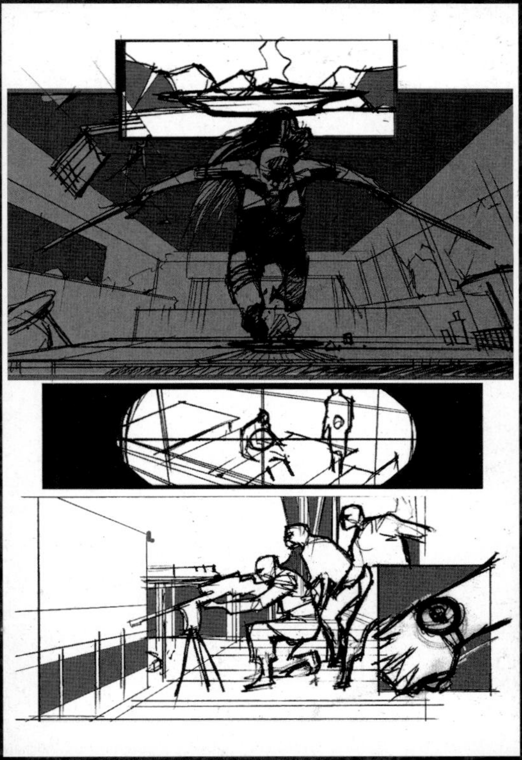

ISSUE 1 PAGE 3 SKETCH

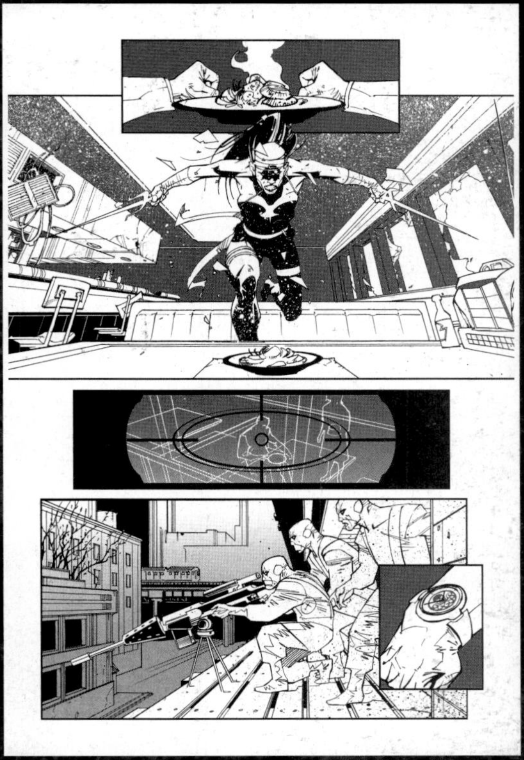

ISSUE 1 PAGE 3 INKS

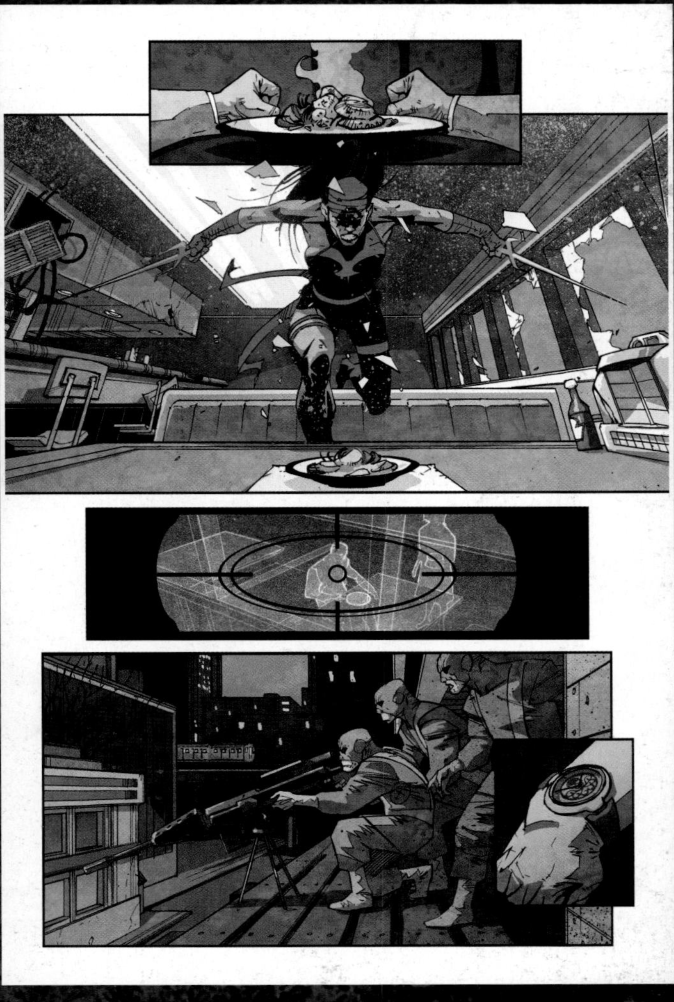

ISSUE 1
PAGE 3 FINAL

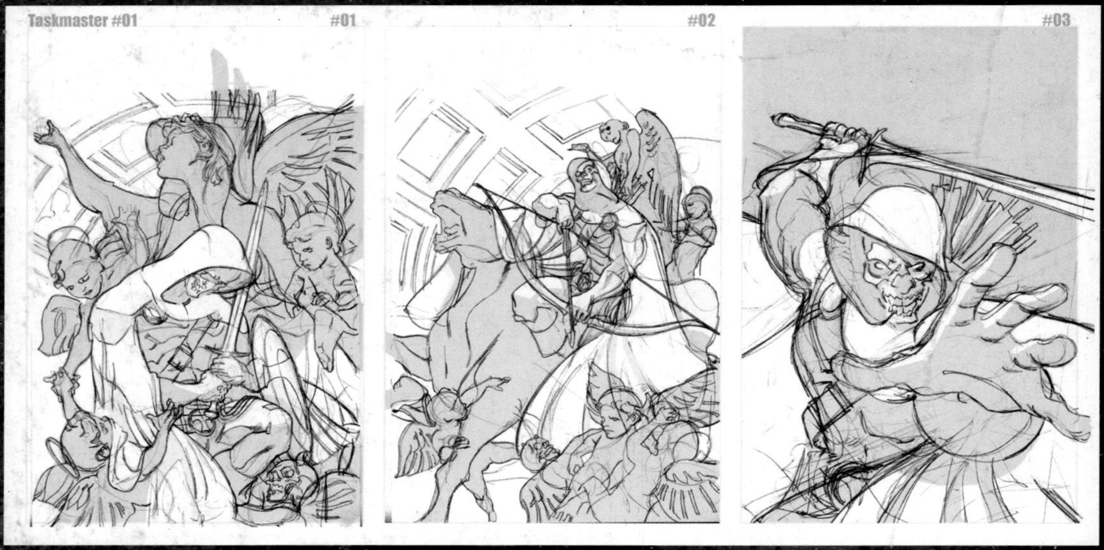
Taskmaster #01
#01
#02
#03

ISSUE 1 COVER SKETCHES BY **GREG TOCCHINI**

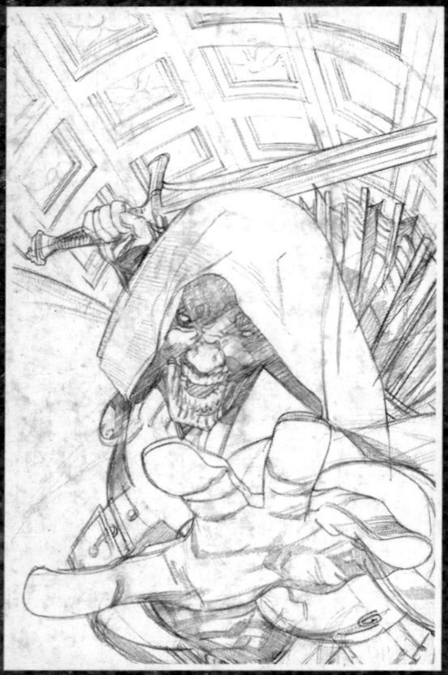

COVER PENCILS

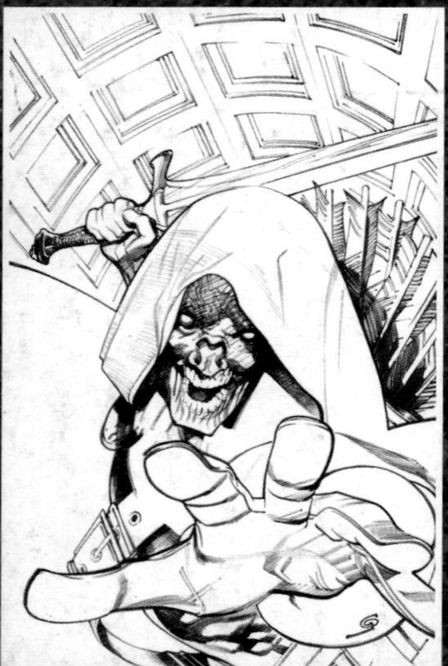

COVER INKS

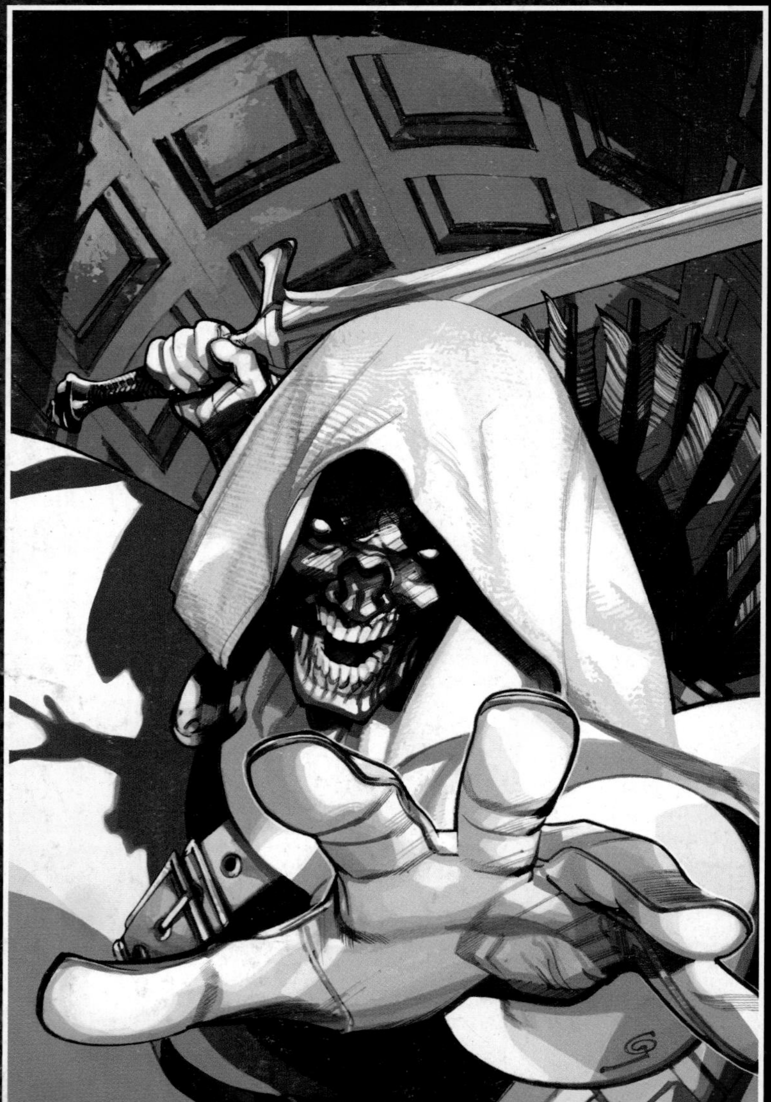

COVER FINAL